Philip Ro

Continuum Studies in Contemporary North American Fiction

Series Editor: Sarah Graham, Lecturer in American Literature, University of Leicester, UK

This series offers up-to-date guides to the recent work of major contemporary North American authors. Written by leading scholars in the field, each book presents a range of original interpretations of three key texts published since 1990, showing how the same novel may be interpreted in a number of different ways. These informative, accessible volumes will appeal to advanced undergraduate and postgraduate students, facilitating discussion and supporting close analysis of the most important contemporary American and Canadian fiction.

Titles in the Series include:

Bret Easton Ellis: American Psycho, Glamorama, Lunar Park
Edited by Naomi Mandel

Cormac McCarthy: All the Pretty Horses, No Country for Old Men,
  The Road
Edited by Sara Spurgeon

Don DeLillo: Mao II, Underworld, Falling Man
Edited by Stacey Olster

Louise Erdrich: Tracks, The Last Report on the Miracles at Little No
  Horse, The Plague of Doves
Edited by Deborah L. Madsen

Margaret Atwood: The Robber Bride, The Blind Assassin, Oryx
  and Crake
Edited by J. Brooks Bouson

Philip Roth: American Pastoral, The Human Stain, The Plot Against
  America
Edited by Debra Shostak

Toni Morrison: Paradise, Love, A Mercy
Edited by Lucille P. Fultz

PHILIP ROTH

American Pastoral, The Human Stain,
The Plot Against America

Edited by Debra Shostak

continuum

Continuum International Publishing Group

The Tower Building   80 Maiden Lane
11 York Road   Suite 704
London SE1 7NX   New York, NY 10038

www.continuumbooks.com

British Library Cataloguing-in-Publication Data
A catalogue record for this book is available from the British Library.

ISBN: 978-0-8264-2631-4 (hardcover)
ISBN: 978-0-8264-2227-9 (paperback)

Library of Congress Cataloging-in-Publication Data
A catalog record for this book is available from the Library of Congress.

Typeset by Newgen Imaging Systems Pvt Ltd, Chennai, India
Printed and bound in India

Contents

Series Editor's Introduction

Each study in this series presents ten original essays by recognized subject specialists on the recent fiction of a significant author working in the United States or Canada. The aim of the series is to consider important novels published since 1990 either by established writers or by emerging talents. By setting 1990 as its general boundary, the series indicates its commitment to engaging with genuinely contemporary work, with the result that the series is often able to present the first detailed critical assessment of certain texts.

In respect of authors who have already been recognized as essential to the canon of North American fiction, the series provides experts in their work with the opportunity to consider their latest novels in the dual context of the contemporary era and as part of a long career. For authors who have emerged more recently, the series offers critics the chance to assess the work that has brought authors to prominence, exploring novels that have garnered acclaim both because of their individual merits and because they are exemplary in their creative engagement with a complex period.

Including both American and Canadian authors in the term 'North American' is in no sense reductive: studies of Canadian writers in this series do not treat them as effectively American, and assessment of all the chosen authors in terms of their national and regional identity, as well as their race and ethnicity, gender and sexuality, religion and political affiliation is essential in developing an understanding of each author's particular contribution to the representation of contemporary North American society.

The studies in this series make outstanding new contributions to the analysis of current fiction by presenting critical essays chosen for their originality, insight and skill. Each volume begins with a substantial introduction to the author by the study's editor, which establishes the context for the chapters that will follow through a discussion of essential elements such as the writer's career, characteristic narrative strategies, themes and preoccupations, making clear the author's importance and the significance of the novels chosen for discussion. The studies are all comprised of three parts, each one presenting three original essays on three key recent works by the author, and every part is introduced by the volume's editor, explaining how the chapters to follow engage with the fiction and respond to existing interpretations. Each individual chapter takes a critical approach that may develop existing perceptions or challenge them, but always expands the ways in which the author's work may be read by offering a fresh approach.

It is a principle of the series that all the studies are written in a style that will be engaging and clear however complex the subject, with the aim of fostering further debate about the work of writers who all exemplify what is most exciting and valuable in contemporary North American fiction.

Sarah Graham

Acknowledgments

I am profoundly grateful to all those who have aided me in completing this volume. I owe a tremendous debt to the editor of this series, Sarah Graham, for her wise counsel, sensitive reading of the manuscript, and encouragement, and likewise to Colleen Coalter at Continuum Press, for her helpful shepherding of the book. I wish to take this opportunity, too, to thank the friends and colleagues with whom I have had delightful conversations, real and virtual, about Roth over the years, especially David Brauner, Derek Parker Royal, Catherine Morley, Bernard Rodgers, and Tim Parrish. I am grateful to the College of Wooster for supporting me with funding from the Henry Luce III Fund for Distinguished Scholarship, which granted me release time in the fall of 2009 to work on this project. I am indebted to my husband, Jeff Pinkham, for his help in preparing the index to this volume. I give thanks as well to Kathie Clyde, Administrative Coordinator at the College of Wooster, for her help with details of manuscript preparation. This project would not have been so pleasurable without the constant support of friends devoted to the life of the mind and to our work among scholars and students of literature, especially Carolyn Durham, John Gabriele, John Lyon, Jenna Hayward, Nancy Grace, Tom Prendergast, and Mary Mekemson. My deepest gratitude goes to my family—to Jeff, and to my children, Sarah and Michael—for sharing good humor, books, movies, music, and, of course, love.

I gratefully acknowledge permission to reproduce in altered form portions of the review essay by Brett Ashley Kaplan, "Contested, Constructed Home(lands): Diaspora, Postcolonial Studies, and Zionism," which appeared in *The Journal of Modern Jewish Studies* 5.3 (2006), quoted by permission; portions of Andrew Gordon's essay, "The Critique of Utopia in Philip Roth's *The Counterlife* and *American Pastoral*," published in *Turning Up the Flame: Philip Roth's Later Novels*, ed. Jay L. Halio and Ben Siegel, University of Delaware Press, 2005, quoted by permission of Associated University Presses; and portions of the review essay by Timothy Parrish on *The Plot Against America*, which appeared in *Philip Roth Studies* 1.1 (2005), quoted by permission of Purdue University Press. I also gratefully acknowledge permission to quote from unpublished materials in the Philip Roth Collection, Manuscript Division of the Library of Congress. Copyright © by Philip Roth, used with permission of The Wylie Agency LLC.

CHAPTER 1

Introduction: Roth's America

Debra Shostak

Getting People Right

Among the notes that Philip Roth made while he was composing *American Pastoral* (1997) is a terse diagnosis of the seductive, doomed project of fiction-making:

> can't read anyone . . . Never know anyone in life this way. The falseness of fiction—to pretend that we can. The magic of fiction. Life losing its opacity. But could be dead wrong. Assume it is all dead wrong. But it is still [as close] as I can come to understanding. ("Contains Notes" 1)

Roth was directing not only himself as the "I" in these notes but also his alter ego, the fictional novelist Nathan Zuckerman. A similar passage appears in *American Pastoral* itself, when the narrating Zuckerman laments his "astonishing farce of misperception": in thinking about other people, "you never fail to get them wrong." Zuckerman movingly concludes, however, that one should not stop trying: "The fact remains that getting people right is not what living is all about anyway. It's getting them wrong that is living . . . That's how we know we're alive: we're wrong" (35).

It is a reader's good fortune that Philip Roth, born in 1933, has been using the "magic of fiction" for over 50 years to get people right even as his characters get themselves and each other wrong. Roth is now firmly established among the most important contemporary novelists of the later twentieth century in the United States. The author of twenty-seven novels, an autobiography, a memoir, two collections of essays, and assorted short stories, Roth has garnered major literary awards in America ever since the release of his first collection, *Goodbye, Columbus*, which won the National Book Award for 1959. Not only has he earned the National Book Critics Circle Award, the PEN/Faulkner Award (twice), the Pulitzer Prize, and various other prizes, international and domestic, but also the prestigious Library of America is now five volumes into the project of republishing his collected works in authoritative editions, an honor bestowed on just two other living American novelists. In 2006, the editors of the *New York Times Book Review* polled several hundred prominent writers, critics, and editors, asking them to name "the single best work of American fiction published in the last 25 years" (Scott 17). As David Brauner notes elsewhere in this volume, *American Pastoral* numbered among the top five novels identified by the survey; just as important, five other novels by Roth, including *The Human Stain* (2000) and *The Plot Against America* (2004), received multiple votes, more books than the judges singled out for any other writer.

No wonder. Roth's fiction has been consistently diverse, reinventing itself in forms ranging from psychological realism to postmodernism. He has moved from raucous comedy to austere tragedy, in sentences alternately sinuous, crystalline, poignant, and uproarious. Consider Alexander Portnoy, anxiously trying as a child to understand what it means to be a Jew—" 'Momma, do we believe in winter?' "—and, later, declaiming his desperate desire to put "the id back in Yid" (*Portnoy* 37, 236). Or, by contrast, the protagonist of *Everyman* (2006), visiting his parents' graves: "They were just bones, bones in a box, but their bones were his bones, and he stood as close to the bones as he could, as though the proximity might link him up with them and mitigate the isolation born of losing his future and reconnect him with all that had gone" (170). Roth has provoked his readership, digging deep into vexed questions, at times daring political controversy, at times exposing the embarrassments of intimate or forbidden feelings and behavior. He has dismissed decorum to inquire into Jewish identity and the place of the American Jew in the United States. He has peered mercilessly at masculinity, male sexuality, and the fortunes and misfortunes of the male body. He has challenged complacencies concerning the writer's obligations to his family and community. Roth has also directed his piercing gaze toward the relationship between what he calls "the written and the unwritten world" (*Reading* ix), that is, the slippery connection between fiction and the reality it purports to represent. He has entranced and offended his readers, perhaps in equal measure, by his transgressions against taste and both ethnic and gender sensibilities—by his willingness, that is, to tell what Ross Posnock has called, in the title to his book, "rude truths."

This volume offers brilliant new readings of three of Roth's most powerful and challenging novels from the last decade and a half. Together, *American Pastoral*, *The Human Stain*, and *The Plot Against America* take as their starting point "America" as place, culture, political environment, and idea. Set at a range of American crisis points—the 1960s, the 1990s, and the 1940s, respectively—each scrutinizes American history and selfhood, especially the identities of those whose origins are not wholly white, Christian, and European. Each novel imagines a character who is blindsided by the contradictions that exist between the democratic promise to the American individual and the actuality of group and institutional practices governed by nonegalitarian ideologies. *American Pastoral*, for example, tests the ideal of cultural assimilation for ethnic Americans. Roth explodes the myth that the United States offers its citizens opportunities for wholesale self-reinvention—an explosion that occurs quite literally in the text with the ignition of a bomb. *American Pastoral* portrays the passionate commitment of many mid-century Jews, often just a generation away from immigration, to the mythic promise in the United States that material prosperity offers a sure avenue to reinvention as "Americans." Nathan Zuckerman tells the story of Seymour "Swede" Levov, a golden boy of the Newark Jewish community, who flourishes according to the terms of American success—good looks, wealth, athletic prowess, a "good" (i.e., mixed) marriage. Levov's innocence supports his success by erasing the traces of history, specifically his difference from some indefinable norm of Gentile life. Roth draws a lovingly detailed portrait of the good-faith striving of his protagonist to be fully "American"—by building a family, a business, and a house—only to show that the critique of this idealized image that emerged in the 1960s rendered Levov's aspirations intellectually and practically impossible. Zuckerman sets himself the task of reconstructing how Levov's world shatters because his innocent pastoral vision is hollow, delusory, and fatal to a coherent sense of self.

The Human Stain likewise addresses cultural positioning and questions the ideological plausibility of American self-transformation, but specifically in class and racial terms. As in *American Pastoral*, Nathan Zuckerman narrates *The Human Stain*, and the novel makes clear that Zuckerman fabricates a story to help him explain a present fact—in this case, the deaths of Coleman Silk and his lover, Faunia Farley. By representing his characters "passing" racially and socioeconomically, Roth emphasizes that identity is a performance. He complicates the meanings of the African American Silk's performance of otherness by having him invent an identity not only as a white man but as a Jew. Ironically, having replaced one marginalized identity with another, Silk is socially ostracized for racism and dies for his "Jewishness."

Roth also investigates, in his characterization of Faunia, essentialist assumptions about class. Whereas Zuckerman fades from the reader's awareness as the narrator of *American Pastoral*, in *The Human Stain*, Roth brings him back into focus through the novel's framing structure. Zuckerman's efforts to fill impossible gaps in his subjects' pasts underscore the epistemological project of Roth's inquiry in all his "American" books: what are the pressures of history on the American self? Can we come to know people well enough to get them *right*?

The Plot Against America makes Roth's preoccupation with American history most overt by proposing a counterfactual story of a crucial moment in the 1940s, when the United States chose to enter into the European war. He begins with the premise that the anti-Semitic and isolationist aviator Charles Lindbergh beats Franklin Delano Roosevelt to be elected president of the United States in 1940. Roth develops "events" such that, when the fear-mongering administration appeals to its anxious citizenry, fascism is released in American culture and anti-Semitism becomes not just a value but a public policy. Roth represents the implications of this counterhistory through its effects on a Jewish-American family, and he does so by returning to a device he uses elsewhere: he reimagines his own family. Roth depicts the Roths of Newark under the pressures of an anti-Semitic American regime. He exposes many of the most painful consequences of this counterhistory by narrating the novel from the point of view of the young "Philip." Philip experiences the vast historical trauma through the solipsistic concerns of a youthful sensibility struggling to comprehend an inexplicably hostile environment. Roth implies that the possibilities for a fascistic dystopia, averted in actual American history, are submerged potentialities within American culture—for which effects the novel has also been read as an allegory of the present, since Roth wrote it hard upon the election of George W. Bush to the American presidency and the terrorist attacks on the United States on September 11, 2001.

Overview of Roth's Career

Although Roth's turn in these later novels to deep engagement with the particulars of American history and culture may have surprised some of his longtime readers, he clearly had been preparing for them throughout his career. Roth arrived at *American Pastoral*, *The Human Stain*, and *The Plot Against America* as outgrowths of his topical and aesthetic preoccupations. Very roughly—because Roth's trajectory is anything but linear—the fiction can be described according to three periods. The early work—from *Goodbye, Columbus* through the restrained Jamesian realism of *Letting Go* (1962), the naturalism of *When She Was*

Good (1967), and even the ranting confessional monologue of *Portnoy's Complaint* (1969)—adheres to the conventions of realism. These novels and stories explore how social and psychological conditions constrain the development of an autonomous selfhood. *Portnoy's Complaint* also registers Roth's movement toward the second phase, typified by generic experiments, frequently metafictional, which he continued from the early 1970s to the mid-1980s and beyond. Beginning with the furious satire of *Our Gang* (1971), Roth took on the Kafkaesque fable of *The Breast* (1972), the parodic epic of *The Great American Novel* (1973), and the many-layered reflexive experiment of *My Life as a Man* (1974). He returned to relative realism for *The Professor of Desire* (1977), the prequel, as it were, to *The Breast*, as well as much of the *Zuckerman Bound* tetralogy (*The Ghost Writer* [1979], *Zuckerman Unbound* [1981], *The Anatomy Lesson* [1983], and *The Prague Orgy* [1985]), with the exception of the metafictional framing of *The Ghost Writer*.

With the publication in 1986 of *The Counterlife*, Roth entered a third phase, marked by heightened artistic inventiveness that has lasted well into the twenty-first century. *The Counterlife* initiated a series of playfully serious reflexive experiments that trace back to Roth's novels of the 1970s but take new forms: in the self-conscious framing of *The Facts* (1988), Roth's autobiography covering his youth and early career, in which Nathan Zuckerman talks back to his author; in the theatrical structure of *Deception* (1990), devised wholly around dialogue; and in *Operation Shylock* (1993), a dizzying test of the boundaries between fact and fiction that pits its first-person narrator named Philip Roth against another "Philip Roth," posing as the writer and espousing a political solution to the problems of Jewish identity. Running concurrent to—and often intermixed with—the strains of reflexive writing are Roth's exercises in trenchant realism. While Roth coolly deliberates the autobiography enclosed within *The Facts*, his memoir of his father, *Patrimony* (1991), is a deeply affecting but unsentimental portrait not only of this man of rough wisdom but also of himself as a son.

Nostalgia for the past and the capacity for passionate feeling are then tricked out as rage against mortality and the constraints of social convention in the exhilarating *Sabbath's Theater* (1995), which marks a transition within the third rough phase of Roth's career. Roth turned back toward realism in *Sabbath's Theater*, opening his fiction to more intricate contemplation of how his subjects are situated both in personal memory and in the ideological networks of American history. Indeed, the 1990s and 2000s saw Roth moving beyond the singular focus on the self that dominates the fiction of the 1970s and 1980s, evident in his use of Zuckerman and the avatars of "Philip Roth," toward twin preoccupations. In *American Pastoral*, *I Married a Communist*

(1998), *The Human Stain*, and *The Plot Against America*, the narrative impulse is, to varying degrees, to grapple with the mystery of *others* and to see others both define themselves within and struggle against American history and culture.

Recently, like many artists as they age, Roth has meditated on diminishment, death, and dying. Following upon the outrage, fierce comedy, and Rabelaisian commitment to the life force in *Sabbath's Theater*, he resurrected one protagonist, David Kepesh (*The Breast* and *The Professor of Desire*) to face the decaying of the flesh and fleshly desires in *The Dying Animal* (2001). Roth has seemed to draw inward and hush his tone. If, in 1974, he asserted to Joyce Carol Oates that "Sheer Playfulness and Deadly Seriousness are my closest friends" ("After Eight" 111), he has seemed more inclined in recent years to converse with the latter than the former. *Everyman*, for example, posits an anonymous narrator who, resisting the signals as others die around him, goes to his own death unprepared. *Exit Ghost* (2007) brings to a close Nathan Zuckerman's long career. Zuckerman first appeared in *My Life as a Man*, served as the protagonist and sometime narrator of the *Zuckerman Bound* tetralogy and *The Counterlife*, wrote sternly to the autobiographer Roth about the fallaciousness of "fact" in *The Facts*, and narrated the American trilogy. In *Exit Ghost*, however, Zuckerman confronts the waning of his most precious capacities—the erotic, the artistic, and memory—and, bitterly, cannot reconcile himself to loss. While *Indignation* (2008) returns to the occasionally nostalgic historical project of the 1990s novels, it begins and ends with the wasteful death of its youthful protagonist. Subsequently, *The Humbling* (2009) follows its aging central figure, an actor, toward his suicide after he loses the "magic" of his acting abilities (1).

As this overview of Roth's career suggests, one can trace significant patterns of continuity and change in his subject matter, thematic pre-occupations, and narrative forms. Although he has consistently written about the individual subject, generally positioned as male, American, and Jewish, his attention has moved outward, from the relatively narrow scope of the Newark Jewish community's place at the midpoint of the century, to a much broader canvas on which to paint the concept of American selfhood. He has tested such selves with traumas large and small, private and public, bodily, familial, and cultural. Roth has taken numerous risks, portraying taboo desires in unfettered language and grotesque bodies, making his argumentative characters at times misguided and unlikable, and appropriating forms omnivorously. He has exploited his own persona, thwarting his readers' desire to distinguish autobiography from invention. He has designed new narrative structures and resisted categorization within the formal literary critical schemes of realism, modernism, and postmodernism.

Roth has not done these things in isolation. His work is deeply embedded in the literary culture of Europe and the United States; indeed, the tendency to look narrowly at Roth through the lens of his position as a Jewish-American writer alone, typical of the early criticism of his work, has been supplanted by a far richer texture of reference and intellectual history. As Catherine Morley has suggested, Roth's work must be seen within a web of "transnational and trans-temporal interconnections." She lists a host of writers, in references both "direct and subtle," who compose Roth's patrimony, running from Sophocles and Virgil through Shakespeare, to Hawthorne, Twain, Melville, Flaubert, Tolstoy, and Gogol in the nineteenth century, to Anglo-American and Continental modernists, including Joyce, Mann, Yeats, Genet, and Beckett (*Quest* 35). And that is not to reckon with Emerson, whom Ross Posnock highlights among Roth's forefathers (*Rude Truth*), nor James, who features prominently in *The Ghost Writer*, nor Kafka, who is an unmistakable source for *The Breast*, nor Ellison, to whose *Invisible Man*, as Tim Parrish demonstrates, *The Human Stain* serves as a sequel ("Becoming Black"), nor Kundera, a friend whom he edited for the series he published with Penguin Books in the 1970s and 1980s on "Writers from the Other Europe," nor Edna O'Brien, whom he quotes in the epigraph to *The Dying Animal*. Then there are the mid-century American Jews, Malamud and Bellow, with whom Roth is often linked, and other white male writers who specialize in contemporary American realism, such as Updike. The list could go on; the point is that Roth's writing is firmly enmeshed in Western reading culture and he has forged enlivening connections with his writing contemporaries.

It is possible that Roth's deep culture has helped to open his eyes to his own historical moment. Whatever the cause, he has throughout his career anticipated some of the most complex contemporary cultural issues, representing them in all their contradictions and ironies. In *Goodbye, Columbus* and *Portnoy's Complaint*, for example, he wrote about the politics of ethnic identity—what does it mean to be a Jew in America?—before the concept of "ethnic identity" had truly been formulated, and he helped instigate the revolution in what we could say about sex. In *The Breast*, he wrote about the instabilities of gender and its relation to the body before "gender" became a notable category in the humanities. In *Portnoy's* therapeutic monologue and *The Breast's* Kafkaesque fable of metamorphosis, Roth broke through conventional narrative formulas in order to find expressive forms within which to embrace these complex new questions. In a sense, Roth has written a bookshelf's worth of the novel of ideas—those fictions that bring their argument about public issues to the forefront—but he has disguised them all as realism, or fabulation, or comic exaggeration, or pseudo-autobiography, or postmodern playfulness. He has done so without dogmatism, posing a range of opposing views with utter conviction but without reconcilement, in novels that are by turns outrageously funny, mordantly ironic, and deeply tragic. "Where, in the end, are we supposed to stand?" asked Robert Alter, of *Operation Shylock* ("The Spritzer" 34). Nowhere and everywhere, Roth answers.

The Counterlife as Exemplary Roth

It is that capaciousness—and, perhaps, slipperiness—that has drawn some readers to Roth. Using *The Counterlife* as an exuberant illustration of the directions the fiction has taken since the mid-1980s, I will highlight just a few interconnected concerns that rise to the surface in much of Roth's writing. Topically, he has pursued questions about ethnicity, race, gender, sex, the mortal body, and the politics of Israel and postimmigrant Jewish-American life. Roth returns almost obsessively to the often contradictory means by which we define, invent, and know ourselves and others, as well as persistently addressing how our various positions in the world shape these processes and how they can be represented in narrative forms. *The Counterlife* not only registers a shift in Roth's storytelling ambitions but also is centrally motivated by the ways in which we make selves by telling stories. With energy and glee, *The Counterlife* exemplifies the "astonishing farce of misperception" (*Pastoral* 35) that, Roth claims, lets us know we are alive. Roth offers in its structure a virtual manual for how to get people wrong, rewriting the fundamental facts of his characters in chapter after chapter, each time leading the reader to conclusions that are shattered as we turn the page. Does Nathan Zuckerman's brother, Henry, die on the operating table, for example, or does Nathan? Is Maria really Henry's illicit Swiss lover, or is she Nathan's English lover? Or Nathan's English wife? Who is Nathan in each case? If we cling to principles of narrative coherence and consistency of character, we are doomed to befuddlement—much as we are, Roth implies, if we innocently trust that we can come to understand ourselves and others ever more clearly.

In Zuckerman, who is narrating—indeed, making up—all of the novel's self-canceling events, Roth illuminates how we go about inventing selves. Because he does so in the figure of a novelist, he emphasizes how the invention of self is both a performance and a textual product, the creation of the words we speak about ourselves and those around us.

As Nathan notes, he "made himself *out* of words" (*Counterlife* 208). Roth's formal invention and ideological challenges reach their height in *The Counterlife*. Each chapter *seems* psychologically realistic, but they are embedded within a metafictional structure that, in erasing each chapter's premise of who the characters are and what happens to them, also erases the possibility that we each possess an essential "self." Before our very eyes in these mordantly comic chapters, the post-modern "subject"—a fleeting construction of words and cultural conditions—replaces the transcendent individuality and wholeness of "self" long promised by liberal humanism. Among the delights of the narrative structure Roth chooses for *The Counterlife* is a paradox: the novel makes a case for representation, for the possibility that words can present the world directly to us, within a reflexive form that is hostile to the principle of representation itself.

In probing the different possibilities for selfhood, *The Counterlife* takes on most of the themes I have identified above. For the first time since a brief episode toward the end of *Portnoy's Complaint*, Roth tests the notion of what it means to be a Jew within a global context. Henry runs to Israel to escape from the chaos of his erotic desires into a fantasy of an idealized, transpersonal, historically situated, "Jewish" self. Roth inquires into whether there even can *be* someone called a "Jew," a kind of Platonic Jew, without context: "A Jew without Jews, without Judaism, without Zionism, without Jewishness, . . . a Jew clearly without a home, just the object itself, like a glass or an apple" (324). Nathan's belief that no strings attach to his self is shaken by the possibility that he is irrevocably defined by his "tribal" position, when he encounters anti-Semitism in England sufficient to cause a rift with his Gentile wife and to make him, for once, *feel* like a Jew, whatever that is. Roth's consideration of ethnicity as a determinant of selfhood is also inextricable in *The Counterlife* from the ways in which Henry and Nathan experience their masculinity, male sexuality, and the flesh itself. Each, in one telling or another, risks his life, fatally going under the knife for the sake of his sexual potency; and each becomes sexually embroiled with a "shiksa" (Gentile woman) as a challenge to the constraints of his Jewish manhood.

All this inwardness, self-exploration, even self-laceration may strike some readers as entirely too much navel-gazing on Roth's part, despite his projection of his concerns into fictional characters. Indeed, since fairly early in his career, he has been accused of narcissism, most notoriously in Irving Howe's 1972 "reconsideration" of Roth's work. Howe accused Roth of a "thin personal culture," finding his imagination unnourished by a tradition (73), and of not taking "pleasure in discovering the world's body," including the "varieties of social experience" (69).

A dozen years later, Joseph Epstein chimed in: Roth lacked "a generous spirit" (62), he claimed, and, instead, possessed "an implacable confidence in the significance of [his] own splendid self" (64). Yet these judgments seem narrowly conceived. Roth is in fact deeply nourished by his cultural traditions—both literary and sociocultural—and, while he shows little interest in the natural surfaces of "the world's body," he more than makes up for that deficit by his devotion to the social and psychological dimensions of life in the world. Arguably, Roth is not obsessed with himself so much as willing to cannibalize his perceptions of himself in order to explore the way selves work in the world. His primary concern with how consciousness seeks to make sense of that process is the motive for his narratives and explains why getting people wrong is still so satisfying, since it is the getting that matters in the end more than the right or wrong.

Roth's devotion to the epistemological project of knowing selves and others also explains why he resists singular identification with realism or postmodernism. His exploration of what consciousness apprehends is as much troubled as animated by the contradiction between the premises of realism, according to which reality is verifiably "out there" and representable in language, and those of postmodernism, according to which language is all the reality we have. David Brauner succinctly lays out Roth's range as a writer who "combine[s] characteristics conventionally associated with postmodernist writing (metafictionality, self-reflexivity, intertextuality, plurality, the indeterminacy and instability of both text and self) with many of the attributes identified with realist fiction (an investment in the psychology of character, a commitment to the ideals of liberal humanism, an assertion of the existence of a socio-historical reality external to, and independent of, the text)" (51). Roth's generic experiments have roved between these poles throughout his career. Each mode provides a way of asking central questions about the self: how are we situated in the world and time? How can we know? Are we in control? And can we feel at home in our place or our very skins? Roth seems less interested in trying to reconcile these ideological and narrative modes, however, than in showing how they can at once inhabit the same spaces comfortably and challenge each other.

Consider again *The Counterlife* as a prototype for how Roth will develop these questions in the novels that focus overtly on America, three of which are under discussion in this volume. The title names the fundamental postmodern premise that one can invent multiple selves textually and performatively, within one's language. By implication, one freely constructs selves unmoored from the history of an organism or a tribe or a set of social relations or material circumstances. Zuckerman puts the case baldly: "If there even *is* a natural being, an irreducible

self, it is rather small . . . and may even be the root of all impersonation
. . . in the absence of a self, one impersonates selves" (320). The
materiality of the body in history, however, defeats the utter freedom
of impersonation that Zuckerman idealizes. The Jewish male body,
marked by circumcision, illustrates how the "pastoral," a "womb-dream
of life in the beautiful state of innocent prehistory" (323), is impossible:
the ritual practiced on the body insists that the infant male participate
in Jewish history. Zuckerman must conclude that he is inescapably
a Jew; he cannot avoid being created by conditions outside himself.
That recognition confirms Zuckerman's rejection, as a writer, of the
pastoral genre, which "make[s] readers happy, with everything cozy
and strifeless, and desire simply fulfilled" (317). That recognition also
suggests the power of realism—which insists on the materiality and
historicity of the real—as a mode of knowing and telling.

This concluding moment in *The Counterlife* anticipates the fiction
of the mid-1990s and beyond, which retains traces of postmodernism
in its indeterminate subjects and narrative strategies but also returns
to realism's stance of direct reference to the world. Beginning with
Operation Shylock, Roth increasingly pits his characters—both protagonists and narrators—against the urgencies of history and the material
world. Roth's characters often begin where Zuckerman placed his bets
in *The Counterlife*, with the assumption that an autonomous but not
irreducible self exists, only to be thrown when they find their illusion of
autonomy under assault from the world about them. *Operation Shylock*,
with its doubling, unreadable characters, parodic impersonations, and
paranoid plots, puts the case in terms of "the uncontrollability of real
things" (237), a phrase Roth quotes from Carl Jung and uses to title a
chapter. But whereas the antic inventiveness of Roth's "real things"
serves his bewildering purposes in this novel—where we are tested to
discern "fact" from "fiction," one Philip Roth from another, political
intrigue from fantasy—real things become increasingly vivid and
grounded in the fiction that follows. Like the shaving mug belonging
to his grandfather that Roth longs to have as his father's legacy in the
memoir *Patrimony*, or the cardboard box of Sabbath's dead brother's
personal effects in *Sabbath's Theater*, the simple things and events of
the world are shatteringly replete with meaning in Roth's work from
the 1990s onward. Such things remind us that the seemingly distant
happenings of the wider world are inextricable from who we are.

Roth's America

That the public is the private becomes a central preoccupation in the
"American" novels that are the focus of this volume. Four novels that
follow *Sabbath's Theater—American Pastoral, I Married a Communist,*

The Human Stain, and *The Plot Against America*—register Roth's almost unbroken concentration on significant periods in American history and culture, ranging from the 1940s to the 1990s, interrupted only by the publication of *The Dying Animal* and *Shop Talk* in 2001. Not only do these novels explore in new ways all of the main concerns to which Roth devotes his previous fiction, but they do so within the context of his intimacy with the events and people of the later twentieth century in the United States, and also with an intense sense of place, most often the Newark, New Jersey of Roth's youth. Roth provides a rich texture of real things, drawing on the sensual detail of his memory to celebrate what Catherine Morley has called "the strange beauty of the banal" (*Quest* 12). He writes, for example, in loving specificity about the Newark glove trade in *American Pastoral*; about Coleman Silk's boxing training with Doc Chizner at the Newark Boys Club in *The Human Stain*; about the minerals that "fluoresce" (201) at Tommy's rock dump in Zinc Town in *I Married a Communist*; and about young "Philip"'s prized stamp collection in *The Plot Against America*. When Roth shows the interpenetration of the material world with the self in time, the fiction reveals the common American past in the smallest of things. In a 1989 profile of his friend the artist Philip Guston, Roth extols their "shared delight in what Guston called 'crapola,' starting with billboards, garages, diners, burger joints, junk shops, auto body shops" (*Shop Talk* 135); such "crapola" makes the fiction come alive to document its times. As Zuckerman thinks in *I Married a Communist*, "You flood into history and history floods into you" (39).

Clearly, the history that fascinates Roth is American history from about the time of his birth onward. Although Roth's preoccupation with American culture as such emerged most explicitly in the 1990s, he has always been writing about the United States and what it means to be an American. Even as early as 1960, Roth took up the question when he published the essay "Writing American Fiction," claiming that the contemporary "American reality" was so outlandish that it was an "embarrassment to one's own meager imagination" (*Reading Myself* 176). More to the point, he has insisted that he thinks of himself as an American first and a Jew second. Part of the genius of his work lies in the manifold ways he has exposed those identifying categories, and others, as at once indeterminate and contingent, and inextricably entwined.

Roth has done so especially by returning to the metaphor of the *pastoral* that he introduced in *The Counterlife*. The pastoral offers Roth a unique path into American ideology. The metaphor embraces both the literary iconography of natural harmony, going back to the ancient world, and its transformation, in the United States, into an image of an

Edenic New World of social, political, and spiritual rebirth. Implicit in the image is the burden of choice: one may choose to retain innocence or fall from it. The pastoral appears overtly in *Operation Shylock*, when a Palestinian cynically characterizes the post-Holocaust world of the Jews in America as "The pastoralization of the ghetto" (132), charging that American Jews have been willfully deluded by the possibilities for American bounty and cultural assimilation. A contrastingly nostalgic reference appears in Sabbath's memory of his mother during his childhood, who "hopped and darted to and fro like a bird in a berry bush . . . no less naturally than she dusted, ironed, mended, polished, and sewed" (*Sabbath's Theater* 13–14). That sense of innocent joy in orderly American domesticity marks the pastoral in the novel Roth titled by that name and is figured especially in Swede Levov's fantasy of being a new Johnny Appleseed. What happens to characters who cling to the dream of the pastoral structures each of the three novels addressed in this volume. The American trilogy and *The Plot Against America* all offer antipastoral critiques of American innocence, what David Brauner calls "deconstruction[s] of the Utopian dreams and rituals of purification" (*Philip Roth* 8) typifying the characters' illusions of autonomy. Those rituals, and their failures, serve as the engine of narrative in these novels.

Readers will observe that this volume does not treat *I Married a Communist*, the middle novel of the trilogy. While it would have been an obvious choice to pursue the symmetry provided by the trilogy, I have chosen instead to place *American Pastoral* and *The Human Stain* in conversation with *The Plot Against America*. This seemed important because posing a counterfactual history against the representation of "real" histories starkly illuminates the dreams and nightmares of American culture as Roth has perceived them. Each novel attests to how history is really about what happens to the ordinary man or woman. When the "Herman Roth" of *The Plot Against America*, for example, asserts that "'History is everything that happens everywhere'" (180), Roth can elicit many painful ironies as he shows history happening, brutally, right in the "Roth" household.

At the same time that Roth provides the rich flavor of the times in the things and events of his novels, they remain devoted to two other aims: to uncover the processes of history that make selves and to expose the problems of telling that history. *The Plot Against America* expresses the former most clearly. Philip notes how "the relentless unforeseen was what we schoolchildren studied as 'History,' harmless history, where everything unexpected in its own time is chronicled on the page as inevitable"; hindsight only disguises the "terror of the unforeseen" that is felt as it is happening (113–14). To capture the terror of the unforeseen, Roth repeatedly questions within his storytelling strategies how knowledge is linked with power. The uncontrollability of real things matters most because the real cannot be foreseen; Roth thus uses his narrators to emphasize that the problem of knowing the stories they want to tell parallels their actors' inability to govern events. Zuckerman meditates on his blindness in telling the stories of Swede Levov and Coleman Silk, for instance, and in *The Human Stain* freely admits that he must make things up. Likewise, Roth narrates *The Plot Against America* from the memories of a child who cannot see beyond the anxieties and desires of his immature perspective. These unstable narrators, traces of Roth's earlier generic experiments in postmodernism, enable him to present realistic "histories" even as he undercuts the stability of what we can pretend to know about—or control in—our own histories.

The scholars who have generously contributed to this volume are among those who have been most centrally engaged in rethinking Roth's *oeuvre*. Picking up on many of the thematic and formal threads I have summarized here, they continue to expose the complexities, subtleties, and ambiguities that make Roth's fiction among the best that has been produced in the United States since the late 1950s. Our hope is that the reader will enjoy participating in this further deepening and widening of the understanding of recent American fiction. Perhaps, too, readers will be inspired to turn back to some of Roth's earlier work to see where this view of Philip Roth's America began, in all its density of insight.

Part I

American Pastoral

Introduction

American Pastoral is the story of two men. Foremost, Roth tells the tale of Seymour "Swede" Levov, whose beautiful, exemplary life unravels tragically through the force of history and his own good faith. The Swede signifies for Roth all the light and hope of the Jewish postimmigrant generation in the United States at the middle of the twentieth century: "[H]e loved America. Loved being an *American*" (*Pastoral* 206). The Swede believes in America because it promises individuality freed from the past and a will to choose. It promises, too, that hard work, determination, and material prosperity will bring him a fresh and vital identity in the world—and that, once fulfilled, these promises will make him an American who happens only incidentally to be a Jew. The Swede follows the command captured in the title of Johnny Mercer's popular song of the 1940s, "Dream," four lines of which Roth quotes in the novel's epigraph. Roth has questioned the dream before, however. Late in *Sabbath's Theater*, for example, Mickey Sabbath wraps himself in an American flag as a gesture of defiance and grief. Yet the Swede lacks Sabbath's saving irony when he, too, if metaphorically, drapes himself in the American flag. It is ripped away when the Swede faces the violence underlying the social, economic, and cultural system to which he has innocently dedicated himself, a violence that exists not just on the streets of American society in the late 1960s but also buried within his family and the aspirations on which he has built his home and selfhood.

American Pastoral is secondarily the story of Nathan Zuckerman, the writer who yearns to explain how a man so blessed with good fortune could have had such bad luck. In trying to make sense of Seymour Levov's life, Zuckerman runs up against the mystery of other people— how it is impossible to know, let alone tell, the truth, because others' lives and motivations remain stubbornly inexplicable. So he is left to invent a plausible tale. Through Zuckerman and his storytelling, Roth thus opens up essential questions not just about the consequences of intransigent American ideologies but also about the meaning of history. "History," of course, has a peculiarly double sense: it is both what happens and the story we tell about what happens. Roth at once exposes the gap that opens up between these two meanings and, in the narrating figure of Zuckerman, attempts to bridge it, as we all do, through imagination, detective work, and the possibilities alive in the words we speak.

Critics have paid considerable attention to these features of *American Pastoral*. Roth's readers have been alert to the complexities and contradictions in what he has to say about America, giving special attention to two framing metaphors Roth invokes in the title and section titles. The first is the homegrown metaphor of the American dream. At least since F. Scott Fitzgerald's *Great Gatsby* appeared in 1925, the image of the American dream has expressed the aspirations of American citizens seeking to better their lives through material success (see MacArthur; Schur; and Stanley). The second is the metaphor of the American Eden, the pastoral image preceding the paradise lost (see Brauner; McDonald; Morley, *Quest*; and Posnock, *Rude Truth*). With its ancient lineage, the metaphor arrived on the shores of the New World to describe the reborn identity of its population of European immigrants and pioneers. This was the American Adam, as R. W. B. Lewis famously described the classic figure of nineteenth-century fiction—not unlike the Swede's Johnny Appleseed fantasy. Roth, some argue, sees the 1960s as a turning point in American history and myth, and thus he tempts the Swede to fall from innocence, like the original Adam, so as to explode the dream in radical violence.

The criticism on *American Pastoral* falls roughly into two other thematic categories. Beginning with Roth's critique of American culture, critics have explored how the novel represents the individual's capacity to remake a self. Ethnic identity may constrain the exercise of such freedom, and for Roth's Jews, like Seymour Levov, the costs of pursuing the assimilative ideal—to invent and inhabit a wholly "American" identity—may include inauthenticity, exile, the disintegration of the home, and a void of self (see Hogan; Parrish, "End of Identity" and "Ethnic Identity"; Royal, "Fictional Realms"; Rubin-Dorsky; and Schur). Other critics, inquiring into the narrative tasks of both Roth and Zuckerman, attend particularly to the storyteller's challenge to represent the world, its people, and their past in discourse stripped of fictionalizing tendencies (see Bernstein; Johnson; Parrish, "End of Identity"; and Royal, "Fictional Realms").

The three chapters that follow offer fresh angles of approach to these concerns. For David Brauner the crucial insight is that, contrary to most readings of *American Pastoral*, the novel is less about the 1960s than about the web of necessity and consequence woven across 60 years of American history. Brauner demonstrates that the novel does not simply tell an individual's history; instead, it presents a meditation on historiography, on the problems of constructing a coherent story of the past, and on history as an idea. Noting how Roth's characters allegorize varied philosophies of history—alternately as the unknown, as a deterministic force, and as a static condition—Brauner argues that the novel aims to undermine reductive views of history and human agency.

Andrew Gordon surveys the contradictions implicit in Roth's American theme, especially his simultaneous embrace and rejection of the pastoral ideal. Tracing the utopian idea of the pastoral back to its classical roots, to its rebirth in Emerson's optimism, and to Roth's exploration of the idea in *The Counterlife*, Gordon brings to the surface the contrary darkness lurking in the image of the American dream. Roth, Gordon argues, at once adheres to a utopian dream and undermines the untenable fantasy of upward mobility and rational action inherent in such utopianism.

Jennifer Glaser considers the double-edged fantasy in more overtly Freudian terms, examining how the domestic ideal the Swede pursues disguises the terrors at the heart of American national identity and history. Focusing especially on the historical repression of ethnic and racial difference, figured in the Swede's disavowal of his Jewish past, Glaser explores how the uncanny erupts in *American Pastoral* into disorder within the domestic sphere—literally within the Swede's iconic house in the country, and figuratively within the family he, as a "New Jew," has constructed around him.

These chapters intersect fruitfully at a number of points. All three address the ways in which *American Pastoral* is deeply embedded in American history, and in literary history in general. Both Gordon and Brauner see the novel's version of the 1960s in relation to twentieth-century American history, running from the 1940s onward. Glaser takes a psychoanalytic view of the incursions of the past into the present in both individual consciousness and the "unconscious" of a culture, expressed in its ideology. Gordon and Glaser, who both nod to *Gatsby*'s influence on Roth, identify the home as the poignantly contested space that is, for the likes of the Levovs, pastoral no more. And Brauner, like Glaser, explores the novel's insight into how we know and tell the past, or fail to do so. Each chapter uncovers Roth's multiplicity of vision, including his contradictions and ambivalences, to mark the fullness of his portrait of the pastoral illusion that was America.

CHAPTER 2

"What was not supposed to happen had happened and what was supposed to happen had not happened": Subverting History in *American Pastoral*

David Brauner

Critical Reception

American Pastoral is one of Philip Roth's most feted novels. Winner of the Pulitzer Prize for fiction in 1998, a year after its publication, more recently the novel came fifth in the *New York Times* list of the "Best American Fiction of the Last 25 Years," compiled in 2006 on the basis of responses from "prominent writers, critics, editors and other literary sages," who were asked to nominate "the single best work of American fiction" published during that period (Scott 17). It is also one of Roth's most controversial books, interpreted by some critics as a repudiation of his earlier work and a damning indictment of the so-called permissive society, but read by others as a restatement of previous convictions and a stout defense of liberal values (for a useful summary of the ways in which the novel polarized reviewers along political lines, see Tanenbaum 42–3). Critical responses to the novel's three central characters—the narrator, Nathan Zuckerman; the protagonist, Seymour "The Swede" Levov; and his daughter, Meredith "Merry" Levov—and to the relationship between them have similarly been polarized. Most critics follow Timothy Parrish ("End of Identity"), Derek Parker Royal ("Pastoral Dreams"), and Debra Shostak (246) in emphasizing the parallels between Zuckerman and Seymour, an identification that Ross Posnock sees as "vitiating Roth's portrayal of the sixties" (*Rude Truth* 103), but for others Seymour is less Zuckerman's alter ego than his antithesis, whom he finally condemns for his naivety and complacency (Brauner 160–72). Likewise, many critics have alleged that Zuckerman (and, by extension, Roth) represents Merry reductively as what Robert Boyers calls a "cartoon of adolescent rebellion" (39) and Mark Shechner, similarly, a "cartoon insurrectionist" (*Up Society's Ass* 159; see also Neelakantan "Monster" 58 and Tanenbaum 45), but for Aliki Varvogli "the narrative structure aligns Zuckerman with Merry and not with the Swede" (109) and Catherine Morley agrees, suggesting that "Merry's story . . . represents a bid for freedom and self-expression on the part of both the writer and the female protagonist" (*Quest* 102).

On one point almost all critics are unanimous, however: *American Pastoral* is about a particular decade in U.S. history—the 1960s. If Sandra Kumamoto Stanley and Brian McDonald situate the novel in the Adamic tradition of the classic American pastoral, while Monika Hogan and Richard Schur see it as a parable about the struggle of immigrant Jews to become fully assimilated Americans, they converge in their view that, as McDonald puts it, *American Pastoral* "focus[es] on the tumultuous historical events of the sixties" (30) and, as Schur claims, that it "offers a seemingly realistic account of the 1960s" (19). Although there is heated debate about its political perspective and a divergence between those who, like Kathleen MacArthur, argue that the novel is concerned primarily with "the trauma of the Kennedy assassination and the ensuing cultural turmoil" (16) and those, such as Todd Gitlin, who view it as a response to the protests against the Vietnam War (193–203), there is a wide consensus that at the heart of the novel is a reconsideration of the sixties. However, in this chapter I want to contest this consensus, first, by suggesting that there are compelling arguments for situating the novel in a number of different historical contexts, and, second, by proposing that *American Pastoral* is preoccupied with history as an abstraction, and with the problems of historiography, as much as with a particular historical period.

Origins of *American Pastoral*

The question that follows the assumption that *American Pastoral* is about the 1960s, for many commentators, is why, at this particular juncture in his career, in the 1990s, had Roth chosen to return to the era which had brought him fame and notoriety as the author of *Portnoy's Complaint* (1969)? Debra Shostak explicitly invokes this conjunction when she suggests that *American Pastoral* "by implication offers a much-delayed critique of *Portnoy's Complaint*, but without urging readers to condemn the impulse toward freedom and understanding represented by the earlier novel's breakthrough into speaking the unspeakable" (5). Mark Shechner similarly sees the novel as in part "a delayed response to the sixties" (*Up Society's Ass* 162). Characteristically, Roth had his own explanation for what Shostak and Shechner term this "delay." In a series of interviews, he presented *American Pastoral* as the first of an "American trilogy" of novels that also comprises *I Married a Communist* (1998) and *The Human Stain* (2000; see, for example, "Zuckerman's Alter Brain"). Although these novels have no common characters apart from Nathan Zuckerman, who narrates all of them, Roth suggests that they form a trilogy on the basis that each is framed by a moment of historical crisis in postwar American history: *The Human Stain* by the attempted impeachment of Bill Clinton; *I Married a Communist* by the anti-Communist witch-hunts of the House Un-American Activities Committee; and *American Pastoral* by the Vietnam War. Many critics have followed Roth's lead and written about *American Pastoral* as part of the American trilogy (see Royal "Pastoral Dreams"; Brauner; Morley *Quest*).

However, it is equally legitimate to read the novel not as the start of a series of 1990s novels but as a sequel, or companion-piece, to a series of novels that Roth published in the 1970s, at the time when he first began working on the manuscript that was eventually to become *American Pastoral*. In his initial review of the novel Mark Shechner speculated that perhaps Roth "had drafted parts of *American Pastoral* a good many years earlier" (*Up Society's Ass* 162) and in her book *Philip Roth—Countertexts, Counterlives* (2004) Debra Shostak confirmed that Roth had indeed begun work on the novel in 1972, rejecting a series of alternative titles for it, including "The Diary of Anne Frank's Contemporary," "A Businessman's Sorrow (Anne Frank in America)," "Ordinary Dreams," and "How the Other Half Lives," before finally settling on *American Pastoral* (124). The subtitle of the second of these anticipates Roth's 1979 novel *The Ghost Writer*, where Nathan Zuckerman imagines a counterlife for Anne, in which she survives the war and lives a secret existence in America as Amy Bellette. However, the first title also finds its way into another of Roth's 1970s novels. In *My Life as a Man* (1974), the protagonist author, Peter Tarnopol, summarizes the events of one of his short stories, titled "The Diary of Anne Frank's Contemporary," in which a young American boy, disoriented by his family's change of address, fears that his mother has been captured by invading Nazis. Later, he realizes with relief that "we are Jews who live in the haven of Westchester County, rather than in our ravaged, ancestral, Jew-hating Europe" (*My Life as a Man* 245).

In this context, the novel can be seen as engaging, thematically, with some of the same territory as *The Great American Novel* (1973) and as presenting, in formal terms, some of the problems that also plagued the composition of *My Life as a Man*. Sandra Kumamoto Stanley points out that, in an interview about *The Great American Novel*, Roth "describes the 1960s as a 'demythologizing decade' in which 'the very nature of American things yielded and collapsed overnight,'" language which certainly seems to prefigure *American Pastoral* on a number of different levels (1). The connections between *American Pastoral* and *My Life as a Man* are manifold: both books had a long and difficult gestation, in which Roth's problems with point of view and authorial distance manifested themselves in a series of drafts that moved from the first person to the third and back again (see Shostak 241). Whereas in *My Life as a Man* this struggle to reconcile a subjective, intimate viewpoint with a more objective, distanced perspective mani- fested itself in a complex structure that shifted, and blurred the bound- aries, between first- and third-person narration (see Brauner 51–63), in *American Pastoral* Zuckerman's first-person narrative collapses into the third-person narrative of Seymour Levov's life and is absorbed by it.

American Pastoral as Historical Novel

In historical terms, too, *American Pastoral* can be seen as a novel as much about the perils of what, in *My Life as a Man*, Roth described as being "Serious in the Fifties" (a subject that Roth returned to more recently in *Indignation* [2008]) as about the pitfalls of 1960s permissive- ness. At one point, Zuckerman describes Seymour as "someone who excitedly foresaw, in perfect detail, the outcome of his story . . . looking ahead into responsible manhood with the longing of a kid gazing into a candy-store window" (*Pastoral* 192). The poignancy of this passage resides not just in the fact that the ironically named Seymour ("see- more") in fact fails absolutely to envisage the catastrophe that ensues when he does become a responsible husband and father, but also in the yearning with which he anticipates not the adolescent transgression that the delights of the candy-store might conventionally symbolize but rather its antithesis: "responsible manhood." As Seymour's brother, Jerry, notes, with characteristic acerbity, Seymour is "[f]atally attracted to responsibility" (72), possessed of what Zuckerman calls a "strange spiritual desire to be a bulwark of duty," infatuated by what—in another context—Zuckerman calls "the stupendous satisfactions of being a dependable person" (329).

If, as I have been suggesting, *American Pastoral* is as much a product of the 1970s as the 1990s, and as interested in the sensibility of a genera- tion of Jews who became men in the 1950s as in that of their children who grew up in the following decade, it should also be remembered that the novel in fact begins by juxtaposing two other decades of American history: the 1940s and the 1980s. The opening pages of the novel make quite clear that the quasi-deification of Seymour "The Swede" Levov by the Jewish community of Weequahic, New Jersey, is partly a response to the historical circumstances in which he grew up. Prodigious though his athleticism is (he excels at all three of the premier American sports, football, baseball, and basketball), he is feted as much for what he symbolizes as for his feats on the sports field. As Zuckerman himself puts it: "The elevation of Swede Levov into the household Apollo of the Weequahic Jews can best be explained, I think, by the war against the Germans and the Japanese and the fears that it fostered" (4). In other words, Seymour distracts his elders from their anxieties about the fate of those "beloved sons" who were "far away facing death" (80) and perhaps also, as Debra Shostak suggests, of the European Jews:

> Although it remains unspoken by Nathan, the implication that hovers behind this urge to forget is that the Swede gives the American Jews license to repress their knowledge of what was happening to the European Jews. If they can forget themselves as Jews, they can forget the image of the docile, feminized Jewish man who, in failing to resist gentile oppression, troubles their own self-image. (101)

For Shostak, then, the Swede becomes a paradigm of the athletic, all-American male—the perfect antidote for the guilt and shame associated with the Jewish victims of the Holocaust, who are at once far removed from, and at the same time intimately connected, with the American Jews of Weequahic. Whether Shostak is right, or whether, as Monika Hogan argues, the Swede embodies not the healthy, whole, virile Gentile, male body, but its antithesis—what she calls, after Anne Cheng, the "racial-ethnic-hypochondriac[al body]" (Hogan 2)—Zuckerman insistently juxtaposes Seymour's achievements with descriptions of wartime engagements. Sometimes he implies a connection between the two: "Marines of the Sixth Division captured Sugar Loaf Hill, May 14, 1945—three more doubles for the Swede in a winning game against East Side—maybe the worst, most savage single day of fighting in marine history" (*Pastoral* 209). At other times he explicitly makes that connection:

> He was fettered to history, an *instrument* of history, esteemed with a passion that might never have been if he'd broken the Weequahic basketball record . . . on a day other than the sad, sad day in 1943 when fifty-eight Flying Fortresses were shot down by Luftwaffe fighter planes. (5–6)

In each case he invokes "history" by name.

Zuckerman also self-consciously enlists "history" at the start of the speech that, like the eulogy to Henry Zuckerman that begins *The Counterlife* (1987), he includes in the novel but never actually delivers at the occasion for which it was composed (in this case his forty-fifth high school reunion). He refers to the immediate postwar era as "the greatest moment of collective inebriation in American history" (40), a time at which "the clock of history [was] reset and a whole people's aims limited no longer by the past" (41). There is of course an implicit warning in Zuckerman's diction that this euphoria will be short-lived— "inebriation" is invariably followed by a hangover and the reference to clocks being reset has ominous connotations of the "year zero" concept endorsed by the architects of the French Revolution and the Khmer Rouge regime in Cambodia. Moreover, it immediately follows Zuckerman's dinner with Seymour—initiated by Seymour, who writes to his brother's former classmate to ask for help in writing a memoir about his father—that takes place during the 1980s, at which Seymour bemoans the decline of Newark from its zenith in the 1940s as " 'the city where they manufactured everything' " to its current nadir as " 'the car-theft capital of the world' " (24). Seymour's nostalgia for the golden age of Newark and dismay at its decline itself echoes—but in terms of the structure of the novel anticipates—the views of his father, Lou Levov, on the fate of the city, which he expresses at some length at the dinner party held in 1973 with which the novel concludes.

This final section, "Paradise Lost" (alluding, like the first two sections, "Paradise Remembered" and "The Fall," to Milton's epic poem and to its main source, Genesis) also begins by locating itself in relation to a pivotal episode in American history: "It was the summer of the Watergate hearings" (285). In *Our Gang* (1971), Roth's fantastical satire on Richard Nixon that preceded by two years the Watergate scandal and the president's resignation that it precipitated, Nixon, having been assassinated, takes to his comeback trail in Hell, running for the post of chief devil. In this sense, the opening of "Paradise Lost" returns us to the 1970s not only in terms of the larger national history, but also in terms of Roth's career. Just as Nixon is depicted in *Our Gang* as a Satanic figure, so in *American Pastoral* he is cast in the role of the serpent in the garden: the agent of corruption who despoils the new Eden of America. Reaching for a historical rather than allegorical frame of reference, Lou Levov compares him to Hitler, calling him a " 'real fascist' " who " 'would take this country and make Nazi Germany out of it' " if allowed to proceed unchallenged (287). Later, Lou's rhetoric takes an apocalyptic turn as he reflects on all that he has witnessed in the postwar era: " 'I sometimes think that more has changed since 1945 than in all the years of history there have ever been. I don't know what to make of the end of so many things'" (365). In his essay, "Monster in Newark: Philip Roth's Apocalypse in *American Pastoral*," G. Neelakantan identifies a "stridently apocalyptic" tone running through the novel (56). This seems to me to be overstating the case but certainly there is in Lou's diction ("the end of so many things") an eschatological inflection that is echoed in the mocking, nihilistic laughter of Marcia Umanoff that concludes the book. There is also, in Lou's musing on the radical acceleration of history in the postwar era, an implicit echo of Zuckerman's paradoxical statement, earlier in the novel, that history is "a very sudden thing" (87). In the rest of this chapter I want to focus on these aspects of history in *American Pastoral*: history, that is to say, not as the events of a particular period or the narrative account of an era but as a more abstract concept, an idea, an ideology. In doing so, I will also suggest that several characters in the novel may be seen as allegorizing different facets of history: Seymour representing history as an unknown and unknowable force, Merry representing history as determinism, and William Orcutt III, a neighbor of the Levovs, representing history as stasis.

History as Idea

Toward the end of *American Pastoral*, there is a detailed description of the food and drink that has been laid on for the Levovs' dinner party, at which the guests argue over Watergate and the other scandal of the time, the pornographic film *Deep Throat*, oblivious of the revelations with which Seymour is struggling to come to terms, after his meeting earlier in the day with Merry: that Merry has not only been responsible for the bombing of the Old Rimrock post office that had killed a local doctor but also for subsequent acts of terrorism that had resulted in three further fatalities; that Merry had been sheltered by her former speech therapist, Sheila Salzman (with whom Seymour had enjoyed a brief affair in the aftermath of Merry's flight from home), for several days after the Old Rimrock bombing; that Merry had been raped on several occasions during her years on the run; and that she has now become a Jain, living a life of extreme asceticism and self-denial behind a veil designed to ensure that she does no harm to airborne micro-organisms with her breath. During the course of the evening, Seymour makes a further discovery: that his wife, Dawn, is having an affair with Bill Orcutt, their next-door neighbor. Earlier in the evening, inadvertently referring to the centerpiece of the dinner as "Merry's big beefsteak tomatoes" (292)—rather than Dawn's, as he had intended to—Seymour had broken the tacit agreement not to speak of his disgraced fugitive daughter. However, the "large platters of the beefsteak tomatoes" that adorn the dinner table are not the only reminder of the elephant in the room; there are also "the half a dozen bottles of the Swede's best Pommard" that "he had laid down for drinking in 1973" (363). Earlier in the evening when Seymour had gone down to the cellar to retrieve the wine

> he had found 1/3/68 inscribed, in his handwriting, in the spiral notebook he used for recording the details of each new purchase . . . "1/3/68" he had written, with no idea that on 2/3/68 his daughter would go ahead and outrage all of America. (364)

This is a significant episode on a number of levels. First, the wine here can be read as a metaphor for the novel itself: like the Pommard, *American Pastoral* was "laid down" for many years before being disinterred, having matured in the intervening years. Second, it represents the impact that Merry's bomb and subsequent flight have had on Seymour: the wine was acquired, stored, and logged at a time of optimism, when Seymour was able to anticipate enjoying it. The very fact of it being "laid down" for drinking in five-years' time bespeaks a certain confidence, a faith in the future that is belied utterly by the events that follow, so that Seymour's rediscovery of the bottles becomes an act of mourning for this lost time of innocence, the time before what the novel itself calls "The Fall." Finally, the fact that Seymour entered the wines in his log book exactly one month before the bombing graphically demonstrates that history is indeed a "very sudden thing," that you can never be prepared for the moment when, as Zuckerman puts it, "the strong arm of the unforeseen comes crashing down on your head" (36). That word "unforeseen" is a key term in thinking about history in *American Pastoral*. On the one hand, it seems to connote the opposite of what is conventionally understood by the word "history": because, by its very nature, history is always written retrospectively, it can never be surprising, its outcome will always be foreseen. On the other hand, if history is viewed from the other end of the process—as events that will become history—then it is always likely to be unforeseen, since it is often the most startling events that are accorded the greatest prominence in history.

It is this paradox that Zuckerman is alluding to when he announces, in the wake of Merry's bombing, that:

> [h]istory, American history, the stuff you read about in books . . . had made its way out to tranquil, untrafficked Old Rimrock . . . and, improbably, with all its predictable unforeseenness, broke

helter-skelter into the orderly household of the Seymour Levovs
and left the place in a shambles. (87)

Merry's bombing is both "the stuff you read about in books," part of a
national historical narrative that seems inevitable with the benefit of
hindsight, and also a bolt from the blue that shatters the domestic
harmony of the Levovs. The oxymoron "predictable unforeseenness"
echoes one of the novel's epigraphs, taken from a William Carlos
Williams poem: "the rare occurrence of the expected . . ." ("At Kenneth
Burke's Place," Williams 107). If, as Williams counterintuitively suggests, the things that we expect to happen don't usually happen, then
the corollary must be that most things that happen are unexpected.
In this sense, Merry's bombing is paradoxically both predictable and
startling.

Most critics of the novel have argued that Roth's vision of history in
American Pastoral is essentially deterministic. Debra Shostak argues
that "history . . . [is] the principle that shapes self and other and that
compels storytelling" in his fiction of the 1990s (233); Derek Royal
suggests that in the American trilogy Roth "write[s] the individual
subject into the fabric of history, and in doing so he illustrates that
identity is not only a product of, but also a hostage to, the many social,
political, and cultural forces that surround it" ("Pastoral Dreams" 186);
and Mark Shechner observes that "in Roth's fictional world this natural
all-American guy [Seymour] doesn't stand a chance; he will have to
be inducted into history" (*Up Society's Ass* 104). Certainly, this is the
line taken by the various iconoclasts who populate the novel. From
Rita Cohen, Merry's self-proclaimed disciple and possible lover, who
justifies her blend of extortion, sexual taunting, and political diatribes
by insisting on her aim to " 'introduce [Seymour] to reality' " (*Pastoral*
143); to Jerry Levov, who tells Zuckerman that Seymour " 'took the kid
[Merry] out of real time and she put him right back in' " (68); to Marcia
Umanoff, another guest at the 1970s dinner party, who patronizes Lou
Levov by telling him how " 'delightful' " she finds his " 'delusions' " (354);
to Merry herself, who rehearses the mantra that " 'everything is political' " and berates her father for caring only about " 'life out here in little
Rimrock' " (105); to all, there is a sense that the Levovs, father and son,
inhabit an ahistorical, utopian dreamworld—" 'glove heaven' " (277),
as Jerry puts it—from which they are destined to be ejected by the
irresistible force of history.

The structure of the novel also ostensibly supports this deterministic
view of history: because Zuckerman (like the reader) first hears from
Jerry about Seymour's death from cancer, and about the bomb that had
imbued his family with "notorious significance" (85), before he decides

to recreate imaginatively the life that preceded it, there is a sense of teleological inevitability about the narrative that follows. Yet near the end of the novel Zuckerman observes that Seymour's fate, far from being predictable, is the product of "deviancy": "Improbably, what was not supposed to happen had happened and what was supposed to happen had not happened" (422). The question of what causes Seymour's life to deviate from the path that it was "supposed" to follow is at the heart of the book.

History, Allegory, Fiction

American Pastoral is the most interrogative of Roth's novels: almost every page of the novel contains a question and on many the most frequent form of punctuation is the question mark. The novel ends with two rhetorical questions—"And what is wrong with their life? What on earth is less reprehensible than the life of the Levovs?" (423)— but the novel's "central mystery: how did Merry get to be who she is?" has no obvious answer. Seymour's compulsive, tautological reframing of the question—"What *is* the grudge? What *is* the grievance?"; What then was the wound? What could have wounded Merry?" (138, 92)— reveals both his bewilderment and his belief that there must be some originary cause for Merry's behavior.

Seymour advances two theories for Merry's radical turn, both of which are based on the fashionable, Freudian notion of a traumatic event that is repressed as a psychological defense mechanism. At one point in the novel Seymour recalls Merry witnessing, at the age of 11, the self-immolation of Buddhist monks protesting against the corrupt regime of South Vietnamese president Diem and becomes convinced that "he has unearthed the reason for what happened" (152). However, he had earlier cited another incident from Merry's eleventh year as the moment of trauma: an episode in which his daughter, suffering now from a severe stutter, had implored him to "kiss me the way you k-k-kiss umumumother" (89). Unsettled, Seymour initially responds by stuttering a refusal "N-n-no" but is then overcome by remorse at his insensitivity and compounds his initial crime by kissing "her stammering mouth with the passion that she had been asking him for" (91). The memory of the kiss haunts Seymour, and he returns to it on several occasions, asking himself "Could *that* have done it?" (174) and "Did it have to do with him? That foolish kiss?" (240). Indeed there are insinuations of incest in the way that Rita Cohen invites Seymour to have sex with her by parodying Merry ("'Let's f-f-f-fuck, D-d-d-dad'" [143]), in the euphemisms employed by Sheila Salzman when she explains to Seymour why she did not contact him when Merry sought refuge with her after the bombing ("'sometimes you start to believe the worst about people . . . I just thought she was so fat and so angry that something very bad must have gone on at home'" [375, 378]), and in Merry's barbed response to Seymour's warning that New York is a "'dangerous city'" where she could "'wind up getting raped'": "'Girls wind up getting raped whether they listen to their daddies or not. Sometimes the daddies do the raping'" (111). However, when Seymour asks Merry "'who made'" her detonate the bomb at Old Rimrock, she responds simply by saying: "'Lyndon Johnson'" (247).

It is unclear which—if any—of these explanations account for Merry's radicalism, or if, as Aliki Varvogli has argued, Merry is "a symbol for the forces of history" (108), so that her actions should be understood in allegorical rather than psychological terms. Certainly, when Zuckerman wonders at how "the daughter and the decade blast[ed] to smithereens his [Seymour's] particular form of utopian thinking" (*Pastoral* 86), the apposition and alliteration of "daughter" and "decade" reinforces the notion that the former is an agent of the latter rather than an autonomous individual—that she is more the product of political than personal history. Yet in spite of its allegorical elements, *American Pastoral* is essentially, in Zuckerman's own words, a "realistic chronicle," albeit one that is paradoxically "dreamed" (89). As such, it implicitly rejects both determinism—whether psychological or historical—and allegory, in favor of a more complex representation of reality. In fact, the novel might be read as a critique of reductive views of history and the human subject.

The novel begins with Zuckerman recalling, and colluding in, the mythologization of Seymour Levov: the ungrammatical opening sentence—"The Swede"—immediately presents him as a phenomenon rather than a person. During the course of the novel he is compared to John F. Kennedy, to the baseball-prodigy protagonist of John R. Tunis's *The Kid from Tomkinsville*, and to the American folklore figure, Johnny Appleseed. This has led many critics to see him as a quintessentially American hero, a symbol of the nation itself: for Kenneth Millard he represents "an ideal of American selfhood and nationhood" (Millard 245), for Brian McDonald his "tragedy . . . mirrors the American tragedy that was Vietnam, his desperation and suffering reflecting the violence done to the consciousness of the whole nation" (32), and for Derek Royal he is simply "a stand-in for America itself" ("Pastoral Dreams" 201). Yet there is an equally insistent emphasis on Seymour's unexceptional nature. At one point Zuckerman reminds himself that Seymour was "actually only another of our neighborhood Seymours" (20), possessed of an "utterly ordinary humanness" (72) or, as he puts it elsewhere, with a characteristic oxymoron, "all the attributes of a monumental ordinariness" (81). According to Jerry, too, Seymour was "completely banal and conventional" (65).

As it turns out, however, Seymour is no more an everyman, or a Joe Schmoe, than he is an all-American hero or demigod (89). Just as Zuckerman qualifies what he calls in another context the "willful excursion into mythomania" (55) with which he glorifies the Swede, he soon has to acknowledge that his subsequent impression of Seymour as "a person of apparent blankness and innocence and simplicity" (74), the "embodiment of nothing" (39), is equally flawed. Conceding that he was "[n]ever more mistaken about anyone in my life" (39), Zuckerman rejects both the superhuman and "superordinary" (86) versions of Seymour that he had initially proposed, recognizing instead that Seymour is "another assailable man" (89). The rest of the novel is dedicated to pursuing "the revelation of the interior life that was unknown and unknowable" (80), a paradoxical pursuit that results in Zuckerman's presence as narrator being effaced completely, in favor of an omniscient third-person narration that often shades into free indirect discourse, so that the distinction between Seymour's view and the narrator's becomes blurred. The fact that Zuckerman does not reappear at the end of the novel suggests that his fictionalized history of Seymour's life takes precedence over the factual version (within the terms of the larger fictional framework) and, by implication, that all history is inflected by the subjectivity of its author.

The "unknown and unknowable" nature of "the interior life" manifests itself not just in Zuckerman's struggle to imagine himself into Seymour's consciousness but in Seymour's own difficulties in interpreting the behavior of others. Betrayed, as he sees it, by his daughter, wife and (erstwhile) mistress, Seymour laments that he lacks the "skill or capacity" "to penetrate to the interior of people" (409). His frustration at being unable to see metaphorically into the heads of those closest to him expresses itself at times in violent fantasies in which he literally breaks into their craniums, as when he imagines "collid[ing] with [his father's] skull . . . to split it open as bloodlessly as he could to get at whatever was inside" (295) or "bludgeon[ing]" Sheila Salzman "over the head" with a framed photograph of Dawn's prize cow, Count (373), or "slamming Orcutt's head against the flagstones" (381). Conversely, he sometimes feels so angry that "he feared that his head was about to spew out his brains" (256). The disturbingly visceral quality of these images—contrasting starkly with the image of Seymour as a "gentle giant"—ironically reveals a hinterland to Seymour that is just as opaque to the outside world as those that he belatedly discovers in his family and friends.

The other recurring trope that is used to signify the impossibility of gaining access to the hidden motives and thoughts of other people is that of the mask. Sometimes the mask is literal, as in the veil with which the Jain Merry covers her face; sometimes it is metaphorical, as in the mask that Seymour "learns to live behind" (81) in order to conceal his suffering or the alias—Mary Stoltz—that Merry assumes while on the run; sometimes it is somewhere between the two, as in the "new face" that the plastic surgeon gives Dawn that actually covers up some of her old features as well as figuratively providing a façade beneath which the trauma of Merry's bomb can be obscured. For Richard Schur, these masks are a facet of what he sees as the novel's postmodernism, creating "the illusion of closure when it may merely be the bottom of one fantasy" (23). It seems to me, however, that they provide a symbolic link between the impenetrability of individual subjectivity and the opacity of history. The connection between them is suggested by two passages in the second chapter of the novel.

The chapter begins with a four-page speech that Zuckerman "didn't give at my forty-fifth high school reunion, a speech to myself *masked* as a speech to them" (44, my emphasis). Later in the same chapter he finds himself gazing at his old contemporaries "as though it were still 1950, as though '1995' were merely the futuristic theme of a senior prom that we'd all come to in humorous papier-mâché masks of ourselves as we might look at the close of the twentieth century" (46). The implication here is not simply that the changes wrought in the faces of his classmates by age—by the action of history, in other words— are akin to the metamorphoses accomplished by putting on grotesque masks, but also that history, like a mask, superimposes a new reality over the old, rather than effacing it. The reference to "the close of the twentieth century" invokes all the grand and horrific events that have come to define the hundred years between 1900 and 1999, but the revelations of personal history that take place at the reunion—notably those pertaining to Seymour's life and death—serve as a reminder that personal histories are as predictably unpredictable as the material that forms the basis of history books.

Ultimately, it is this vision of history as dynamic, fluid, and startling— history as embodied in Seymour himself—that prevails in *American Pastoral* over a more teleological version of history, represented by the Levovs' neighbor, Bill Orcutt, the adulterous architect and purveyor of paintings "that looked like they didn't look like anything," "pictures of nothing" (323). When the Levovs first move to Old Rimrock, Orcutt takes Seymour on a guided tour of the local county, delivering a "historically edifying" lecture (303), a "lesson in American history" (306) that revolves around his own ancestors, who had settled in the area in the eighteenth century. Seymour feigns interest although he finds it "deadly" because he feels that Orcutt is essentially, as he tells Dawn, "a good guy" (304). Later, however, when Seymour is inveigled into participating in a weekly touch-football game, he finds that Orcutt "began to use his hands . . . in a way that the Swede considered cheap and irritating, for a pickup game the worst sort of behavior" (380–1). On the third occasion that Orcutt does this, Seymour decides to teach Orcutt a lesson of his own, "dump[ing] him" with "a single, swift maneuver" that leaves Orcutt "sprawled in the grass at his feet" (381). Looking at his prostrate neighbor, whom he had once admired for being "no stranger to . . . the great historical drama of this country" (322), he now notes, with satisfaction: " 'Two hundred years of Morris County history, flat on its ass' " (381). For Seymour at this moment, Orcutt represents history itself—which is to say, the kind of atrophied history that entrenches the interests of a privileged, WASP elite, symbolized by the tombstones of previous generations of Orcutts that form the centerpiece of Orcutt's guided tour. In this respect, the bomb that destroys the Old Rimrock post office, though it shocks and dismays Seymour, might be said to display the same iconoclastic spirit that moves Seymour to dump Orcutt on the seat of his pants, as might the satirical laughter of Marcia Umanoff, whom the narrator brands the "professor of transgression" (365) (an echo of the title of another of Roth's 1970s novels, *The Professor of Desire* [1977]) and who "relish[es], as some people, *historically*, always seem to do, how far the rampant disorder had spread" (423, my emphasis).

American Pastoral, then, is not the conservative and certainly not the neoconservative novel that some critics have wanted it to be, nor for that matter a defense of liberalism, but rather a characteristically ambiguous and complex novel. In terms of literary history, it can be situated either, according to its publication date, as a novel of the 1990s, the first installment of Roth's American trilogy, or, taking into account its genesis, as an extension of the formal and thematic issues with which Roth grappled in the 1970s. In terms of its subject matter, too, its historical focus is wider than has generally been recognized. It can be read as a novel about the 1960s, but in fact it also deals in some detail with the 1940s, 1950s, 1970s, and 1980s. Finally, however, what is most distinctive and most interesting about history in *American Pastoral* is how the novel interrogates the semantic, philosophical, and political implications of the term itself. In this sense, *American Pastoral* is as much concerned with historiography as it is with history. As such, it pulls off the rare trick of being at one and the same time a powerfully affecting historical novel, a family drama, a tragedy, and a novel of ideas.

CHAPTER 3

The Critique of the Pastoral, Utopia, and the American Dream in *American Pastoral*

Andrew Gordon

By titling his 1997 novel *American Pastoral*, Philip Roth is announcing epic ambitions: he intends this work to be not only a family chronicle but also a meditation on the pastoral, on utopian dreams, and on the nature of American identity, American history, and the American dream. Writes Bonnie Lyons, "The very title of the book . . . suggests that a whole period of American history [postwar America from 1945–65] can be seen as a collective pastoral, a beautiful and fragile bubble bound to burst" (Lyons 126). The novel moves in concentric circles: at its center is the disintegration of the family and loss of illusions of Seymour "Swede" Levov, who grew up in the 1930s and 1940s in Weequahic, the Jewish section of Newark, inherited his father's Newark glove factory, married the Irish-Catholic Dawn Dwyer, Miss New Jersey of 1949, and moved in the 1950s to Old Rimrock in rural New Jersey. In a larger sense, the decline of the Levovs goes along with the crumbling of the city of Newark in the late 1960s and early 1970s, with race riots in the inner city and the loss of its industrial base. In the largest sense of all, the dissolution of the family and the urban decay mirror the decline of America in that same period, from the presidency of Lyndon Baines Johnson to that of Richard Nixon, from the counter-cultural chant "Hey, hey, LBJ, how many kids did you kill today?" during the Vietnam War to the protestations of "Tricky Dick," President Nixon, that "I am not a crook!" The Swede's pastoral illusions about America begin to dissolve in 1968 as a result of his daughter's violent protest against the Vietnam War, and the novel ends with the final nail being driven into the coffin of the Swede's marriage and family five years later, in 1973, during a long dinner party at his home during the Watergate hearings, when presidential corruption and the popular pornographic movie *Deep Throat* have become the topics of middle-class dinner table conversation.

Roth and the Pastoral

Some Versions of Pastoral is the title of a critical work by William Empson, and Roth, in *American Pastoral* and many of his other novels, has been concerned with deconstructing some contemporary versions of this pastoral. Roth's satiric, subversive bent makes him an antiutopian and antipastoralist who questions idealistic longings and validates perpetual struggle, complexity, and uncertainty in both life and art. Nevertheless, in *American Pastoral*, despite his demolition of the American dream, Roth paradoxically ends up clinging to certain pastoral ideals, contrasting the wonderful lost America of his Newark childhood in the 1940s to the fallen America of the 1960s and 1970s.

The pastoral was originated by the Greek poet Theocritus and the Latin poet Virgil, who wrote poems about the lives of shepherds ("pastor" is Latin for "shepherd"). The traditional pastoral is "a deliberately conventional poem expressing an urban poet's nostalgic image of the peace and simplicity of the life of shepherds and other rural folk in idealized natural settings" (Abrams 202). Empson expands the definition of pastoral to include, according to M. H. Abrams, "any work which opposes simple to complicated life, to the advantage of the former" (Abrams 203). In other words, any pastoral contains an element of utopian longing.

In *The Counterlife*, Nathan Zuckerman's lover Maria tells him: "The pastoral is not your genre . . . Your chosen fate, as you see it, is to be innocent of innocence at all costs" (*Counterlife* 317–18). What she says of Zuckerman is equally true of Roth. Like Zuckerman, Roth constantly fights his own tendency to be attracted by pastoral illusions of innocence, which are persistently appealing: defeat one and another emerges in its place. Again, as Maria tells Nathan, "I think that you are embarrassed to find that even you were tempted to have a dream of simplicity as foolish and naive as anyone's" (318). Roth sees us all as fiction-makers and forces us to reconsider the nature of the utopias we all script. He rejects all these as fantasies of innocence, retreats to the womb. The only utopia Roth will allow is that of fiction-making itself: the power of the human mind endlessly to imagine and to reimagine our lives.

The Counterlife constructs and then deconstructs a series of "pastoral myths" (322): an escape to Switzerland, or to Israel, or to

England. Each myth is a counterlife that constitutes a utopian dream of innocence:

> at the core is the idyllic scenario of redemption through the recovery of a sanitized, confusionless life. In dead seriousness, we all create imagined worlds, often green and breastlike, where we may finally be "ourselves." Yet another of our mythological pursuits. (322)

The "green and breastlike" world alludes to "the fresh green breast of the new world" evoked at the end of F. Scott Fitzgerald's 1925 novel *The Great Gatsby* (182). Gatsby foundered on his utopian dream, his American pastoral; Gatsby was a perpetual adolescent, "borne back ceaselessly into the past," as Fitzgerald's novel's last line states (182). The utopian dream is of a life without confusion, a life of blissful innocence that can only be found in the past, not in the present or future. As Derek Parker Royal writes, "Seymour Levov, much like Jay Gatsby, reaches out for an idealized version of American life, one that will allow him to escape from any predetermined notions of identity and reinvent himself on his own terms" ("Pastoral Dreams" 190). By moving from the Jewish section of Newark out beyond the suburbs and into the supposed rural simplicities of Old Rimrock, New Jersey, Swede Levov is trying to blend into America. But he is reaching for the impossible, for "an idealized version of American life." Like Gatsby, in seeking to find himself through immersion in "a sanitized, confusionless" America that never existed, the Swede loses himself.

Roth suggests that these "pastoral myths" represent a retreat not simply back to the past but all the way back to the womb: "the womb-dream of life in the beautiful state of innocent prehistory" (323). Only in the womb can we find a "sanitized, confusionless life." Many of Roth's heroes yearn "to be taken off to the perfectly safe, charmingly simple and satisfying environment that is desire's homeland" (322), the original utopia of the womb. Roth sees the utopian dreams and the desire for the simple life of the pastoral as tempting and quite understandable, but also as fundamentally puerile.

According to Ross Posnock, *American Pastoral* deals with "assimilation as sacrifice that entails identifying America as a WASP nation founded on a myth of pastoral innocence" (*Rude Truth* 90). Through the novel, Roth critiques that myth of pastoral innocence and shows that Swede Levov sacrifices his identity for the wrong dream. If, as Roth suggests in many of his novels, our identities are fictitious and we all live through fiction, then our goal should be to reject inferior fantasies and to imagine better fictions. For Roth, whose temperament is fundamentally oppositional, such fictions will be tense, unresolved, and even mutually contradictory. Although Roth never spells out what the right dreams might be, *American Pastoral* is clear about the disastrous consequences of living out the wrong ones.

The novel ends with the Swede lost and questioning. The Swede's tragedy is that, having devoted his life to the wrong dream, once it is revealed as a fantasy, he has nothing with which to replace it. As Posnock suggests, "Lacking the capacity to fashion a counterlife, he is doomed" (*Rude Truth* 109). For Zuckerman, the Swede was as good as dead in 1973, when, bereft and devastated, he lost his illusions. We know that the Swede lives over 20 years after this point, but Zuckerman is not interested in narrating those years, which he envisions as a masquerade, with the Swede pretending to be the same man but having lost the myth of pastoral innocence which had sustained him.

The American Dream as Utopian Fantasy

In *American Pastoral*, Roth tackles the American dream as the ultimate American utopian fantasy. Carol Iannone notes in a review of *American Pastoral*, "To many a literary imagination, America represented from its inception a New World Eden where the American Adam faced boundless possibility and infinite, open-ended opportunity" (Iannone 55). But against this Emersonian optimism, there has always been a tragic counterstrain in American literature, one represented by such authors as Melville, Hawthorne, Dreiser, or Mailer. Iannone notes further that "in Roth's *American Pastoral*, the grain has darkened still further . . . no less than the end of the American dream itself, destroyed, even as it comes most fully to fruition, by its own offspring" (55).

In *American Pastoral*, the narrator Nathan Zuckerman attends in 1995 the forty-fifth reunion of his Newark, New Jersey high school class, the Weequahic High class of 1950. Seeing all his aged classmates after so many years and learning there of the death of his childhood hero, the school's most famous athlete, Seymour "Swede" Levov, of the class of 1945, puts Zuckerman into a sad and nostalgic state of mind. He ponders post-World War II American history and how it had affected his generation, and he thinks about the loss of the Swede, the greatest of his generation of Jewish-American children and grandchildren of immigrants, "the boy we were all going to follow into America, our point man into the next immersion, at home here the way the Wasps were at home here" (*Pastoral* 89).

The Swede loses his innocence in the late 1960s through the actions of his daughter Merry. She sets off a bomb in their rural hometown post office/general store to protest the Vietnam War, thereby killing a beloved local physician: "the daughter and the decade blasting to smithereens his particular form of utopian thinking, the plague America infiltrating the Swede's castle and there infecting everyone. The daughter who transports him out of the longed-for American pastoral and into everything that is its antithesis and its enemy, into the fury, the violence, and the desperation of the counterpastoral—into the indigenous American berserk" (86). If the Swede, who was "our Kennedy" (83), has like JFK been ambushed by history, cut down by sudden, random violence (he is an indirect victim of his daughter's bomb) then what has become of the American pastoral and the American dream for Zuckerman and his entire generation?

To pursue the question, Roth allows multiple meanings of the pastoral to resonate in *American Pastoral*. For example, Michiko Kakutani observes that, in the novel, Roth has split two sides of himself, "the optimistic strain of Emersonian self-reliance" versus "the darker side of American individualism . . . the American berserk" into Swede and his daughter (Kakutani C11). The pastoral seems to emerge from that Emersonian, optimistic strain, so it is as if Roth's "darker side" is critiquing the pastoral. Because Roth likes to leave the tensions in play, the novel ends not with a resolution of the two sides—American pastoral versus American berserk or counterpastoral—but with a question. Roth also critiques several versions of the pastoral, to address a range of social and economic conditions in America. Elizabeth Powers cites two examples: "Dawn's cattle farm, recalling the occupations of traditional literary herdsmen, but also the Newark Maid Glove Factory over which Seymour presides, which stands in for the pastoral economy, one based on transmission of generational skills" (Powers 136). Finally, the novel invites an allegorical interpretation, as the titles of the three books of *American Pastoral*—"Paradise Remembered," "The Fall," and "Paradise Lost"—allude to yet another version of pastoral: Milton's epic poem *Paradise Lost* (1667). William Empson considered *Paradise Lost* a pastoral, with the Garden of Eden the original pastoral dream world. *American Pastoral* can thus be viewed in one light as a Miltonian allegory in which Swede is the American Adam, living in blissful innocence—or willful denial—in the supposedly unspoiled garden of rural New Jersey (the Garden State) with his wife Dawn, until the serpent enters the garden and ruins everything.

The Dream of Jewish Assimilation

The central pastoral dream Swede Levov attempts to live out, however, is the immigrant dream of becoming a totally assimilated American by moving to a small town. Many of Roth's novels deal with the dilemma of Jewish-American masculine identity in the late twentieth century—the challenge for a Jewish man to assert his potency according to the terms of American success, without sacrificing ethical responsibility. The Swede's solution to that dilemma is to attempt to transform himself into an all-American man by marrying Dawn, Miss New Jersey, and becoming a country squire. The Swede, born Seymour Levov, a son of the Newark Jewish ghetto, moves in the 1950s into rural New Jersey. "What was Mars to his father was America to him—he was settling Revolutionary New Jersey as if for the first time. Out in Old Rimrock, all of America lay at their door. That was an idea he loved. Jewish resentment, Irish resentment—the hell with it" (*Pastoral* 310). He imagines that in post-World War II America, the younger generation has moved beyond all the old prejudices and resentments, so that now "people can live in harmony, all sorts of people side by side no matter what their origins" (310–11).

Zuckerman later explains that this American pastoral of egalitarian peaceful coexistence is an illusion that can be sustained only momentarily, in brief rituals such as the all-American holiday of Thanksgiving: "A moratorium on all the grievances and resentments, and not only for the Dwyers and the Levovs but for everyone in America who is suspicious of everyone else. It is the American pastoral par excellence and it lasts twenty-four hours" (402). But the Swede glories in such ordinary, small-town American pastimes as being able to walk from his home into the small town to pick up the paper at "Hamlin's general store, with the post office inside, and outside the bulletin board and the flagpole and the gas pump—that's what had served the old farming community as its meeting place since the days of Warren Gamaliel Harding" (317). Entering this scene, which might have been painted by the illustrator Norman Rockwell, gives the Swede the illusion of being all-American, of belonging in Old Rimrock. In fact, the Swede never truly belongs in "rock-ribbed Republican New Jersey." In the 1920s, in the Harding era, the Ku Klux Klan, who included Jews among their racial and ethnic enemies, burned their crosses in Old Rimrock (309).

In exploding the Jewish dream of assimilation to small-town America, Roth writes in the tradition of another Jewish-American novelist, Nathanael West. In West's 1933 novel *Miss Lonelyhearts*, the urban hero goes for a pastoral retreat, a weekend in the country. He "drove into Monkstown for some fresh fruit and the newspapers. He stopped for gas at the Aw-Kum-On Garage and told the attendant about the deer. The man said there was still plenty of deer at the pond because no yids ever went there. He said it wasn't the hunters who drove out the deer, but the yids" (West 37–8). It is not far from the rural Americana of "the Aw-Kum-On Garage" in Monkstown to Hamlin's general store in Old Rimrock. Ironically, it is this same general store that Swede's daughter Merry later blows up. The daughter, who represents the American berserk, explodes her father's American pastoral.

In his assimilationist delusions, the Swede even imagines himself as Johnny Appleseed, the legendary sower of the American countryside. "Johnny Appleseed, that's the man for me. Wasn't a Jew, wasn't an Irish Catholic, wasn't a Protestant Christian—nope, Johnny Appleseed was just a happy American. Big. Ruddy. Happy. No brains probably, but didn't need 'em" (*Pastoral* 316). The Swede attempts to live out this American legend. Writes Timothy L. Parrish, "As Johnny Appleseed, Swede can imagine himself as the progenitor of the America he now inhabits: ancestor and inheritor all at once" ("End of Identity" 136). But this is pure fantasy; in Old Rimrock, the Jewish Swede is neither ancestor nor inheritor. His Wasp neighbor Bill Orcutt is, and Orcutt, "Mr. America," will also inherit Dawn, the Swede's wife (*Pastoral* 385). The Swede is not Johnny Appleseed but an American Adam who bites into the apple, has his eyes opened, and is forever exiled from Eden.

The Swede's pastoral dream of American assimilation, of raising a family in an old stone house in the country, was first concocted when he was a teenager. Like Fitzgerald's Gatsby, who attempted when he was 17 to transform himself into a WASP by anglicizing his name from James Gatz to Jay Gatsby, the Swede remains true to his adolescent reinvention of himself. And when they are grown men, the puerile dreams to which they cling lead them both to disaster.

The Swede's hotheaded brother Jerry is the only one who dares to tell him the truth: because the Swede swallowed American fantasies whole, he never grew up. Jerry calls the Swede "'The boy who never breaks the code'" (*Pastoral* 274); even though the Swede is middle aged, he calls him a boy. He tells him, "'You think you know what a man is? You have no *idea* what a man is . . . You think you know what this country is? You have no *idea* what this country is. You have a false image of *everything*'" (276). Jerry's diagnosis of the Swede recalls Biff Loman's judgment of his father, Willy, in the Requiem to Arthur Miller's play *Death of a Salesman* (1949)—the iconic story of the American dream: "He had the wrong dreams. All, all, wrong" (221).

First Fidelity Bank

Perhaps the novel's bitterest critique of the American Dream, or rather of the fantasies that upheld this unsustainable dream, takes place when the Swede waits for his outlaw daughter Merry, who, five years after the bombing, is living under an assumed name, in filth and danger, in the Newark slums. As the Swede waits on a street corner,

> he could see the skyline of commercial Newark half a mile away and . . . the most reassuring words in the English language . . . ten stories high the huge, white stark letters heralding fiscal confidence and institutional permanence, civic progress and opportunity and pride . . . : FIRST FIDELITY BANK.
>   That's what was left, that lie. First. *Last.* LAST FIDELITY BANK. From down on the earth . . . where his daughter lived even worse than her greenhorn great-grandparents had, fresh from steerage, in their Prince Street tenement—you could see a mammoth signboard designed for concealing the truth. A sign in which only a madman could believe. A sign in a fairy tale. (*Pastoral* 236–7)

Like the legend of Johnny Appleseed, "First Fidelity Bank" is another prop in the American dream, another inferior fiction, a fairy tale by which people live their lives. In this novel, the dream of assimilation and upward mobility of American immigrants runs in reverse, so that after four generations in Newark, "his daughter lived even worse than her greenhorn great-grandparents."

As the Swede's life is falling apart at the dinner party in 1973, with all the things he has learned that day that he could not possibly talk about in front of his friends and family—including the return of his crazy daughter Merry, who has murdered three more people with her bombs and twice been raped; the affair he has just discovered that his wife Dawn is carrying on with their neighbor, the architect Bill Orcutt; and the Swede's own brief fling with Sheila, Merry's speech therapist, who, he has just learned, harbored Merry after the bombing—while all this is repeating in the Swede's head, Dawn is talking to their guests about a trip to Switzerland. In point-counterpoint, we read the narration of the Swede's guilty, anguished thoughts —"*She killed three more people! You could have prevented that!*"—together with Dawn's babbling about Swiss cows and the barns and how it was all "Very clean and very nice" (414). The reality of the Swede's torment as all his hopes are punctured and his life spins completely out of control is ironically juxtaposed with Dawn's pastoral illusions. The Swede has woken up to cruel reality while Dawn retreats into fairy tales, seeking an "uncontaminated life" while cheating on her husband (385). "Last Fidelity Bank," indeed!

Aside from the glove factory, the cattle farm, the Gentile wife, the small town, and Johnny Appleseed, the nexus of the pastoral dream, for Zuckerman if not for the Swede, lies in the Newark ghetto of his childhood in the late 1940s. Sylvia Barack Fishman writes, "the truly elegized and unsullied 'Paradise Lost' of the story turns out to be the earlier existence that Levov shared with Zuckerman and the other Jewish progeny of Weequahic, in their baseball-besotted youth" (25). According to Erik Lundegaard, "[t]he constricting social mores that have been used to such comic effect in previous Roth novels are seen here through the soft focus of nostalgia—whether Roth's or narrator Zuckerman's, we don't know" (M3). If the 1960s and 1970s are hell in *American Pastoral*, then the 1940s are heaven. Roth mines a rich vein of nostalgia. In "Paradise Remembered," the 62-year-old Zuckerman becomes overwhelmed with nostalgia at his high school reunion. The souvenir *rugelach* offered at the reunion remind him of the *rugelach* his mother used to bake. "By rapidly devouring mouthful after mouthful of these crumbs whose floury richness—blended of butter and sour cream and vanilla and cream cheese and egg yolk and sugar—I'd loved since childhood, perhaps I'd find vanishing from Nathan what, according to Proust, vanished from Marcel the instant he recognized 'the savour of the little *madeleine*': the apprehensiveness of death." In the end, though, Zuckerman cannot escape his aged self, "having nothing like Marcel's luck." He further recognizes the comic irony that this "wolfish intake of saturated fat" is no good for his heart (*Pastoral* 47).

American Pastoral is a death-haunted novel. As in *The Counterlife*, *The Human Stain*, and *Exit Ghost*, Zuckerman faces impotence and his own mortality. "Let's speak further of death and of the desire—understandably in the aging a desperate desire—to forestall death, to resist it, to resort to whatever means are necessary to see death with anything, anything, *anything* but clarity" (*Pastoral* 47). Zuckerman realizes that the nostalgic desire to return to the past is a way to avoid thinking about death. Childhood becomes the ultimate pastoral dream. Nevertheless, even though Zuckerman knows that nostalgia is futile, and, in the case of the fatty *rugelach*, counterproductive, he still indulges in it. Zuckerman also narrates the story of a counterhero who can suffer the fate he fears: the Swede, a double who will die from the same prostate cancer that has rendered Zuckerman impotent and incontinent. This becomes another way to displace the fear of decline and fall, of aging and death.

The Utopia of a Rational Existence

The final utopia that *American Pastoral* deconstructs is "the utopia of a rational existence" (*Pastoral* 123). The Swede, who lived devoted to order and reason, repeatedly "learned the worst lesson that life can teach: that it makes no sense" (81). Roth laces the narrative with repetitions of the Swede's astonished recognition: "Yes, at the age of forty-six, in 1973, almost three-quarters of the way through the century that with no regard for the niceties of burial had strewn the corpses of mutilated children and their mutilated parents everywhere, the Swede found out that we are all in the power of something demented" (256); "It is not rational. It is chaos. It is chaos from start to finish" (281); "The old system that made order doesn't work anymore" (422). From such a bleak novel, it is thus surprising that one critic decided that Roth "loves the right things. His parents, his relatives, his hometown. His baseball and his country" (Schiller 54). And this is true. It is the decline and fall of all the things that he, like the Swede, holds dear that infuriates him: "Roth isn't merely saddened but maddened by what he sees happening to his country" (Kemp).

American Pastoral is therefore structured as a tragedy, a story of decline and fall. Such a narrative trajectory implies that things were once better. According to Roth in the novel, America has declined from the relative order, reason, and progress of the 1940s and 1950s into the anarchy, irrationality, and lust for destruction of the 1960s and 1970s. Writes Robert Boyers of *American Pastoral*, "The nostalgia for the 'country that used to be' is so palpable in this novel that it virtually immobilizes the imagination of reality . . . Once, not long ago, according to this narrative, everybody had it good, or good enough. But many Americans suddenly went unaccountably crazy" and wrecked it all for no reason (41). It is as if Roth has taken his own self-division— between the "paleface" and the "redskin" ("On *The Great American Novel*" 82–3), between the side that craves order and reason and the side that desires only to shock and outrage—and projected it onto America, playing it out in the division between the Swede and Merry, between parent and child, and between the past and the present.

Blame It on the Sixties

Despite his apparently thorough and unrelenting critique of pastoral myths and utopian illusions, in *American Pastoral*, Roth suffers from a blind spot. Like many conservative social critics in America today, he wants to blame it on the 1960s. But Roth gets the 1960s wrong. Sixteen-year-old high school students like Merry were not the mad bombers; college and graduate students were the most militant. Todd Gitlin, who was in SDS (Students for a Democratic Society), notes that "Merry explodes prematurely," bombing the post office in Old Rimrock in 1968, two years before the extremist Weathermen faction of SDS began their bombing campaign (202). Mark Shechner compares

American Pastoral to Saul Bellow's "novel-cum-diatribe of 1970, *Mr. Sammler's Planet* which . . . takes a jaundiced view of youth culture, of revolutionary romanticism, and of libertine sex" (*Up Society's Ass* 159). He calls the novel "politically thin," with "cartoon insurrectionists in Merry Levov and her comrade in firearms, Rita Cohen" (159). Finally, he notes the absence in the novel of any mention of 1960s rock music, the soundtrack of the youth rebellion. Such disparities make Zuckerman's "realistic chronicle" of the 1960s less convincing (*Pastoral* 89).

There is also a contradiction in Roth's thinking. A central idea portrayed in *American Pastoral* is that, starting in the 1960s, a disorder spread like a plague throughout the country, ruining the cities, decaying morality, and finally destroying the American family. But if this is true, then it is not true, as the novel elsewhere argues, that life makes no sense and never did. Because the novel also implies that, once upon a time, in America and in Weequahic in the 1940s, things were better and life made sense. But "the old system that made order doesn't work anymore" (422). Through his nostalgia for a vanished America, for the supposedly good old days of his youth, Roth ends up reinforcing another pastoral myth. It remained for Roth to correct that nostalgic image in *The Plot Against America* by returning to the Weequahic neighborhood in the 1940s and showing how, with just a slight twist, his childhood paradise could be turned into a nightmare.

CHAPTER 4

America's Haunted House: The Racial and National Uncanny in *American Pastoral*

Jennifer Glaser

An Uncanny Generation

Philip Roth's *American Pastoral* begins with a rhapsodic rendering of the high school heroics of its protagonist, Swede Levov. By the end of the novel, however, the Swede's life is in shambles, his formerly "impregnable" home destroyed by a bomb detonated by his politically radical young daughter and penetrated by a predatory male suitor in love with his wife (237). The fact that the third act of Roth's tragedy takes place almost entirely in the fortresslike confines of Levov's stone farmhouse sets up the formally tragic nature of the novel, culminating in the destruction of the great man, the Swede, and the metaphorical house of Levov.[1] In its portrayal of a domesticity finally and fully undermined by the chaos it has sought to conceal, part III of *American Pastoral* is also the fruition of what I see as one of the novel's central, and most undertheorized, concerns: the uncanniness of post-1960s America. Most explicitly, Roth's novel functions as an exploration of the domestic uncanny, the terror lurking at the heart of the most conventional family home. It also, however, engages with the uncanny on a broader level, by exploring the many specters that haunt the larger tribes of race and nation. These two mutually constitutive discourses of the uncanny— the racial and national—shadow the universe of Roth's novel and provide the archetypical American author with a way to meditate on questions of home and homeland, Jewish identity, and larger concerns about the path of the nation in the wake of Vietnam.

American Pastoral is narrated by Nathan Zuckerman, the character Roth refers to as his "alter brain." As Zuckerman makes clear from the opening pages of *American Pastoral*, he views Swede Levov, his high school idol, as not simply an individual, but a type of individual, one that is gradually growing as extinct as the dodo bird in a post-Vietnam, morally relativistic America. This depiction of the Swede is continuous with Roth's own increasing preoccupation with "dealing with the historical moments in postwar American life that have had the greatest impact on [his] generation" ("Zuckerman's Alter Brain" 8). Roth emphasizes his interest in the generational response over the individual one by beginning *American Pastoral* at Zuckerman's high school reunion— an event that allows him to cast a retrospective gaze upon his own peer group and speculate about the meaning of their particular American experience 45 years after graduation.

At the reunion, Zuckerman's idealized memories of the past collide with the much more complicated realities hidden beneath the cheery 1940s' façades of his classmates—a precursor to the exploration of the uncanny return of the repressed that occurs throughout the novel. *American Pastoral* is itself the collision between different ideas of the past and how to write about the past—the mock reunion speech that celebrates Zuckerman's classmates versus the true stories that most speech elides, one of which will become the focus of the novel. At the reunion, Zuckerman first discovers the complexity of the Swede's story—a narrative that highlights the disjuncture between the writer's perception of others and their own experiences, what Zuckerman calls "this terribly significant business of *other people*, . . . so ill-equipped are we all to envision one another's interior workings and invisible aims" (35).

Months before the reunion, Zuckerman had met the Swede and found him disturbingly blank, all "surface" (23). At his reunion, the writer learns that there was more to the man than the impeccable façade he showed to the world. There, Zuckerman discovers that the Swede is dead and that his life had been a far more tragic one than Nathan imagined, his perfect record besmirched by the terrible crimes of his daughter, Merry, who blew up the local post office to demonstrate her commitment to the antiwar movement.

Zuckerman's early description of the Swede as a man of surface and not depth paves the way for Levov's unraveling. All the Swede "care[s] about is skin. Ectoderm. Surface. But what's underneath, [he doesn't] have a clue" (137). Much of *American Pastoral* is a meditation on the darkness that lies in wait for those who most aggressively refuse to see the shadows in their own lives. The Swede is a haunted man in Zuckerman's imagining, a man "awakening in middle age to the horror of self-reflection"—a malady that Roth suggests is epidemic during the immediate postwar era (85).

Zuckerman's interest in discovering what exists behind Swede Levov's uncanny blankness catalyzes his writing of the book-within-a-book that comprises *American Pastoral*. This sense of the uncanny pervades the narrative in myriad ways, especially in relation to the role of what Roth calls the "indigenous American berserk" (86) that constitutes his description of national and personal haunting. Freud defines the uncanny as "that class of the frightening which leads back to what is known of old and long familiar" (930). In search of the etymology of the German word for the uncanny, *Unheimlich* ("unhomely"), Freud seeks out the manifold meanings of its root word, *Heimlich* ("homely"), a word that is usually perceived as its binary opposite. Despite its common usage, the term *Heimlich*

> is not unambiguous, but belongs to two sets of ideas, which, without being contradictory, are yet very different: on the one hand it means what is familiar and agreeable, and on the other what is concealed and kept out of sight. (933)

Heimlich is most commonly defined by its associations with the home; that which is *Heimlich* is deemed, like the family hearth, "not strange, familiar, tame, intimate, arousing a sense of agreeable restfulness and security as in one within the four walls of his house" (933). Freud reminds us, however, that *Heimlich* also refers to that which is "kept from sight, so that others do not get to know of or about it" (933); at the heart of what we consider most "homely" or comfortable is the possibility for both secrecy and terror. Recognizing the fact that these two terms are not entirely opposing—that both the most familiar/homely and the most uncanny/strange experiences are constituted by their being veiled in secrecy—Freud argues that "what is *Heimlich* thus comes to be *Unheimlich*" (933). In *American Pastoral*, Swede Levov's most *Heimlich* of lives comes to be *Unheimlich* precisely because of what he tries to keep from haunting its well-lit corridors.

Freud suggests that the uncanny emerges as a result of repression:

> if every affect belonging to an emotional impulse, whatever its kind, is transformed, if it is repressed, into anxiety, then among instances of frightening things there must be one class in which the frightening element can be shown to be something repressed which *recurs*. (944)

The uncanny need not have been "originally frightening"; instead, what is frightening in the experience of the uncanny is the fact that an object once repressed has returned to haunt the present (944). Freud suggests thus that the "uncanny is in reality nothing new or alien, but something which is familiar and old-established in the mind and which has become alienated from it only through the process of repression" (944).

Acculturation and Its Discontents

Although it differs significantly from the eighteenth- and nineteenth-century texts most often associated with the uncanny, *American Pastoral* shares many of their constitutive features. The novel details how Swede Levov, "the household Apollo of the Weequahic Jews," builds what looks to the outside world like the perfect life, only to have it destroyed by what he has long since repressed (4). By the end of *American Pastoral*, he finds the name and life he has built decimated, "the plague America infiltrating the Swede's castle and there infecting everyone" (86). The novel thus focuses not just on "the Swede's castle" and the permeability of his family home to chaos, but also on the "plague America," the particular national disease infiltrating homes across the country at the time of Merry's radicalization (86). Much of the novel explores just what makes the Swede's home so susceptible to this imagined contamination—namely, the disavowal of the past, particularly the Jewish past, that leaves Merry without a clear identification. Central to the novel is an idea of racialized Jewishness disavowed. Timothy Parrish argues that the character of Swede Levov "was born to make the transformation that Zuckerman has struggled so ardently for in his life and art: to become an American who happens to be a Jew" ("End of Identity" 133). At the same time, Roth makes it clear throughout *American Pastoral* that this casual acculturation is not as seamless as it appears. By evincing the "counterpastoral" effects of the Swede's embrace of radical individualism, Parrish contends that "Roth in a sense completes his assimilation story by rendering judgment upon its naïve hopefulness" (*American Pastoral* 86, "End of Identity" 133).

Moreover, neither the Swede nor his wife, Dawn, can fully escape their roots. The repressed otherness of their lower middle class, ethnically marked youths returns to haunt the present. In her exploration of the uncanny, Terry Castle points out that "the more we seek enlightenment, the more alienating our world becomes; the more we seek to free ourselves, Houdini-like, from the coils of superstition, mystery, and magic, the more tightly, paradoxically, the uncanny holds us in its grip" (15). While Castle is partially referring to the uppercase "Enlightenment" here, she is also invoking the more personal ways in which the uncanny recovers what the project of enlightened humanism would rather efface—difference, the dark underbelly of universalism. In *American*

Pastoral, the Swede is portrayed as the endpoint of a genealogical line of immigrants who have fully embraced the American project of assimilation and radical individualism. Although the novel details the Swede's particular struggle to maintain his family in the face of violence and rupture, it also tells the tale of the third-generation American population of immigrants who have erased ties to their racialized Jewish pasts in order to become more fully American.

A number of critics have noted that race stages an uncanny return for those who seek to escape from it. Gwen Bergner writes that

> [r]acial identity is inherently uncanny because consolidating a coherent identity as either black or white requires that aspects of the other term be repressed, disavowed, or projected as radically external to the self. If that repression, disavowal, or projection wavers, the externalized aspect of self resurfaces so as to produce an uncanny sensation. (66)

Although Bergner is referring to the racial binary system of black and white, her theorization of the results of "repression, disavowal, or projection" holds equally true for the Jewish protagonist of *American Pastoral* (66). Swede Levov is not unlike Coleman Silk, the African American man attempting to pass for white in Roth's *Human Stain*. Both men seek release from the anchor of their racial or ethnic identity, both resent the shackles of the "*E pluribus unum*," "the coercive" pull of racial and familial affinity (*Stain* 108). Most strikingly, both men come to a tragic end because of the rejection of their identities. Roth suggests that even the heartiest repression cannot prevent a return of biographical fact.

Not only does Merry's violent despair remind the Swede that to disavow his racial heritage carries costs, but he also encounters the uncanny in the form of the national history that disrupts his cheerfully ahistorical/pastoral life and makes him "history's plaything" (87). In *The National Uncanny*, Renee L. Bergland argues that America and the terrain of American literary history have been haunted by the presence of disavowed ethnic others, most particularly Native Americans. In *American Pastoral*, we are greeted by another form of the national uncanny, the infiltration of the depoliticized (and often de-ethnicized) American dream by the realities of the Vietnam War and the generational and political fault lines it uncovers.

Appropriately, the Swede is greeted by many instances of both the racial and national uncanny in the privacy of his own home. Anthony Vidler calls the uncanny "a domesticated version of absolute terror, to be experienced in the comfort of the home" (3). He describes "its favorite motif . . . [as] precisely the contrast between a secure and homely interior and the fearful invasion of an alien presence" (3). *American Pastoral* focuses on the paradoxical nature of the home as a space of containment and safety, as well as an arena for secrets and danger, much as Vidler and Freud's definitions do. The dinner party the Swede and Dawn host in their home near the end of the novel proves an important indicator of Roth's interest in the uncanny duality of homelife. Traditionally a marker of civility, the dinner party atmosphere quickly devolves into chaos. The Swede's guests include his parents; Bill Orcutt, the architect and Wasp paragon who is seeking to build a new home for the Swede at the same time that he is having a covert sexual relationship with the Swede's wife; Orcutt's alcoholic wife Jesse; Sheila, Dawn's former speech teacher and the Swede's former lover; the Swede's childhood friend, Barry Umanoff; and his professor wife, Marcia.

History intervenes at the party, where "conversation . . . was about Watergate and *Deep Throat*" (344). The Swede's parents obsessively watch and discuss the Nixon impeachment hearings. The group talks about the recent release of *Deep Throat*, the pornographic film sweeping mainstream viewing audiences during the early 1970s. While the Swede and Dawn try to steer conversation to the mundane—the scale model of the new home they are building, ironic sign of both the importance and the failure of the idea of home in the landscape of *American Pastoral*—the other dinner guests are preoccupied by taking sides in the burgeoning culture wars. Not surprisingly, Roth depicts Marcia Umanoff as a proponent of the film—a mark of the place often reserved for academics in satirical portraits of the New Left. The Swede's father, Lou Levov, becomes a particularly active critic of *Deep Throat* and the shift in American culture it portends. He is soon joined in his critique by Orcutt, who says that the film is emblematic of the age and its "[a]bnormality cloaked as ideology." To Orcutt, the era is one of "perpetual protest. Time was you could step away from it, you could make a stand against it" (347). He contends that "the grotesque is supplanting everything commonplace that people love about this country. Today, to be what they call 'repressed' is a source of shame to people—as not to be repressed used to be" (348). Orcutt's speech is undercut by the fact that his private morality does not match his public show of scruples. The Swede has only recently walked in on the man having sex with his wife.

Moreover, his sentiments about being "repressed" collide with the amount of repression going on at the table (348). Orcutt is avoiding recognition of his wife's alcoholism, the Swede is ignoring his wife's infidelity, and Lou Levov is pretending that the world has not changed at all since the time of his own vaunted youth. Most remarkable, however, is the suppression of the subject that undergirds the entire scene: the story of the Swede and Dawn's daughter, Merry, and her decision to bomb the local general store in order to protest American involvement in Vietnam. The Swede recognizes that "*Deep Throat* had never been the real subject anyway. Boiling away beneath *Deep Throat* was the far more disgusting and transgressive subject of Merry" (380). Unlike Dawn, who has recently undergone a face lift in order to erase the history of pain her daughter has inscribed on her face, the Swede is haunted by his absent child. Merry's suppressed story exists beneath the surface of dinner party chatter. The Swede is seeking to hide her chaotic return as a shattered version of her former self from the guests at his home. His decision to maintain this secret emphasizes the power of lies and evasions throughout the novel. The final pages of *American Pastoral*, however, suggest the impossibility of keeping these realities out of the home, a pastoral space no more.

Disorder and At-Homeness in America

The image of a house penetrated by world-historical events is a fitting ending for a novel that delves into the *Unheimlich* hidden at the heart of the *Heimlich*. It also refers back to a pivotal scene in the novel, one of many in which the Swede revisits the past to attempt to find the key to Merry's violent behavior. *American Pastoral* functions as an epistemological detective story with multiple levels of sleuthing work put forth to discern the motivation for her collapse and that of the Levov family line. While Nathan Zuckerman seeks a narrative commensurate with the task of explaining the tragic fall of high school hero, Swede Levov, Swede is engaged in a similar search for the motivations for his daughter's own dystopian swing into disorder.

In search of a reason for Merry's bombing of the local village general store, the Swede lands upon the images of self-immolating South Vietnamese monks that were disseminated on the evening news during the early days of the war. Merry, just 11 years old, had nightmares for weeks after witnessing the graphic images coming

> [o]ut of nowhere and into their home, the nimbus of flames, the upright monk, and the sudden liquefaction before he keels over; into their home all those other monks . . . ; into their home on Arcady Hill Road the charred and blackened corpse on its back in that empty street. (153–4)

The repetition of the phrase "into their home" emphasizes the Swede's strong belief in the sanctity of the private sphere of the family as a bulwark against the vicissitudes of world events. This dichotomy between the purported safety of home and the danger of the outside world threatening to permeate the boundaries of the domestic recurs throughout *American Pastoral*. It is again exemplified in Merry and the Swede's argument about the teenager's politically motivated trips into nearby New York City, a space that the Swede defines in contrast to the security of their tiny hamlet of Old Rimrock. Ironically, however, it is from the "safety" of her own home and in Old Rimrock that Merry plans and commits her gravest crime—a bubbling up of the *Unheimlich* into the *Heimlich*.

Fundamental to the universe of *American Pastoral* is this interest in home and the complexities it hides. Why can parents raised during and just after World War II not impart the feeling of security (both in the home and in the nation) that they'd experienced growing up? Does America function as an ideal home for diasporic Jewry, a long-term preoccupation of Roth's?[2] How can immigrant Jews inscribe themselves into the narrative of American life? Most prominently: Can the Jews' at-homeness in America exist alongside an equal sense of Jewish difference? Might Jews be too at home in America? Does their sense of the *Heimlich* nature of the nation mask something *Unheimlich*?

In fact, what draws Zuckerman to the Swede's story is precisely his high school hero's at-homeness not just in his own body—the athlete's grace that leaves the young Nathan breathless—but in America. The Swede was

> at home here the way the Wasps were at home here, an American not by sheer striving, not by being a Jew who invents a famous vaccine or a Jew on the Supreme Court, not by being the most brilliant or the most eminent or the best. (89)

This sense that the Swede was at home, not because of his exceptional Jewish brain, his Jewish difference, but precisely because of his sameness, his "isomorphism" to Wasp America, is what makes him seem to his many Jewish admirers "our point man into the next immersion" (89). Zuckerman's self-conscious use of the language of the playing field to describe the Swede's at-homeness in America has something to do with his body, too. The Swede is remarkable to Weequahic's Jewish population because he has not only been assimilated in the traditional immigrant sense; he has somehow been fully incorporated into the American body politic and the model of healthy American masculinity that so many Jewish men fail to attain. He does everything in "the ordinary way, the natural way, the regular American-guy way" (89). More problematically, the Swede experiences Jewishness as a pathology of sorts. When he is later recruited for a local synagogue, the Swede contends that he goes

> "into those synagogues and it's all foreign to me. It always has been. When I had to go to Hebrew school as a kid, all the time I was in that room I couldn't wait to get out on the ball field. I used to think, 'If I sit in this room any longer, I'm going to get sick.' There was something unhealthy about those places." (315)

The unhealthiness of "those places" is directly contrasted to the spheres in which the Swede is successful—the sports arena and the workplace. For the Weequahic Jews, the Swede's successful and healthy masculinity de-Judaizes him and makes him their "point man" into Americanness and whiteness.

American Pastoral articulates a number of preoccupations fundamental to Jewish-American writers during the postwar era. The Swede, the Gentile-seeming high school sports hero whom Zuckerman worships from childhood, embodies—in his "tall, blond, athletic" form— the tension between sameness and difference experienced by so many Jews in America.[3] The Swede, with his ability to slip between Christian and Jewish worlds with ease, has an "unconscious oneness with America." Free from "striving," "ambivalence," and "doubleness" (20), he is Roth's New Jew, ironic corollary to Alain Locke's "New Negro." If Swede Levov were a character in one of Roth's earlier novels, he would no doubt have functioned primarily as a peripheral figure, someone to be satirized: the white-bread Jew, the "Swede" in a Hebrew's clothing. However, emerging as the centerpiece of Roth's ambitious and historically engaged *American Pastoral*, he clearly possesses a more allegorical role. Here, the Swede illustrates a central tenet of postwar Jewish identity: "the contradiction in Jews who want to fit in and want to stand out, who insist they are different and insist they are no different" (20). As Roth makes increasingly clear in *American Pastoral*, the Swede marks a turning point in Jewish consciousness—as well as a shift in the consciousness of Jewish-American writers, including Roth himself. In post-1960s America, no longer does the Jew embody an immutable difference.

Representing this difference—whether through the perversion of Alexander Portnoy in *Portnoy's Complaint*, the physical abjection of Nathan Zuckerman in *The Anatomy Lesson*, or the class-conscious striving of Neil Klugman in *Goodbye, Columbus*—has long been Roth's theme. However, in *American Pastoral*, Jewish difference is something far more fluid, a racial identity that can be donned and doffed with comparative ease. Jews such as the Swede are exceptional in the American racial landscape precisely because, unlike African Americans, they can be "different" and "no different" at the same time (20). The Swede represents a shift in Jewish-American history from a time of anxious striving to a period of postwar prosperity when Jews prided themselves on having a special relationship to America that buttressed their sense of difference while maintaining their faith in the nation.

This Edenic scenario does not last, however. In *American Pastoral*, Roth depicts the postwar years in America as a gradual expulsion from paradise with distinct racial undertones. The Newark race riots first destroy the idyllic world of Swede Levov, where Jews can be both Jewish and American with equal fervor. With the rise of identity politics and the conflict between Baby Boomers and those born during the Depression, America enters a period of decline. Central to this dystopian vision is the Swede as a figure who stands in for America precisely because of his unselfconscious embrace of a pre-racially separatist form of ethnic identification. Roth, however, is not without ambivalence in his depiction of the Swede. Although Roth is brutal in his portrayal of Merry, throughout *American Pastoral* he clearly emphasizes that the Swede's acculturation and the lack of an authentic identity he imparts to his daughter are partially at fault for her attraction to violence and disorder.[4] And, in his discussion of the Swede's name—"this Swede who was actually only another of our neighborhood Seymours, whose forebears had been Solomons and Sauls and who would themselves beget Stephens who would in turn beget Shawns"—he foreshadows the extinction of a distinct Jewish genealogical line (20). The Swede's renaming is necessary for his transformation from an average Jewish boy into a Wasp simulacrum. The Swede's was

> an old American nickname, . . . bequeathed in a gym . . . He carried it with him like an invisible passport, . . . forthrightly evolving into a large, smooth, optimistic American such as his conspicuously raw forebears—including the obstinate father whose American claim was not inconsiderable—couldn't have dreamed of as one of their own. (207–8)

The Swede's renaming not only provides him with an "invisible passport" to a realm far outside the confines of Newark, but it also provides him with access to whiteness, the decidedly un-Jewish "Swede-ish" identity his name invokes.

This decimated genealogy is in direct contrast to that of William (Bill) Orcutt III, the Swede's foil in *American Pastoral*. When Dawn and the Swede first move to Old Rimrock, Orcutt takes it upon himself to give the young city-raised couple a tour of the area. During this tour,

Orcutt focuses particularly on tracing the trajectory of his own family's genealogy—an ancestral line that stretches back to pre-Revolutionary War America and collides with many American greats along the way. In contrast to the Levov line, the Orcutt family's story is "'a lesson in American history'" (306). Orcutt's natal myth is already inscribed into the mythology of the nation. But, even in this moment of seeming self-effacement—with the Swede marveling at the authentic Americanness of the Orcutt lineage—his repressed past emerges to haunt the present. When Orcutt mentions Morris County, his family's home for hundreds of years, the Swede can't stop thinking about his dead Uncle Morris, his father's beloved brother. Orcutt's recitation of national history is challenged by the Swede's Jewish-inflected personal history. This moment emphasizes the impossibility of ever fully effacing the past at the same time that it recalls a scene in Roth's later novel, *The Plot Against America*, when the character "Philip Roth" visits Washington, D.C., with his own America-obsessed father. Trekking to the Lincoln and Washington monuments, Roth's father provides his own subterranean history of the United States while giving his sons a tour of the nation's capital. This tour, alongside Orcutt's in *American Pastoral*, suggests that beneath national history is always a far more plural, hybrid tradition of narratives—the private family stories that always triumph over the universality of national myth.

Despite the Swede's seeming comfort in his own body, he experiences a certain degree of racially- and class-inflected anxiety when taking this tour with Orcutt. Seeking to implant himself into the American landscape, he begins to fantasize himself into the role of Johnny Appleseed—casting seeds onto the ground to become, literally, more rooted in the national geography. The Swede also seeks permanence in America through the home he buys in Old Rimrock. The eighteenth-century stone home not only imparts a feeling of security to the Swede and his young family, but also affords them a purchase on an authentic Americanness. The house is the emblem of the Swede's American dream realized. As Zuckerman relates, the rural stone house has had a lengthy career in the Swede's dreamlife. Traveling to a faraway baseball game during his high school days, the city-raised Swede Levov catches a glimpse of "a large stone house with black shutters set on a rise back of some trees": "the first house built of stone he'd ever seen, and to a city boy it was an architectural marvel" (189). The Swede garners much of his identity from the stone house he and Dawn inhabit during their marriage. When Dawn expresses disdain for the house and drafts Orcutt to design them a new, modern dwelling, the Swede, most notable for his unflappable neutrality throughout much of the book, takes it personally. The Swede relates that "[w]hen he overheard her telling the architect . . . that she had always hated their house, [he] was as stunned as if she were telling Orcutt she had always hated her husband" (189). The Swede identifies the house with himself and Dawn's attempt to escape from him and their marriage, but he also identifies the house with the past, both the long-ago past that Orcutt's family maintains in the area and the recent past in the form of Merry's history. Unlike Dawn, the Swede seeks to maintain this tie to the past and Merry's Edenic childhood.

The power of the house is also connected to its location in a rural part of New Jersey that functions in direct contrast to the more urban areas in which the Swede and Dawn grew up. The Swede's decision to live in Old Rimrock, its name and Wasp pedigree significant because it provides his family with a portal into the very bedrock of white Americana, proves the only choice he has ever made that challenges his father's point of view. Lou Levov believes that the couple should live in the suburbs just outside Newark, an area of upwardly mobile sons and daughters of working-class Newark immigrants and a place where young Merry can grow up around Jews. For the Swede, "[n]ext to marrying Dawn Dwyer, buying that house and the hundred acres and moving out to Old Rimrock was the most daring thing he had ever done" (310). The Swede's decision to challenge his father emerges from his explicit desire to escape the confines of Jewish identity into what he perceives as an authentic American space. He contends that "[w]hat was Mars to his father was *America* to him—he was settling Revolutionary New Jersey as if for the first time. Out in Old Rimrock, all of America lay at their door" (310). Roth's focus on the capacity of a house to convey national identity and class mobility—to be the realization of the American dream—alludes to and rewrites Fitzgerald's *The Great Gatsby*. Zuckerman, like Fitzgerald's narrator Carraway, records the decline of fortunes that the great house portends for the tragic protagonist of his story.

The Old Rimrock house is the culmination of the Swede's fantasies of Americanness, but it is also the site of the uncanny return of all he has sought to suppress in his flight from difference. The Swede explicitly links his decision to live in the Old Rimrock house with his choice to marry outside the Jewish faith, asking "'Why shouldn't I be where I want to be? Why shouldn't I be with *who* I want to be? . . . That's what being an American is—isn't it?'" (315). Deciding "where [he] want[s] to be" and with whom is fundamental to the ideal of American individuality that the Swede embraces; despite his absolute obeisance to familial duty in most respects, in these decisions he is caught in the dialectic between "descent" and "consent," inheritance and choice, the antipodes that Werner Sollors sees as central to the symbology of American identity and American literature. The Swede begins to wonder if Merry was harmed by his choice of place and faith. Near the end of *American Pastoral*, the Swede recalls Lou Levov's prediction about Merry. After hearing that Dawn had covertly had his infant granddaughter baptized, the Swede's father couldn't "shake the conviction that what lay behind Merry's difficulties all along was the secret baptism: that, and the Christmas tree, and the Easter bonnet, enough for that poor kid *never* to know who she was" (389). Although the Swede once eschewed his father's ominous reading of Merry's mixed heritage, he retrospectively gives credence to the idea that her lack of a fixed identity led to her endless—and increasingly dangerous—search for an ontological index, a marker of where and to what group she belonged. He and Dawn "raised a child who was neither Catholic nor Jew, who instead was first a stutterer, then a killer, then a Jain" (386). Merry's attraction to extremes comes, he fears, from her parents' attempts to raise her as a blank slate, free from the bonds of ethnic and class identification from which they have fled. Their attempt to bring up Merry free from the fetters of their own pasts has backfired. The Swede begins to wonder if "[a]ll the wrongness that he had locked away in himself, that he had buried as deep as a man could bury it, had come out anyway"—a return of the repressed that haunts all of the Levovs (386).

There are other signs, too, that Merry represents the uncanny, "all the wrongness that he had locked away." Seeking the origins of his daughter's behavior yet again, Swede happens upon the memory of an act of symbolic incest, a prolonged kiss between father and daughter during a beach vacation. The Swede returns to this image throughout the novel to explain his daughter's future anger, but also to examine the impulses that might have existed beneath the careful façade of perfect father and husband he maintained over the years. The Swede is forced to confront these incestuous feelings and his own imperfections when he encounters Merry's proxy and uncanny double, Rita Cohen. After she goes on the run, Merry sends fellow militant Cohen to the Swede to ask for money and prized items from her childhood, and, according to Rita, to seduce him. Although she looks nothing like Merry, Cohen emerges as an uncanny reminder of the lost child to the Swede, functioning as Merry's double at the same time that she reminds Swede of the ugliness of an ethnic identity he has left behind. At times, Rita seems a figment of the Swede's imagination; like Merry, Rita is deeply invested in showing him his wrongness, the internal demons he has carefully kept at bay. She invites him to a hotel room and tries to seduce him, displaying her genitalia to the unflappable Swede. When the Swede gets an erection, he feels himself at odds with his idea of himself, but also strangely reminded of his flirtation with young Merry; Rita's sexuality is a frightening reminder of both his daughter and his own inappropriate desires.

Cohen also functions as an uncanny reminder of the Jewishness the Swede has left behind. Her curly hair and Jewish name remind him of the many young American Jews involved in radicalism at the time. To the Swede, Rita and Merry are seeking in radical politics the identity afforded by the Jewish diasporic past. As Lou Levov puts it: "Once Jews ran away from oppression; now they run away from no-oppression" (255). In addition to sharing this uniquely Jewish motivation for violence, Rita shares with Merry her anger, articulating the absent girl's rage against her parents. Rita asserts that Merry's anger at her parents arose from recognizing the force of her mother's hatred—the disgust Dawn felt when confronted with her daughter's stutter and her distinctly unfeminine attributes. Even more shockingly for the Swede, according to Rita, Merry believes that her mother hated her because "she's [the Swede's] daughter. It's all fine and well for Miss New Jersey to marry a Jew. But to raise a Jew? That's a whole other bag of tricks." According to Rita, the Swede had a "shiksa wife," but not a "shiksa daughter" (138). Despite her official lack of religious identification, Merry somehow retains a marked Jewish difference; a tall, blond girl, she is still somehow not a "shiksa daughter." Merry's adolescent weight gain functions as a repudiation of conventional Wasp standards of beauty, the very same ideals that helped her mother win Miss New Jersey. More strikingly, however, her unremitting stutter undermines her family's attempts at all-American fluency and likens the young Merry to her Yiddish-accented grandparents and great-grandparents, the first Levovs in America. When Merry becomes politicized, she even more overtly marks her difference from her parents and their ideals. She ventriloquizes the militant speech of the Black Panthers and paints the word "honky" on her bedroom wall, adopting a racialized otherness that is not explicitly Jewish inflected, but that proves disturbing to her parents nonetheless. According to the Swede, Merry was "[a]lways pretending to be somebody else. What began benignly enough when she was playing at Audrey Hepburn had evolved in only a decade into this outlandish myth of selflessness" (242).

It is Merry who reminds her parents that they, too, are impersonators who have self-consciously rejected their own pasts. Dawn disavows her working-class Irish roots and becomes a Miss America finalist. When her daughter contaminates her life with violence, she decides to leave the Swede, to purify herself and her past by marrying Bill Orcutt, "Mr. America" (385). From his first appearance in *American Pastoral*, Swede Levov, too, is identified with forgetting—the central mechanism of the uncanny. He functions as a figure of forgetting in a dual manner. During wartime, when many of Newark's fathers, sons, and husbands are fighting and dying abroad, Seymour's triumphs on the sports field function as a potent talisman against recognition of death. This forgetting works on more than one level. As Debra Shostak points out:

> although it remains unspoken by Nathan, the implication that hovers behind this urge to forget is that the Swede gives the American Jews license to repress their knowledge of what was happening to European Jews. If they can forget themselves as Jews, they can forget the image of the docile, feminized Jewish man who, in failing to resist gentile oppression, troubles their own self-image. (101)

Forgetting themselves as Jews involves more than just a disavowal of offstage genocide. It also necessitates a forgetting of self entirely—the Swede's eerie depersonalization and "oneness with America" (*Pastoral* 20).

The pastoral that Lou Levov and his forebears have given birth to is not the one they had imagined. They had set into motion the "flight of the immigrant rocket, the upward, unbroken immigrant trajectory from slave-driven great-grandfather to self-driven grandfather to self-confident, accomplished, independent father to the highest high flier of them all, the fourth-generation child for whom America was to be heaven itself" (122). They had intended to design a "utopia of a rational existence" that would allow their sons and daughters to choose their affiliations and fully embrace the civil religion of Americanness (123). These Jewish immigrant forefathers had not imagined the return of unreason that the "fourth-generation child" might bring to the "heaven" of America, the eruption of madness into reasonable existence that Terry Castle describes as being at the heart of the uncanny.

In *American Pastoral*, Merry Levov becomes just such an uncanny child, uninterested in the transmission of tribal knowledge and the American dream espoused by her parents and grandparents. She marks the "disruption of the anticipated American future that was simply to have unrolled out of the solid American past," in which "each generation's getting smarter—smarter for knowing the inadequacies and limitations of the generations before" (85). This progressive view of history was predicated on

> each new generation's breaking away from the parochialism a little further, out of the desire to go the limit in America with your rights, forming yourself as an ideal person who gets rid of

the traditional Jewish habits and attitudes, who frees himself of
the pre-America insecurities and the old, constraining obsessions
so as to live unapologetically as an equal among equals. (85)

Roth portrays Merry's madness as the direct result of her family's
decision to create a perfect American subject, free from the shackles
of the past, "the pre-America insecurities" and the responsibilities that
come along with them. By doing so, he does not suggest that maintaining a Jewish identity, or any identity for that matter, is necessary to
prevent descent into madness. Instead, he contends that this sort of
madness is an unavoidable remnant of the ways in which we all deal
with the question of the past. Beginning with Nathan Zuckerman's high
school reunion and his memories of the vaunted Swede Levov, the
novel ends with a meditation on the different ways in which the past
evades our attempts to erase it. To the Roth of *American Pastoral*, the
past is inescapable, a repressed entity that always returns to haunt the
personal and national landscape. It is in the terrain of this struggle,
rather than in Old Rimrock and the genealogical posturing of Bill
Orcutt, that he situates the true America.

Part II

The Human Stain

Introduction

As Jennifer Glaser demonstrates, the tragic consequences of the history that Roth presents in *American Pastoral* are illuminated by Freud's notion of the uncanny. Freud worked from the principle that repressed thoughts must, disconcertingly, return to conscious experience. Swede Levov's fascination for Nathan Zuckerman derives in part from his uncanny blankness and from how his evasion of his past and culturally defined identity requires an act of concealment, even from himself—such that the violence that occurs to him seems unforeseen. Such concealment of the stains that make the individual impure and hence human is central to the premise of *The Human Stain*, whose repressed material is also knotted into America's troubled racial and ethnic history. Like *American Pastoral*, *The Human Stain* presents a view of America, offered in the story of Coleman Silk and framed by that of his biographer, once again the writer Zuckerman; and likewise, the narrator's inventions echo the protagonist's process of remaking his own life. But whereas Zuckerman fades out as an embodied presence less than a quarter of the way through *American Pastoral* and does not return, he remains visible to the end of *The Human Stain*. Zuckerman assigns himself the task of historiography, his curiosity about Coleman turned to dedication upon the death of his friend. The unraveling of secrets becomes the engine of narrative in *The Human Stain*, fueled, as in *American Pastoral*, by Zuckerman's imagination when he lacks knowledge of other people's secrets. Roth thus uncovers many ironies. The chapter title "Everyone Knows," for example, threatens the power of the social network over the individual; the confident assertion, however, obscures how impossible it is to reckon with either public histories or private secrets.

The novel is bursting with secrets past and present—secrets held, secrets told. Coleman, professor of Classics and dean of Athena College, possesses several. Most crucially, like the Swede, Coleman represses his past and his identity—a light-skinned African American, he succeeds for most of his adult life in passing as a Jew. He also keeps his current life a secret, conducting an affair with the seemingly unlikely Faunia Farley. Working as a custodian at the college, she has secrets, too, a secret of past socioeconomic privilege, a secret tragedy, and a secret literacy. Similarly, Coleman's nemesis at the College, Delphine Roux, silences the story of her French family as well as her present longings for romance. Even Zuckerman has his secrets. He gives no reason for his flight from life into the habits of a recluse nor for his reversal, once he pursues the story of the friend who "danced me right back into life" only to let "all the world's malice [come] rushing in" (*Stain* 45).

Some critics have contemplated the novel's form, including Zuckerman's construction of himself in the tale he tells (see Royal, "Plotting") as well as Roth's debt to classical tragedy, especially Sophocles' *Oedipus the King* (see Bakewell; Sánchez Canales; and Carlos del Ama). More have addressed the politics of *The Human Stain*, notably how it responds to the phenomenon of "political correctness" that dominated the culture wars of the 1990s in the United States, which Roth invokes in the opening pages with reference to the "purity binge" (*Stain* 2) of the impeachment proceedings against President Bill Clinton (see Boxwell; Medin; Podhoretz; and Safer, "Tragedy"). Most critics, however, have concentrated on the novel's complex representations of identity. Of particular interest are the intersections and slippages Roth illuminates within the discourses of race and ethnicity. Some readers have thus inquired into Coleman Silk's choice of a Jewish identity as the guise in which to perform his invented selfhood, suggesting that Roth finds in the vexed question of what constitutes "Jewishness" a useful metaphor for the indeterminacy of identity (see Glaser and Kral). In considering Coleman's choice to pass as white, many other critics have observed in Roth's presentation of selfhood the tensions between the fixities of racial classifications and a postmodern model, according to which we perform our identities; critics give special attention to the trope of racial passing (see Franco; Kirby; Maslan; and Rankine) and identify the writer Anatole Broyard, who passed as white for his entire career, as a possible source for Roth's characterization of Coleman Silk (see Kaplan).

That very issue of racial passing leads Dean Franco to inquire in this volume into how identity depends on the contradictory relations between social recognition and individuality. As in David Brauner's analysis of *American Pastoral*, Franco identifies a crucial problem of storytelling, concerning who may have the authority and access to tell another's story. And as in Glaser's treatment of that earlier novel, Franco finds the repressed material of race to constitute a terrifying cultural secret. Franco notes that, in the act of racial passing, one can "write" a story of the self, presupposing that race is distinct from being. He focuses on how Zuckerman's attempt to know and tell Coleman's secrets is an act of recognition, or perhaps misrecognition, with ethical implications. Closely analyzing an intimate scene between Faunia and Coleman, Franco demonstrates that Roth's metaphor of *vision* stands for recognition of social identity, of a secret self that, taken as essential, would weaken the premise upon which Coleman has wagered his life, that selves are stories we invent.

Catherine Morley devotes her chapter to that process of creation, arguing that the American myth of purity underwrites the assumptions that one may make about inventing both identity and texts. Like Brauner's chapter on *American Pastoral*, Morley's focuses on the parallel writing of histories—Zuckerman's writing of Coleman's history, and Coleman's rewriting of his own. Morley attends to the interpenetration of real and imagined happenings, fact and fiction, evidence and conjecture—all the elements of history that fill in the blanks and tell the secrets of identity in *The Human Stain*. Emphasizing that, like history, self-presentation is in the end a matter of words, Morley points also to other words that provide Roth with an inescapable literary context, noting his allusions to *Oedipus the King*, Homer's *Iliad*, James Joyce's *A Portrait of an Artist as a Young Man* (1916), and his own *Ghost Writer*. Fitzgerald's *The Great Gatsby*, too, shadows this novel, as Gordon and Glaser found it to shadow *American Pastoral*.

Such intertextuality is the starting point of Gabrielle Seeley and Jeffrey Rubin-Dorsky's chapter. Meticulously examining the echoes of Hawthorne's *Scarlet Letter* to be found in *The Human Stain*, Seeley and Rubin-Dorsky return to the secrets both Franco and Morley explore and, like Franco, to how such secrets bring out conflicts between an individual's autonomy and the community. The chapter underscores the punishing self-righteousness inherent in the community's assumption that "Everyone Knows" and, like Morley's chapter, questions the "fantasy of purity" (242) that is the standard against which Hawthorne's and Roth's protagonists are measured, a standard belied by the stain that makes us human. Unlike Franco, for whom it remains an open question whether the truth of the self may exist beyond public recognition, Seeley and Rubin-Dorsky conclude that *The Human Stain* rejects the fulfillments Hawthorne predicts for the future of America. For them, Roth's vision of the potential for Americans to live freely, according to their own nature and in consonance with the American mythos inscribed by Emerson and Thoreau, is very dark indeed.

CHAPTER 5

Race, Recognition, and Responsibility in *The Human Stain*

Dean Franco

If I take note of your race, gender, or visible sign of religion, am I taking you more or less seriously than if I regard you as a singular individual? Or, does taking note of your individuality mean precisely that I catalogue your race, gender, religion, and so on? Does a self even exist apart from social identity? The question is tricky because it depends on what we think the signs of identity mean. Identities are either regarded as limitations to be overcome, expressions of group- or self-consciousness to be fully realized, or pragmatic indices of experience, the stuff that shapes our selves. Answering the question depends on how you view the outcome of social battles for group-based recognition waged by minorities and feminists in the United States during the late 1960s and 1970s, and the evolving culture wars—political fights for recognition in public institutions and universities—of the 1980s and 1990s. During the past three decades, we have developed a complicated, if sensitive, grammar for identities, so that identity is a culturally salient, salutary, yet still vexing mode of political recognition. If I am expected to see your "race" it means I should know about your experiences as a raced person, in the here and now, and it also means I should know your history. In this way, public identities are also pedagogical: putting an identity out there in public helps advance understanding about a group, lessening the chances of further discrimination. However, the critical relationship one must have with one's identity, almost as if with an object, guarantees that the political recognition gained is also a form of misrecognition because identity subsumes the whole self. So, what about the *ethics* of recognition? If you announce your social identity as the most prominent part of your self, are you not asking that others, too, foreground a historical and social construct as fundamental? Though the United States as a society has become ever more competent in negotiating the politics of identity en masse, we stumble when it comes to recognizing individuals, calling people "half black" or "half white," relying on a grammar of ratios that can barely begin to describe the experiences and inner lives of individuals so named. This very problem of recognition is embedded in the word itself, which as a noun means "re-knowing," or the confirmation of what was already presumed to be true. You may want recognition, but you need me to give it. Between people, recognition originates with one saying to the other, "yes, you are what I thought you were all along," a pronouncement that either validates or condemns, with occasionally disastrous results.

The tension between public, social identity and individuality is at the core of Philip Roth's 2001 novel, *The Human Stain*, in which identity is like a subscript, transcribing the lives of its characters, often without their knowledge. In the novel's present-time of 1998, social identities offer useful shorthand for gaining recognition, but also promote mis-recognition; or better, identity is the very point at which recognition meets misrecognition. Occasionally, awfully, misrecognition is attended by sanctimonious condemnation, and we long to cry out, as Roth's character Nathan Zuckerman does on behalf of a scandalized Bill Clinton, "A HUMAN BEING LIVES HERE" (3). It is this tension between a presumptive public knowledge and an individual's private sense of self that animates the plot of *The Human Stain*. The novel's initial scene of recognition is between Nathan and Coleman Silk. Nathan has retreated to the mountains of western Massachusetts to live and write in quiet seclusion, out of the public eye and away from the tumult of social life. Coleman has lived as an outspoken dean of nearby Athena college, until his fall from power over his alleged use of a racist term. The fallout includes his angry resignation and his wife's subsequent death, which he blames on the stress of the scandal. Still in the grip of rage and grief, Coleman storms in on Nathan, with whom he is barely acquainted at the time, and requests that he write a book about his life. "If [I] wrote the story ... nobody would believe it" (11), Coleman admits, raising a central question of the novel: who can tell the story of a life? Coleman explains that he is too close to his own story, a familiar paralyzing condition. At the same time, Coleman's story is already in circulation. "Everyone knows," as Coleman's successor in the dean's office, Delphine Roux, puts it (38). The story being told about Coleman is the exposure of his old-fashioned, white patriarchal racism. Coleman has slurred two African American students, calling them "spooks." Never mind that the students had never attended his class and that Coleman had no idea of their race. If they never came to class it was evidence of

Coleman's intimidating elitism and the need for his political correction. So the story goes, but when Coleman attempts to tell his own version, he is thwarted, and though we never learn a word of his own failed manuscript's contents, its title, "Spooks," signifies the impossibility of finding a vocabulary or a narrative arc about himself that is not already commandeered by others.

Recognition

So far, Coleman's problem illustrates the general difficulty of finding a public language for private experience, but readers know that it is more complicated than that. Coleman Silk lived his last 50 years as a white Jewish man, but he spent his first 20 as a black man. Notice how easy that sentence went down, lubricated with the clever preposition "as"—as in "living *as* white" and "living *as* black." With race, seeming is at least as real as being, and being is just as contingent as seeming. When the narrative springs the secret and the reader learns that Coleman is passing, the revelation comes with specificity and a sudden backstory, giving a disproportionate relevance to the past in the present. Sympathetic readers will feel the absurdity of charging Coleman with racism—"*he's not racist, he's black!*"—but ironically we have more claim on this defense than he does. To claim that identity late in the day would be difficult, and announcing race against the grain of popular under-standing may well be impossible. While "race" telegraphs history, it still relies on optics; a man who has convincingly passed as white and Jewish may not be able to contravene visual evidence. Even Nathan, when he sees Coleman fully enraged after the death of his wife, describes him as looking brown-hued, "bruised and ruined like a piece of fruit" (12). Later, at a more temperate moment, he does better by Coleman, noting him as one of those yellowish-skinned Jews who could pass for black (15–16). Presuming Coleman to be white, Nathan interprets his light tan skin in a several ways, but somehow "black" remains outside the frame of plausibility.

Part of the difficulty in telling one's story is that the elements of storytelling, including the narrative arc of a life, the terms of identity, the very terms of recognizability, precede us all; they are generic, yet they are all we have to tell our story. Judith Butler explains the predicament this way:

> The norms by which I seek to make myself recognizable are not precisely mine. They are not born with me; the temporality of their emergence does not coincide with the temporality of my own life. So in living my life as a recognizable being, I live a vector

of temporalities, one of which has my death as its terminus, but another of which consists of the social temporality of norms by which my recognizability is established. These norms are, as it were, indifferent to me, my life, and my death. ("Giving" 26)

Starting with "temporality," the familiar but seemingly pointless question we all receive on one birthday or another—"how does it feel to be eighteen/forty/sixty?"—suggests that our life's temporality is marked by distinct states of being. Eighteen is not simply a number, it means something socially and culturally, as do forty, sixty, and so on. Yet the most common answer to these questions is something like "I don't know, I feel the same," indicating how our internal sense of being is not just out of sync but of a different ontological order from the social meaning of age. Surely the same could be said for other markers of our identity, including gender and race, which have aggregate social meaning. We will never be anyone but our selves, yet we express ourselves in a public and presumably common language, taking a great leap of faith that we are both intelligible and true in our account of others and ourselves. Coleman and his clandestine lover Faunia Farley, with their 40-year age difference, do not conform to the predictive temporality of "age," wherein men of a certain age are socially unacceptable as companions for much younger women. There is not even a publicly sanctioned language for the relationship, and so existing outside the accountability of language, Coleman and Faunia lead "unlivable" lives, to quote Butler from another context (*Bodies* 3).

No wonder that Coleman tells Nathan he cannot write his own memoir. The very structure of memoir writing as a look backward predicts a story's end, quite contrary to the life the still warm and breathing author is living. We say he is "too close" to the experience, but what we mean is simply that he is still living, has not yet counted his story as finished, and so cannot relinquish its telling to a set of terms not his own. Death is the scripted terminus of every one of our stories, and it may be the structuring reality—the given that determines the coherence of everything else—but it is precisely the part of our story that we cannot authentically tell. Let's be honest: ordinarily, we push the fact of our inevitable death so far outside the frame of our lives that it has little to do with identity matters. Identity may be cultural, or ethical, or political, but death is death. Only retrospectively, when the story of a completed life is told, do we need to figure the relation of death to the role identity played in the life lived. For Coleman, however, identity is not fixed and in fact it is only one of several ways in which he lives a protean life, from passing as white, to his affair with Faunia. Commenting on the assistance he gets from Viagra, he tells Nathan "[t]hey should have called it Zeus," a wry line that suggests how, like other mortals who receive assistance from the gods, Coleman lives beyond mortal temporality, beyond social morality (32).

Passing

Even as a young man, Coleman knew that he lived within a set of narratives not of his own making. Thus, though his sister Ernestine insists that "Coleman never in his life chafed under being a Negro," he nonetheless revolted at the prospect of living as part of a collective identity, a "we" (324–5). Rather, the raw singularity of the "I" was what thrilled him most (108). But how to live outside of the "we," how to be an individual "I" and still be recognized? Early in his life Coleman lived in a paradox of blackness. His father was originally an optician but lost his business during the Great Depression and spent the rest of his life as a Pullman porter. The career shift, from self-made professional to working-class staff, thematically correlates with Coleman's own ambitions: a refusal of a racial- or class-based identity (Pullman porter was both), in favor of one unique, individualistic, and precise (ironically, inverting his father's calling, Coleman's singularity depends upon blurry vision). The bluntly aggregate term "Negro" would seem to have nothing to do with Coleman, who learned to regard himself as " 'neither one thing or the other' " (98). What Coleman does not understand when he throws off the "we" for the raw singularity of the "I" is that singularity and individuality are not the same thing. No one can sustain singularity because the singular person is by definition beyond recognition and thus subject to misrecognition. Public language may be inadequate for describing the personal self, but that will not stop others from telling the story of your life anyway. While in the Navy, Coleman chooses to quit blackness, yet is nonetheless found out. A white prostitute guesses his secret one night when he is on shore leave: "You're a black nigger, ain't you, boy?" (180). Her certainty underlines how Coleman cannot live without a public identity, while hinting at what whiteness will come to mean throughout the novel. The being of whiteness is the unmasking of blackness, or brownness, or "yellow," to hearken to Les Farley, Faunia's traumatized, Vietnam-veteran ex-husband. Whiteness exists as the very boundary and hence the exposure of "race" itself. Coleman knows this intuitively from boxing under the presumptive identity of a white man who, against the wishes of one promoter, declares that he "[wouldn't] carry no nigger" (117). Use of the racial epithet establishes Coleman's whiteness at this moment, as does his profane suggestion of whiteness as a meritocracy—an announcement that contravenes Coleman's own youthful experience of how white folks engineer their social privilege (86).

After his early, failed experiment in the Navy, Coleman learns that "passing" is not the same as hiding, nor even is it pretending. Rather, passing involves the free play of expectations, the narrative deployment of public perception, and the summoning of misrecognition. A person passing is fluent in the gestures, habits, and assumptions people have about race based on their own social location and social grouping. Passing is not, therefore, passive, not simply looking like a member of another race. On the contrary, passing exploits just how much physical variation there is in any racial or ethnic grouping, thereby destabilizing the very concept of "race." A group of intellectual white folks might assume that the tan-skinned classicist in their midst is white, and his deployment of cultural capital would confirm that presumption. Passing rejects identity as a state of being, and is instead reliant on—or produces—an "epistemology of the closet," Eve Sedgwick's phrase for gays passing as straight, but appropriate for a discussion of racial passing as well.[1] Passing, like closetedness, assumes that race is separable from being, and that it can be managed, and hidden away. Before marriage, Coleman tries passing with Ellie, a sophisticated, light-skinned African American woman, who is canny enough about racial gamesmanship to ask Coleman

> "What are you anyway?" Right out she spots something and goes ahead and says it. But now the sweat is not pouring off him . . . "What am I? Play it any way you like," Coleman says. "Is that the way *you* play it?" she asks. "Of course that's the way I play it," he says. "So white girls think you're white?" "Whatever they think," he says, "I let them think." (133)

The key phrase is "let them think," which though seemingly a passive project, in fact would involve a sophisticated awareness of the codes of whiteness and the narrative arrangement of a white life. For instance, Nathan thinks Coleman is Jewish, and Coleman "lets" him—but provides a gloss of a backstory about his parents, neighborhood, and name to float Nathan's assumption. The effect is to broaden the spectrum of racial being. Not only black, white, and Jewish, but also fair-skinned Jew, tan-skinned Jew, and so forth. Race becomes less a reified fact and more a contingent variable. When Coleman is charged with racism, his indignation resonates with popular and academic professions of a postethnic and postracial America made by reactionary and cosmopolitan critics alike. Having seemed to escape race, Coleman is shocked to find how much it still matters in 1998.

The Human Stain ends with a barbed dismissal of the reigning politics of race, spoken by Ernestine, Coleman's younger sister, on the day of Coleman's funeral. Her sensible, winning speech may herald the end of political correctness and thereby posthumously exonerate Coleman, but its occasion, Coleman's funeral, implicitly condemns Coleman's unearnest identification. That is, rather than work above-board to critique the veracity of race as a mode of recognition, Coleman deploys the limitations of recognition, including the utter fallibility of public assumptions about identity, as his method of passing. Through Ernestine, the novel arrives at its central insight: Coleman was the victim of the present-day reigning politics of recognition, pejoratively known as political correctness, but Coleman's own cynicism was ultimately an irresponsible and unethical form of storytelling. The novel's route to this final revelation takes in a much wider circuit, namely, the ethical problem of being responsible for the stories we tell about others and that others tell about us; where private lives interface with public identities, recognition is at once a political and ethical phenomenon. Coleman is the victim of misrecognition insofar as his intent toward the missing students was certainly not racist, but he also peddled a false story about his life and family so that he could "pass" as white and Jewish. If Ernestine's common sense is the high road, above the political traffic of race, then Coleman's passing is, if not the low road, at least an ill-fated end-run around race, the passing lane that delivers him right into the very jam he was trying to avoid. As Nathan puts it, "[b]uried as a Jew . . . and if I was speculating correctly, killed as a Jew. Another of the problems of impersonation" (325).

Being Jewish

Popular professions of a postracial society notwithstanding, in public life someone will always be there to say, "I know what you are." There is no living outside of identity. Intuiting this, Coleman chooses what is perhaps the most suitable and accurate identity for him, namely, being Jewish. Arriving at the "four freest square miles in America" (135), Greenwich Village, at precisely the moment when Jews of his generation (and Roth's) were arriving to take in and up the intellectual scene, Jewish or Jew-*ish* may be just the right term to describe Coleman, for Jews were increasingly regarded as liberated, intellectual, ambitious, and racially ambiguous. In fact, "Jewish" has been an ethnically protean identity in the west for at least two centuries. As Daniel Itzkovitz explains,

> During the late nineteenth and early twentieth centuries, many commentators struggled with baffling questions of how to under-stand and categorize the Jews: in an astonishingly wide range of

journalistic, literary, and social-scientific texts, the image of "the Jew" developed out of a set of paradoxes—Jews were both white and racially other, American and foreign, deviant and normative, vulgar and highly cultivated, and seem to have an uncomfortably unstable relation to gendered difference—all of which made them seem at once inside and inescapably outside of normative white American culture. (38)

After World War II, with the waning of restrictive anti-Jewish quotas at universities, and the growing intolerance for public anti-Semitism, along with the increasing value of cultural pluralism, intellectual Jews found academia and the professions of political and cultural commentary to be fertile fields for sowing the seeds of a truly hybrid Jewish-American. No longer anxious about assimilating *into* American culture, third-generation American Jews were instrumental in changing the culture itself, making a place for themselves within it precisely by making it more Jewish.

In the early twentieth century, influential pragmatist thinkers argued that the formation of a Jewish state in Palestine would strengthen American Jews' sense of cultural identity and thereby make Jews an even more integral part of America's cultural pluralism (see Obenzinger). By the 1950s this integration had been achieved, and by the 1960s, when Jewish contemporaries of Coleman Silk were becoming leading figures in art, entertainment, cultural commentary, and academia, Jews were regarded by many Americans as the "model minority," the ethnic group that best maintained cultural particularity, while contributing its own cultural genius to America at large.[2] As Jonathan Freedman argues, during the twentieth century,

> [T]he series of representations created by Jews and Gentiles alike, on the fly, out of their mutually constitutive and destabilizing encounters with each other, helped crucially to shape the stories and the meta-stories U.S. culture tells about race, ethnicity, and gender, and their shifting relation to normative and counternormative identities in a rapidly changing America. (6)

In the middle of the twentieth century, the launch of the magazine *Commentary*, along with public sympathy for Israel and the dissemination of information about the Holocaust, including the Broadway staging of *The Diary of Anne Frank*, made Jewishness a very public, very recognizable identity. However, the protean nature of Jewishness, celebrated and sent-up by Jewish artists and comedians as at once a religion and a culture, a nationality (Israel) and an American ethnicity, lent Jews an insider-outsider status in America, and gave Jews a deconstructive claim on "identity" itself.

It is no wonder that many Jews, who had been historically supportive of civil rights and social equality for African Americans, were turned off by Affirmative Action programs that relied on racial identification (see Herberg). American Jews had successfully liberated themselves from racialization and knew "identity" was a social construction. American Jews may not have thrown off the "we" of people-hood that Coleman Silk flies from while a "Howard Negro," but as early as the mid-1950s they had publicly pluralized that "we"; by 1960 the leading Jewish-edited journals were aptly named *Commentary* and *Dissent*, characterizing the Jewish commitment to multiple-voiced political praxis (*Stain* 108). Most importantly, the popularity of Jewish actors, musicians, comedians, and writers in the 1950s and 1960s meant that Jewishness was a publicly held, publicly performed identity, thus making Jewishness a fine vehicle for racial passing.

Narrative Recognition

Only Nathan suspects that Coleman has a secret, and he probes it upon his death. Nathan's desire to learn about Coleman's real life is not yet more presumptive "knowing" of Coleman but an attempt to plumb the depth of unknowability itself and so to take stock of the complexity of a life. Representing that complexity without reducing it involves destabilizing the very frames of the known—that is, blurring fact and fiction. Nathan is as postmodern an author as Roth is, and his narrative in *The Human Stain* is comparable to Roth's earlier novel *Operation Shylock* (1993). In *Operation Shylock*, Roth merged historical record with fictive invention to create two competing possibilities of a Jewish life, all while cloaking the mechanics of fiction (the novel was billed as a "confession"); *The Human Stain* puts its fictionality upfront, however. The novel provides endless detail about Coleman's life, but only at the end do we learn how Nathan knows so much, from long conversations with Ernestine and a visit to the Silk family home. At the same time, there is much here that neither Ernestine, Nathan, nor anyone but Coleman and Faunia could ever know, and this is where imagination, craft, but also a sense of responsibility comes in. Nathan is not just filling in the blanks with fiction but using fiction to arrive at a more complex and truer account of Coleman's life than Coleman himself would give. Late in the novel, Nathan explains how he began the novel the reader holds, *The Human Stain*:

> Out there at his grave, where everything he ever was would appear to have been canceled out by the weight and mass of all

that dirt if by nothing else, I waited and I waited for him to speak
. . . And that is how all this began: by my standing alone in a
darkening graveyard and entering into professional competition
with death. (338)

Nathan's audacity to revivify Coleman is matched by the frank
admission, "[n]ow that I knew everything, it was as though I knew
nothing" (333), but also the wise reflection that

For all that the world is full of people who go around believing
they've got you or your neighbor figured out, there really is no
bottom to what is not known. The truth about us is endless. As are
the lies. Caught between, I thought. (315)

The last sentence is spare for Roth, and though it is Coleman who is
caught between truth and lies, the absence of a subject in the sentence
suggest that this is the social condition of us all. In this way, without
saying that Coleman is an "everyman," his predicament of living
according to a script not of his own making is in fact universal.

If telling Coleman's story is to "enter into professional competition
with death," Nathan is not the only one competing. The anonymous
blogger "Clytemnestra" (possibly Delphine) folds Coleman into a fem-
inist agenda-pushing tale of rapine patriarchy, while Coleman's children
use his funeral as a podium for recuperative myth-making. At Coleman's
funeral Nathan observes a ceremony performed to redeem and recast
the meaning of his life. The funeral is orchestrated by Coleman's sons,
who refuse to discuss Faunia with Nathan, telling him, "This cheap
little cunt has nothing to do with anything" (308). Instead, the choreog-
raphy, location, music, and speakers—notably, the African American
Herb Keble, who publicly confesses he was wrong for not supporting
Coleman during the "spooks scandal"—amounts to a "purifying ritual"
(285). Intolerably incorrect in life, Coleman is compared to Thoreau
when dead (310). No wonder Nathan thinks of Coleman's sons as
Hollywood executives (308). Nathan resists the fable-making, but his
own attempt to tell Coleman's story comes after the funeral's conclusion,
when he meets Ernestine and learns the secret. Coleman's death, rather
than giving teleological shape to his narrative life—that is, beginning,
middle, end!—makes Coleman appear to Nathan "not just an unknown
but an uncohesive person" (333). Though Nathan admits—insists—
that the truth of a person is so complex, layered, contradictory, and
frequently hidden as to elude firm knowledge, Coleman's charisma
and mystery, and the subsequent fabrication of his life upon his death
returns Nathan to Coleman's original charge, that he must write the story

of his life. When first pressed with the task, Nathan was indignantly dismissive, but confronted by all the retroactive, bad storytelling, he becomes indignantly responsible.

Nathan's competition with death, then, is not an attempt to bring Coleman back to life but to deconstruct the scripting of Coleman's life according to a simple teleology; death puts a punctuation mark at the end of a life's sentence, suggesting linearity, coherence, and completion, and this is the very sentence Nathan aims to deconstruct. When Nathan avowedly assumes responsibility for Coleman's story late in the novel, readers may realize for the first time that this is Nathan's and not Roth's novel, and that the narrative exposition, Coleman's backstory, and especially the intimate details of his relationship with Faunia combine what Nathan knows to be fact with what can only be fiction. By disguising the mechanics of fiction-writing until late in the text, Nathan weaves Coleman's story in with his own growing interest in Coleman. The narrative technique puts Nathan on the periphery of Coleman's story, cloaking his authorial centrality. In this way, Nathan can demonstrate the social meaning of "race" for Coleman while permitting an intimate and personal space of racelessness for his character and friend.

Nathan further occludes the story's narrativity by allowing the putatively illiterate Faunia the most significant insight into Coleman. During a moment that is at once the height of their bliss and the limit of their public isolation, Faunia tells Coleman, "Close all the doors, before and after. All the social ways of thinking, shut 'em down. Everything the wonderful society is asking? . . . Fuck all that" (229). I am referring to the moment in the novel when Coleman commands Faunia to dance for him. Both are naked, after a night of steamy sex, and each is on the cusp of falling in love with the other. Coleman hits "play" on his bedside CD player, and Artie Shaw begins blowing out his rendition of "The Man I Love." While Faunia dances, the reader is given a high-definition blazon of her body, including her "graying yellow hair," her skin "scarred in half a dozen places, one kneecap abraded like a child's," and "very fine threadlike cuts half healed on both her arms and legs" (226). Her "hands [are] roughened, reddened," her body is "a little greasy from the hours before," and she is covered in "spots where she's been bitten and stung, a hair of his, an ampersand of his hair like a dainty grayish mole adhering to her cheek" (226-7). This amalgam—the scars and scrapes, the hair and fluids—is where the body meets the world, and it is the lived experience of being human. Up till this point in the novel, the phrase "human stain" has yet to be defined, and if it previously suggested skin pigmentation, or race, here we see that "stain" is something more like "experience," the messy and mess-making experience of being human.

Roth highlights the abject body here—the private and socially shameful aspects of the body that have no socially sanctioned place or language in public life—and in doing so suggests that Coleman and Faunia are in fact dwelling in abjection, literally outcast from the sphere of the social, as Faunia would have it. Indeed, at the culmination of her dance, Coleman jokingly asks Faunia, "'who can get out of this alive?'" and the question punctuates the scene as not only private, and not only socially unacceptable, but wholly unlivable (231).

Faunia wisely assesses Coleman while she dances, seeing in his gaze a desire for her to "claim" him (227). Giving himself over to Faunia is Coleman's free fall into love with her, and she feels it too, the "connection," but unlike him she resists it, and it is at that point that her interior monologue breaks through, telling Coleman simply, "I see you" (226, 228). The line is simple enough, suggesting that she sees him falling for her, but it also has deeper resonance as a statement of recognition: I see who and what you are, without judgment, and crucially, without scripted expectations. On the contrary, she spends the rest of the dance demanding that he not fall in love, that he hold onto nothing but this moment of joy and thrill, that he refuse the typical outcomes of love, including a straight relationship, social approval through marriage, and a narrative life. It is by pushing back against these scripts, by dwelling in precisely what is abject—the hair, the fluids, the aged and marred bodies—that Faunia refuses the social, and in doing so she alone can see Coleman for what he is: not his race or any of his other secrets, but that self that precedes and exceeds the social and public scrutiny that would require secrets in the first place.

Faunia's seeing Coleman is an antinarrative optics, a way of looking through the two-dimensional screen of reductive stories about identity. Seeing Coleman, she sees through both the stories told about Coleman and the story he would tell about himself. Contemplating his "spooks" scandal, she thinks, "publicly humiliated as a racist professor, and what's a racist professor? It's not that you've just become one. The story is you've been discovered, so it's been your whole life" (228). In contrast to this mythic monster, she sees a "baby" for the way he is evidently falling in love with her, and "baby" effectively captures his self prior to the mess of social experience, a self that has neither been hailed by nor resisted the call to socially identify as any one thing. Though she surely does not mean it this way, Faunia's "baby" is indeed the "raw I" that Coleman longs for when at Howard, raw in the sense that he has yet to be assimilated into the stew of the group, or raw in that he has yet to define himself *against* anything else. Later in the novel Nathan conjectures that Coleman told Faunia his secret, though this scene offers not the revelation of secrets but a life beyond the epistemology of secrets and knowing, beyond the penetrating scrutiny that attempts to figure it all out. Telling a secret does not undo the logic that created the secret in the first place. To say, "I pass as white but I was born and grew up as black" may deconstruct the binary of black/white, but it does not create any space outside the binary and only reaffirms its grip. Coleman seemingly does not understand how to live beyond such a logic, and perhaps neither does Faunia, but in the dance it is Faunia who resists the temptation to extend their moment of bliss into social time and some logical structure. By freezing the moment, Faunia sustains their space beyond the social, the symbolically correct, or the temporally predictable.

If Faunia's seeing is against simplistic narrative, it is nonetheless embedded within Nathan's own complex and layered storytelling, itself a narrative written against reductive optics. Faunia's dance for Coleman is one of many events Nathan imagines in his attempt to reconstruct Coleman's life. There is no evidence of Coleman telling Nathan about this dance, and certainly the high-definition detail that characterizes this section can only be Nathan's invention. The dance, orchestrated by Coleman but performed by Faunia, occurs out of both time and social space. Coleman repeatedly hits the "replay" button on the CD player, so the song loops, never fully ending. Added to that, the moment itself reprises the youthful dance of Coleman's first great love, Steena Paulson, who spontaneously danced to Artie Shaw's "The Man I Love," revealing to Coleman "[t]hat big white thing" (115). That phrase, reflecting Coleman's appreciation of the racial borders crossed, likewise links *The Human Stain* to what is arguably an intertext, Ralph Ellison's *Invisible Man* (1952; see Parrish, "Ralph Ellison"). Ellison's novel also begins with a naked white woman dancing for a black audience, though in Ellison's scene, set in Oklahoma City in the 1930s, the dance violently reinforces racial identities and terrorizes the black boys and the white woman. Having broken the ultimate taboo of interracial sexual mingling, both groups become vulnerable to and thereby reaffirm the power of the white men also gathered in the room. If Coleman's gaze on Steena put him in control of "that big white thing," thereby attaining the power of whiteness itself, Faunia's gaze on Coleman during her dance breaks up the power dynamic entirely. Ellison's stripper was terrified, Steena was alternately liberated and abashed by her own performance, but Faunia above all is frank, clear-sighted, and unencumbered by the social scripts that possess all of the others.

Paying attention to the inventiveness of Nathan's narrative may seem to pose a conundrum: How can we say that Nathan gives us a truer portrait of Coleman when he is so clearly fictionalizing? Isn't this more imagination than recognition? And anyway, if recognition is so hard to come by due to the inadequacy of language, not to mention all the competing stories, how can Nathan possibly confer it? The answer, I think, is that while Nathan cannot finally "see" Coleman, because he was deceived like everyone else while Coleman was alive, he imagines someone who can, Faunia. When after the funeral Nathan learns that Faunia is not illiterate after all, and that she kept a diary, he is faced with a person whose secret is her disclosure of secrets, or giving an account of her own life in writing. In this way she is like Coleman, though also his inverse. In terms of the social purchase of identities, Coleman traded up, while Faunia traded down. Still, each possessed a secret self that no one could claim. With Faunia, Nathan has a surrogate, someone who knows what it means to close off "all the social ways of thinking" and who lives in the contingency of a given moment. Indeed, Faunia is also strikingly like Nathan in this regard. He too has chosen to abandon the welter of the social world, living in a small cabin and devoting his days to craft. And he too is trailed by a human stain, figured in his diseased body. As imagined by Nathan, Faunia announces "the human stain" as the mark we leave upon the world, just by being human. More precisely for Nathan, prostate cancer has left him both impotent and embarrassingly incontinent. Amplifying her connection to the abject, Nathan even imagines a small backstory for Faunia, a job she once had cleaning the remains of a suicide from a cabin. That was the worst job she ever had to do, and in the "worst" was the "truth" (340). The equation of the worst with the truth suggests how truth lies outside of the social and the normative, that the truth of being human exists beyond the grammar of recognition.

If Nathan could not see the truth of Coleman, he nonetheless imagines a relationship wherein someone could. By having Faunia say "I see you," Nathan allows that Coleman can be seen, but he also concedes the intimacy and contingency of the moment. It is not replicable, and it is not transferable, not even from character to author. Nathan creates for Faunia and Coleman a private experience and a private language, not one that can be translated for the reader. When Steena danced for Coleman, he saw the political implications immediately, the "big white thing," a phrase intelligible to both Nathan and the reader. With Faunia, Coleman hardly speaks, only to acknowledge that the moment when each sees the human capacity of the other is precisely the moment that marks their death. Faunia may wipe away all the social ways of being and knowing the self, but what is left remains unstated, recognized by only the two.

For all the critical claims made about Roth's postmodern style and autobiographical trickery, *The Human Stain* demonstrates something about the status of knowing and recognizing the other at once simpler and more elegant. Nathan's story does not detail the really real of

Coleman, but asserts that that real exists; Roth's novel does not give the "truth" of passing, but narrates a space wherein that truth may be. If there is something postmodern here, it is the disarming representation of how narrative—that is storytelling—is not just the novelist's occupation, but the very mode of social encounter itself. The corollary to Nathan's assertion that the unknowns of a life are endless is the commensurate urge to fill in those unknowns with caricature and exaggeration at worst, characterization and realistic possibility at best. That is, Nathan's narrative itself is an act of recognition that intends to compensate for all the bad-faith storytelling about Coleman, while Roth's novel professes the importance and integrity of just such an act. Telling or writing the story of a life has consequences for all involved, and so narrative, as a form of recognition, is an ethical act. And the thrust of narrative recognition is not simply in one direction. As Nathan learns in the closing pages of the novel, having written Coleman's story, he too is now exposed, recognized by Les Farley. Indeed, Nathan is so startled by Les's recognition—knowing Les killed Coleman and Faunia, and knowing that Les knows that he knows—that when Les commands Nathan to send him the book, he retreats: "What book?" Les brings him back, reminding him "Your book. Send the book" (360), and the line underscores the novel's final salient insight about recognition: We are always "sending the book," or telling stories about the world, and these very stories expose us and are the basis of others' recognition of us. Coleman, Faunia, and Delphine all attempt to tell stories without being exposed, and though Nathan's story is precisely of their exposure, he forgets the moral of his own tale. No wonder that the novel's closing lines, among the most beautiful in all of contemporary literature, put Les at the center. Out on the ice, all alone with Les, Nathan is the very epitome of exposed. He knows enough about Les and Les about him to obviate any more storytelling, and "the book" is briefly beside the point. Seated at this fishing hole on the frozen lake is "a man . . . like the X of an illiterate's signature on a sheet of paper. There it was, if not the whole story, the whole picture." Les, that is, the "only human marker in all of nature" (361), symbolizes the point where the truth of a life is deposited before its author retreats to a safer, more anonymous life.

CHAPTER 6

Possessed by the Past: History, Nostalgia, and Language in *The Human Stain*

Catherine Morley

Near the end of *The Human Stain* Nathan Zuckerman considers the life and the fate of his recently deceased friend Coleman Silk. Contemplating Silk's unrelenting individualism and his antipathy toward convention, Zuckerman imagines Coleman's life as a Greek tragedy, his friend a great hero of epic proportions undone by the forces that previously seemed at his behest:

> The man who decides to forge a distinct historical destiny, who sets out to spring the historical lock, and who does so, brilliantly succeeds at altering his personal lot, only to be ensnared by the history he hadn't quite counted on: the history that isn't yet history, the history that the clock is now ticking off, the history proliferating as I write, accruing a minute at a time and grasped better by the future than it will ever be by us. The we that is inescapable: the present moment, the common lot, the current mood, the mind of one's country, the stranglehold of history that is one's own time. Blindsided by the terrifyingly provisional nature of everything. (335–6)

By this stage of the narrative Coleman's secret is known to Nathan: his suppressed past, his identity as an African American, his lost family and lost lovers. The revelation of Coleman's secret, however, is not what undoes him. In fact, by the end of the narrative, nobody knows Coleman's secret other than Zuckerman, and whether or not he will reveal it remains undisclosed. Rather, what undoes Coleman are the circumstances of his present, the cultural mores of the premillennial years during which the public mood was charged by revelations of sexual high jinks in the Oval Office. In a way, what undoes Coleman is the fact that he is "out of time," a figure who belongs more to a vanishing past than to a present mired in political correctness, when what Zuckerman describes as "the ecstasy of sanctimony" (2) threatens to overtake the nation. The idea of Coleman as an historical anachronism is compounded by his sister's entreaties to her other brother to forgive Coleman's rejection, to "[s]ee him historically" (327) as someone too driven and too impatient to wait for the civil rights movement. Ernestine's appeal to regard Coleman Silk as out of time, both behind and ahead of his historical moment, is an instructive way in which to approach the novel as a whole: steeped in history, possessed by the past, and resistant to the present. *The Human Stain*, which takes as its central theme the pliability of the past, throbs with historical resonance, with references to events from the execution of Sacco and Vanzetti to the release of Nelson Mandela. Moreover, it encloses a series of intertextual allusions to the classics, to Shakespeare's tragedies, Bataille, Kundera, Mallarmé, Mann, Keats, Kristeva, Ellison, and to any number of writers from the American Renaissance, including Melville, Thoreau, Emerson, Dickinson, and Hawthorne. Even the ghosts of Roth's own fictional creations haunt the novel, which is set in the same Berkshires location as the aptly titled novella *The Ghost Writer* (1979), where we first met young Nathan Zuckerman as he embarked on his literary career.

Forging Destiny, Forging the Past

The return to the Berkshires for the unraveling of Coleman's story is revealing. Just as the events of *The Ghost Writer* were mediated by Nathan Zuckerman, so too are those of *The Human Stain*. In both novels we are presented first and foremost with the writer's consciousness and with a recollection of the writer's interactions with a strong male character (both of whom are in the employ of Athena College) who briefly and partially allows the writer to share in the events of his life.[1] Moreover, both novels use that central figure, E. I. Lonoff and Coleman Silk, respectively, to facilitate an inquiry into the writer's craft. Toward the end of the earlier novel, the young Zuckerman likens himself to Joyce's Stephen Dedalus, taking on the moniker of Nathan Dedalus and assuming the role that Dedalus sets himself at the end of *A Portrait of the Artist as a Young Man* (1916): "I will to encounter for the millionth time the reality of experience and forge in the smithy of my soul the uncreated conscience of my race" (276).[2] It is interesting to take these words, uttered so resolutely by Joyce's alter ego, in the context of those used above to describe Zuckerman's subject. Coleman too is "forging" something, and while it is not the "uncreated conscience of [his] race," it is an individual "historical destiny" distinct from that of his race. In both instances, the use of the word "forge" is deliberately and deliciously ambiguous, implying both creation and falsification. And therein lies one of the central concerns of the novel, indeed, of both novels: the extent to which the author plays fast and free with the details of the past in the creation of fictions.

This, of course, is not a new subject for Roth. From the very beginning, his fiction has incorporated the details of history and aspects of his own biography.[3] Debra Shostak, for example, makes the case for reading Zuckerman and Roth's protagonists in the American trilogy as subject to the deterministic forces of history and locked within its cyclical patterns (230–68). And Derek Royal, among others, has written convincingly of how the "forces of history—American history specifically—threaten to overtake personal freedom" ("Pastoral Dreams" 186).[4] Certainly Roth has always delighted in tantalizing the reader with a dash of personal history woven through his narratives. Royal is right to observe Roth's desire to write the individual subject into the fabric of twentieth-century American history. Much of Roth's later work from *American Pastoral* (1997) onwards is an overt and sustained engagement with the details and textures of postwar American history. But more than this, Roth is interested in the role of the writer in salvaging the individual stories and unofficial histories that get lost beneath the weight of the documented past. He is interested in the various forms of contingency that enter the historical record. *The Human Stain* explores the malleability not only of individual identity but also of history and it examines the means by which the imprint of the author's mind marks the historical material with which he works.

Though ostensibly a secondary character in the novel, the first voice the reader encounters in *The Human Stain* is that of Nathan Zuckerman. The story Nathan reveals is that of his dead neighbor and friend, Coleman Silk. Zuckerman's first impulse is to contextualize his story within the recent historical framework of the Clinton administration during the summer of 1998, when the details of the Lewinsky affair were an international news story. Moving back beyond the recent past, however, Zuckerman grounds his story even deeper, offering the details of Coleman's tenure at Athena College, and likening the post office cleaned by Coleman's lover to a shelter for an Okie family from "the Dust Bowl back in the 1930s" (1). By setting the dead man's story in such an historical context, Zuckerman immediately fastens Coleman's narrative to the wider history of the United States and, for good measure, mounts it with an American flag, which flutters at the end of the novel's opening paragraph. The overall effect is to deliberately place this story, this lost history, within a wider, national, historical context—to salvage Coleman's story from the scrapheap of lost histories. The irony, of course, is that Coleman is a fiction—at many levels. Coleman Silk and Nathan Zuckerman are the fictional creations of Philip Roth. But even at the level of the story, Coleman is a fiction, a self-conceived, self-molded Gatsbyesque character who has reconstituted his past and rewritten his African American racial identity.[5] Zuckerman's position at the edge of the narrative as neighbor, witness, onlooker, and confidante, and as both character and narrator, bears more than a passing resemblance to Fitzgerald's Nick Carraway, who recounts the secrets of Gatsby's life after his death. Like Carraway, it is Zuckerman who "springs the lock" and untangles the past, but the past unraveled by Zuckerman must be tainted, bearing the inevitable human stain of memory and the incursions of the authorial consciousness. Ultimately, what Zuckerman presents to the reader is the "provisional nature of everything," including his own narrative.

From the very outset of the novel, Zuckerman's narrative is retrospective. When the book opens, Coleman Silk and Faunia Farley are both already dead. It is Zuckerman who resuscitates their stories, who breathes life into their narratives, within the context of his own story, the book he resolves to write after their deaths, "The Human Stain." It is interesting that the initial act that undoes Coleman, precipitating his death, is the "Spooks" incident, when he refers to two absentee African American students as "spooks." For by the time we encounter him, Coleman himself is a specter, a haunting presence brought to life by the author. Coleman's ghostly titled memoir, "Spooks," also haunts Zuckerman, urging its own textual substantiation to escape the historical abyss. But Zuckerman's narrative is necessarily a story of shading and inference. There is much that he cannot know, much that he can only guess at.[6] For instance, his futile efforts to attain the diary of Faunia Farley leave him with just two personal encounters with Coleman's lover upon which to build her history. His only encounter with Lester Farley, Faunia's estranged husband, who may or may not be responsible for her and Coleman's deaths, comes some time after the supposed incidents in the Chinese restaurant where the veteran attempts to overcome his post-traumatic stress syndrome. Again, these incidents are filtered through the consciousness of the writer. Delphine Roux's story, her personal history of unfulfilled sexual longing and her dealings with Coleman, can only be conjecture on the part of the narrator. Finally, our clearly unreliable narrator often seems at pains to validate his own stories. But these attempts at validation only add yet another filtering consciousness which frames Coleman's story, since Nathan reveals that much of what he knows of Coleman's final days is second-hand information, learned from former colleagues and family such as Ernestine, Herb Keble, Nelson Primus, and Jeff Silk.

The narrative is inevitably shaped by Zuckerman's consciousness, and, imitating the workings of the human mind, it skips backwards and forwards in time. It revives Coleman and Faunia, and moves through their pasts in a nonlinear fashion, taking us from the revelation of a love affair back in time to the "Spooks" incident, through to the events of his adolescence and young adulthood, which led him to abandon his race, and back again to his rediscovered ardor. While Zuckerman withholds his knowledge of Coleman's racial identity until well into the narrative, it is clear that he has this knowledge much earlier in the text. For instance, shortly after divulging Coleman's big "secret" regarding Faunia, Zuckerman lays on the dramatic irony by disclosing how Coleman had once been identified as an African American in a Norfolk brothel during his U.S. Navy days. Zuckerman revels in the irony of Coleman's expulsion from Athena College on the basis of his racism, deliberately working into his narrative the details of the Vanessa Williams "Miss America" scandal, his reference to Nelson Mandela's release, and the "mythical battle between a home-run god who was white and a home-run god who was brown" (2).[7] Though clearly attempting to document the events as they unfolded from the summer of 1998 onwards, the writer cannot resist inserting the rhetorical flourishes and touches that enrich a narrative. In fact, confounded by the impossibility of precise historical documentation, Nathan admits:

> How do I know . . . ? I don't. I couldn't know . . . I can't know. Now that they're dead, nobody can know. For better or worse, I can only do what everyone does who thinks that they know. I imagine. I am forced to imagine. It happens to be what I do for a living. It is my job. It's now all I do. (213)

Thus the writer's task, it would seem, is salvage and reclamation, albeit with an acknowledgment that deviation from the historical record is inevitable. Zuckerman declares as much by the end of the narrative when Lester asks him about the kinds of books that he writes. Admitting that sometimes he writes "true stories," Zuckerman declines to categorize his current unfinished project, "The Human Stain," as such, telling Lester that he writes about " 'people like [him]' " (356). Indeed, he tells the veteran that the biographical information regarding his PTSD, information shared with the reader at an earlier stage of the novel, is material for "The Human Stain." What we are presented with, therefore, is a meditation on the means by which a writer crafts his materials, how the writer reorders and renegotiates the past, making the static provisional, for the sake of literary artifice.

The Fuzzy Haze of Nostalgia

While the events of Coleman's life—and indeed the lives of those implicated in his story—are subject to the agenda of the author, they are also filtered through the glistening haze of nostalgia and the permeable strands of memory. Shechner has written persuasively about the association between music and nostalgia in *American Pastoral*, linking the Pied Pipers' 1944 hit record "Dream," which precipitates the flow of narrative and unleashes the Swede's story, to the so-called American Dream that slips through the fingers of Seymour Levov (*Up Society's Ass* 164). Music also plays a large part in the unlocking of memory in *The Human Stain*. Significantly titled big band tunes such as "Those Little White Lies" and "Green Eyes" set Coleman into "emotional motion" (14). In other words, the music elicits memories sweetened by rhythm and lyricism. For Zuckerman too this is undoubtedly the case. An appositely titled Sinatra number, "Bewitched, Bothered, and Bewildered," seals the bond of his friendship with Silk in facilitating their dance, which the writer admits brings him "back into life" (45). It is this musically fuelled marriage of men, the sensuous coupling of the impotent writer and the Viagra-charged professor, that awakens in Zuckerman his desire to write, making Coleman's "disaster my subject . . . And ma[king] the proper presentation of his secret my problem to solve" (45).[8] Coleman and Zuckerman become conjoined. Soon after this point in the narrative, Zuckerman begins ostentatiously to make free with Coleman's story, taking up his life and filling in the blank spaces. Recognizing the importance of music to Silk and its life-engendering capabilities, Zuckerman later imagines an erotic scenario in which Coleman's lost lover, Steena Palsson (introduced to the writer via the accidental disinterment of a long buried letter), performs a provocative dance to Artie Shaw's "The Man I Love." Steena's dance is Zuckerman's first real fictional departure in terms of imagining the details of his friend's life. The earlier materials regarding Coleman's boxing career in East Orange and his experiences at Howard are, we are later informed, supplied by Ernestine. But the intimate details of Coleman's relationship with Steena can only be conjecture, informed to an extent, but quite probably an historical untruth. Later still, Zuckerman presents a similar event between Faunia and Coleman, with the same musical accompaniment, and just as Coleman had named the nubile Steena his "Voluptas" (23), so too is Faunia described.

In both cases the events described by Zuckerman are nostalgia-tinged acts of the imagination rather than facts of history, prompted by shards of truth gathered from remembered conversations between the two men. In both "memories," a song enables the couple to attain a physical intimacy, just as a song brings Zuckerman and Coleman together. But the writer cannot have been privy to the words of either woman, to Faunia's claims to be able to "see" Coleman or to Steena's awkward efforts at poetic invention. In fact, Steena's words and observations are surely those of Zuckerman, who after all has carefully observed the sinews of his friend's legs, back, and neck.[9] In using memories of conversations, which themselves comprise memories of past events, in order to write Coleman's story, Zuckerman invents lives for those who would otherwise be written out of history: the man who "passes," the seemingly illiterate, abused woman, and the crazed Vietnam vet. On one hand, one might regard Zuckerman's narrative as the lonely act of a grief-stricken friend overcome with an overwhelming sense of his own mortality. But on the other hand, Zuckerman's action in penciling in the lives of these characters is a profound and deeply political move, a concerted effort to inscribe lost history. Certainly, the workings of nostalgia are undeniable in the soundtrack that suffuses the narrative, which, as Lester observes, comes to an abrupt end when Coleman dies: " 'Guess that music won't be coming from that house on Saturday nights anymore' " (259). But nostalgia and memory work not to blur the past but to facilitate the composition of histories.

The most immediate and overtly political of histories inscribed by Zuckerman is the lost black history of his protagonist. To an extent Zuckerman invents a past for Coleman, offering a narrative explaining his decision to pass as white. But much of the story is provided by Coleman's sister Ernestine, a history teacher. In the process of informing Zuckerman of the events in her brother's life, his struggles with his father and the pain inflicted upon his mother, Ernestine educates Zuckerman on black history. She discusses her despair of "Black History Month," which she feels perpetuates the divide in history between official and alternative versions of the past. She introduces him to black inventors and explorers such as Charles Drew and Matthew Henson, mavericks not unlike her brother in some respects. Ernestine's education of Zuckerman in the facts of black history, in turn, informs his fictional narrative, his version of Coleman's life. And he attributes to Coleman's mother a lengthy sermon on the interracial history of the Silk family and its links to the English colonist John Fenwick, which she delivers to her son on his impending departure from his African American life. Thus, again, a pattern is established of fiction conjoined with the facts of history. Not for the first or the last time, Roth offers a narrative that straddles the fault line between the real and the imagined.[10] Roth's interest in African American history is carried forward from the previous novel in the American trilogy, *I Married a Communist*, in which he suffuses his story of Iron Rinn with aspects of black history, even at times mapping the trajectory of his hero's life on to that of the black activist, actor, and socialist, Paul Robeson.[11] Robeson, most revered for his role as the revenge-driven Othello, even makes a walk-on appearance in the novel, which itself is a story of revenge and retribution. At another level, of course, the novel layers itself historically in terms of the embedded intertext of Ralph Ellison's novel *Invisible Man* (1952), which Roth has acknowledged as an influence upon *him* (see "Writing About Jews" 223).[12]

The novel's palimpsestic associations with *Invisible Man*, while adding yet another historical layer to the text, actually further compound the central paradox of Zuckerman's task of compiling a history out of half-remembered fragments and orts. The central conceit of Ellison's text is the specterlike quality of his protagonist, the nonectoplasmic ghost who guides us through his lives and guises. The power of his narrative and its historical resonance lie in the reader's inability to locate his identity and the ultimate impossibility of allying his story with any official historical narrative. During the interval of a musical recital, Zuckerman observes from afar his friend with his lover:

> [H]e has a secret. This man constructed along the most convincing, believable emotional lines, this force with a history as a force, this benignly wily, smoothly charming, seeming totality of a manly man nonetheless has a gigantic secret. How do I reach this conclusion? Why a secret? Because it is there when he's with her. And when he's not with her it's there too—it's the secret that's his magnetism. It's something *not* there that beguiles, and it's what's been drawing me all along, the enigmatic *it* that he holds apart as his and no one else's. He's set himself up like the moon to be only half visible . . . There is a blank. That's all I can say. They are, together, a *pair* of blanks. (212–13)

If Coleman presents a blank, an emptiness, then Zuckerman sees it as his role to write upon that blank, to fill it in, to inscribe it with his words. The notion of Coleman—or Faunia—as a blank for the writer to inscribe is extended to the end of the novel when Zuckerman encounters Lester on the blank, white, ice lake.[13] The lake is likened to a sheet of blank paper and Lester is compared to the "X of an illiterate's signature" (361). Thus, that what we are left with at the conclusion of the narrative is an "X" upon a vast white canvas, beneath which dark waters turn themselves over in an eternal cycle of renewal, attests to the central difficulty faced by Zuckerman: the impossibility of inscription that does not detract from the mysterious allure of Coleman. His "blankness," his unreadability, is his story. The unfilled, unwritten blank is Coleman's history.

Infiltrating History with Words

This notion of a bewitching "unreadability" recurs throughout the novel, from Faunia's feigned illiteracy to Lisa Silk's remedial work with illiterate children. In both instances the failure or unwillingness to read is closely related to Coleman. When the professor visits his harassed daughter's Reading Recovery classroom he encounters a young child, Carmen, who though unable to formulate simple words on her magnetic canvas is mesmerized by Coleman. Chided by her teacher to regard the classroom visitor as "'invisible,'" Carmen insists that she "'*can* see him'" (158). Though unable to negotiate words, the unsocialized Carmen can read the blank that is Coleman. The episode with Carmen, as mediated by Zuckerman, is conflated with Coleman's interactions with Faunia and descends into a quasi-surreal scene in which multiple, childish versions of Faunia grapple with plastic letters. Later still, while dancing to "The Man I Love," Faunia repeats to Coleman that she too can "see" him and that her ability to "see" him aligns him with her in terms of their unreadable lives, their secrets. For Carmen and Faunia words are redundant. Words are of no use to either, and rather than reveal they seem to muddy the clarity with which they see. While Carmen's illiteracy is real, Faunia feigns her inability to read or to write—another forgery of sorts. Their erotic intimacy is overturned when Coleman attempts to read the Sunday morning newspapers to Faunia—repeating the educative role of his father who had instructed his children to read the daily newspaper at the dinner table—who claims she "doesn't want to be taught" (235). For Faunia words are unnecessary because they are inadequate; they can never convey the brutal realities of her life's history. Indeed, she recognizes their tendency to aestheticize and thereby alter real, lived experience. For this reason, when dancing, Faunia reminds Coleman not to think, not to move beyond the here and now of "[t]he secret little moment" (229) by reading a love story into their intimacy. Faunia resists being subsumed into an overarching narrative and her refusal to read or write is part of this negation of simplistic explanation, her repudiation of the backstory. She is the self-appointed unreadable cipher and ultimately her story remains undisclosed. Thus Faunia, possibly even more so than Coleman, maintains the magnetic blankness that is so irresistible to a writer.

In many ways, Carmen and Faunia are the antitheses of Delphine, the professor of language and literature who manipulates words in an attempt to understand herself and her feelings for the disgraced Dean. When we first encounter Delphine she too grapples with language as she struggles to find words that adequately convey her conception of herself. Tapping the plastic letters of her keyboard alone in her faculty office, she attempts to invent herself with words as she assembles a lonely-hearts advertisement for the back pages of the *New York Times Book Review*. From the first mention of her in Zuckerman's narrative Delphine is associated with words, not unlike her classical namesake who also issues messages while in a state of extreme frenzy.[14] Delphine is the presumed author of the anonymous handwritten words—likened, unsurprisingly, by Zuckerman to a Dickinson poem in their linear deployment—that inform Coleman of the widespread knowledge of his affair. Words and their configuration are Professor Roux's business and as the arbiter of Coleman's dismissal following his alleged misuse of the word "spooks," she fashions her reality with words and puts her faith in them. Unlike the earthy and intuitive Faunia, who mistrusts words for their very malleability, Delphine embraces the mercurial romance of words and their practitioners, fantasizing about Kundera as she figuratively prunes and ameliorates her self-image. The irony is that Delphine, who regards her life as a *bildungsroman* (not unlike the young Zuckerman in *The Ghost Writer*), bears much resemblance to her prey. She too is a self-invented creature, her lonely-hearts efforts a micro-cosmic version of her American dream to escape the weight of her ancestral past. Like Coleman, an "individualist *par excellence*" (311), she buys into the great American myth of escape from Old World trappings and self-invention:

> I will go to America and be the author of my life, she says; I will construct myself outside the orthodoxy of my family's given, I will fight *against* the given, impassioned subjectivity carried to the limit, individualism at its best—and she winds up instead in a drama beyond her control. She winds up as the author of nothing. There is the drive to master things, and the thing that is mastered is oneself. (273)

Delphine makes the ultimate mistake in placing her faith in words, in assuming that she can write her own destiny and rewrite her identity to escape her past. Like Coleman, the similarly "unclassifiable" (271) professor is undone by words. Her handwriting on the initial missive betrays her identity and her carefully sculpted words, seeking a replica of her besmirched former colleague, are disseminated to her entire department. Her mastery of language is an illusion, which even she acknowledges in her realization that she lacks "fluency" (275). The oracular Delphine loses direction of her narrative and her history is infiltrated and possessed by the authorial consciousness of Nathan Zuckerman.

Of course Nathan Zuckerman, dubbed in *The Ghost Writer* Nathan Dedalus, the master forger, is more than aware of the power of words and their capacity to create, fabricate, and destroy reputations, fictions, and histories. After all, his is a life that has been shaped and tainted by the pen; and his is a quest to write the story of a man who occupies both a real and an imaginary world. At the end of the novel, while conversing with Lester Farley on the frozen hilltop lake, the author's consciousness returns to its abiding concern—how to write the past while remaining loyal to his friend, how to tell Coleman's story? In this instance, Coleman's willful self-disguise, his half-revealing of himself, enables the author to portray him as both a fact of history and the result of invention. In many ways, Coleman himself is the self-created embodiment of Zuckerman's story insofar as he is a commingling of real and imagined histories. The inventiveness of the writer in portraying these seemingly opposing forces, therefore, is a necessary element of Zuckerman's narrative, and is flagged as such from the very beginning of the novel with Roth's deliberate insertion of the epigraph from Sophocles' *Oedipus the King*:

> OEDIPUS: What is the rite of purification? How shall it be
> done?
> CREON: By banishing a man, or expiation of blood by blood . . .
> (Sophocles 114–15)

On one level, the epigraph from the ancient Athenian tragedy underlines the novel's theme of the enchanting but unattainable glow of purity of self.[15] On another level, however, one might regard the epigraph as highlighting the means whereby stories come into being—by fusion and textual alchemy rather than as pure acts of the imagination. Just as the epigraph speaks of the impossibility of pure identity by means other than an eradication of the self, its very enclosure at the beginning of *The Human Stain*, a novel concerned with American identity, American lives, and American history, attests to the impossibility of literary purity, the unfeasibility of eliminating ancestry or escaping the past. Thus the epigraph, a transcultural intertext that illuminates the fusion of the created and "factual" elements of Coleman's story, is Roth's deliberate choice; it both bespeaks the tragedy of a man unable to escape "the history he hadn't quite counted on" (335) and illuminates the impossibility of textual purity.

Indeed, just as Coleman is a hybrid character in terms of his multiple racial identities and his real and imagined histories, Zuckerman's narrative itself is a hybrid in its fusion of history and conjecture with the web of allusions that run throughout. The admixture of epic with classical tragedy and the events of recent history at the very beginning of the narrative, where Coleman explores the affinities between the *Iliad* and the troubles of the Clinton administration, underlies the means whereby the world of the literary imagination and the "real" world infect one another. Moreover, Zuckerman seems intent on demonstrating the inevitable entanglement of real and imaginary worlds when he juxtaposes an imagined version of Coleman's explanation of the origins of Western literature's first epic battle with the actual events of the summer of 1998. For Coleman, the collision of the factual and the fabricated is a way of life, his own personal, self-crafted history a tissue of untruths. Yet this series of untruths constitutes the truth of Coleman Silk; the man is his secret, his blankness. And his story, "Spooks" or "The Human Stain," must conjoin the historical "real" and the imagined in order to approximate the "truth" of the man. Both titles are apposite. The "spook," the ghost, is a hybrid entity, an occupant of two worlds, caught between its past, corporeal incarnation and the present landscape of its haunting where it only half lives. The ghost's spectral existence is entirely predicated on its earlier, real, bodily manifestation. It bears the mark of its own humanity. Coleman's spectral existence is predicated on his African American racial inheritance, a past he deposes in favor of an enchanting fiction. Zuckerman's second title, "The Human Stain," with its multifarious implications, is also appropriate to Coleman's story, symbolizing the "stain" of his ancestry, the stain he fears will be exposed in his children's faces. But it is Faunia who best understands the nature of the human stain in her interactions with the tamed crow who swoops upon the heads of the local schoolgirls and later rips up the newspaper clippings recording his misdemeanors, not wanting "anybody to know his background" (240).[16] Faunia, whose very name suggests synthesis (the mythical faun being a combination of human and goat), recognizes the inevitable mark of humanity on everything with which humans come into contact, the impossibility of purity, as it is converse to humanity. The fact that Zuckerman seems to move toward the latter title for his unfinished manuscript indicates his acknowledgment of the impossibility of purity or objectivity in his narrative of Coleman Silk, the indelibility of his "imprint" (242) upon the narrated past of his subject.

The Human Stain takes as its central theme the notion of creation, the workings of creativity, and the means whereby the literary text comes into being. The novel explores the myth of purity and the fallacy of uncorrupted self-creation. Yet for Zuckerman, a writer who has lived and breathed the textual experience, the textual self is both the forged self and the actual self—"[w]riting personally is exposing and concealing at the same time" (345). And there's the rub: where does the "real" self end and the fabricated self begin? Where does the author engineer a swerve from the facts of history so that the processes of narrative invention may begin? Or is the very notion of an untouched, uncontaminated history a fiction in itself? History, in *The Human Stain*, is portrayed as full of gaps and ellipses. Whole histories are lost to the whirligig of time, written out of official records, the stories of people like Coleman Silk, Matthew Henson, Charles Drew, Faunia, and Lester Farley. While at one level Zuckerman sees his task as the necessary retrieval of such histories, at another he realizes that such an act inevitably taints the subject and thereby alters the facts of history. The human stain of the writer holds fast and history is subject to infiltration by words, words that shape, mold, and contain, thereby denying the swirling, chaotic truth of the lived historical experience. And with every word, the writer—himself possessed by the past—is complicit in its disappearance.

CHAPTER 7

"The pointless meaningfulness of living": Illuminating *The Human Stain* through *The Scarlet Letter*

Gabrielle Seeley and Jeffrey Rubin-Dorsky

Careful reading of Philip Roth is its own reward—the writing is exquisite—but if one needs a reason secondary to aesthetic pleasure, then Roth's incisive criticism of modern America is it. He is always writing about America, in the tradition of the greatest American writers. Roth's novel *The Human Stain* explores the fundamental belief in self-creation and self-fulfillment as integral to the American promise of freedom, asking the profoundest of questions: Is there some element of identity an individual has no right to relinquish in order to attain individual freedom? The novel also addresses the poisonous self-righteousness—and the folly—of a seemingly simple phrase that asserts the value of communal solidarity: "Everyone knows." One way to reveal Roth's larger sense of the failures of American culture is to locate Hawthorne's *The Scarlet Letter* as the shadow text for *The Human Stain*, for examining the parallels between Hawthorne's novel and Roth's helps to illuminate Roth's purposes.[1] When the same questions are asked of both texts, the connection becomes clear. For example, one of the primary ones for *The Scarlet Letter* (1850)—why does Hester stay in Salem and endure the torment when she is free to go?—applies equally to Coleman. Certainly, there is a secret lover involved, but the linkage goes well beyond that to their core relationship with the communities they despise but cannot relinquish. Of course there's more: for one, Mark and Pearl as the probers of conscience; for another, Hawthorne's use of the word "stain." In short, reading *The Scarlet Letter* alongside *The Human Stain* reveals just how Roth views the America of the moment in relation to the America of the past. Roth sees that for all the supposed "progress" America has made in the 150 years since Hawthorne wrote, some of the fundamental ways of thinking about individuals and communities remain fundamentally flawed. In what is perhaps his most "traditionally" American novel, Roth underscores "the pointless meaningfulness of living" in America (*Stain* 52).

The "persecuting spirit" and the "ecstasy of sanctimony"

Hawthorne's novel posits oppositions between the individual and the community, between concealment and revelation. Is Hester a rebel or a revolutionary? Should Hester rule her own life or accept the constraints within which her dour and rigid community expects her to live? Is she justified in choosing to keep secrets from Dimmesdale and the community? Roth, too, concerns himself with what he has called the "business of choosing"; his heroes are often in a struggle for authority over their own lives ("Document," *Reading* 27). In a self-conducted 1973 interview, Roth discusses "the problematical nature of moral authority and of social restraint and regulation"—the main theme of *The Scarlet Letter*. "The question of who or what shall have influence and jurisdiction over one's life," he writes, "has been a concern in much of my work" ("Great American Novel," *Reading* 84). In *The Human Stain*, Roth pursues these questions through Zuckerman's account of Coleman Silk, just as Hawthorne examined them in telling the story of Hester Prynne.[2]

Roth litters his novel with both direct and oblique references to his predecessor. Zuckerman describes Coleman's paramour as having "the kind of severely sculpted features customarily associated with the church-ruled . . . colonial women locked up within the reigning morality and obedient to it"; the description hearkens to Hester's fellow townswomen (*Stain* 1). Zuckerman mentions that "Hawthorne . . ., in the 1860s, lived not many miles from [the] door" of the cabin where he is living and working alone (2). "The secret" to living such a solitary life, Zuckerman writes, "is to find sustenance in *people* like Hawthorne, in the wisdom of the brilliant deceased" (44). Later in the novel, perceiving that Coleman and Faunia are doomed, Zuckerman remarks, "[e]veryone on earth does the end differently: this is how the two of them work it out" (203–4). This is a riff on Hawthorne, who has Dimmesdale publicly tell Hester, "thou mayest work out an open triumph over the evil within thee" (Hawthorne 67). Later, Hester ruminates that she may "work out another purity than that which she had lost" (80). Moreover, at the novel's conclusion, Hawthorne has Hester return, after an extended absence, to the scene of her crime to work out "the end" in her own way. In addition, Roth's chapter title "What Maniac

Conceived It?" recalls Mistress Hibbins whispering to Hester, "what mortal imagination could conceive it?" as she reveals her knowledge of Hester and Dimmesdale's clandestine forest meeting (241). At Coleman's funeral, Herb Keble's reproachful speech refers to "the American individualist's resistance to the coercions of a censorious community"; "Hawthorne," he says, "come[s] to mind" (*Stain* 310). From front to back, Hawthorne, especially the Hawthorne of *The Scarlet Letter*, resonates through the pages of *The Human Stain*.

With Hawthorne's ghost hovering above his text, Roth reminds readers of the pleasure Americans—represented not by individuals but by popular opinion—take in indulging "what Hawthorne identified in the incipient country of long ago as the 'persecuting spirit'" (2). Roth fills in the "sordid" details of the America of 1998: the nation, high on piety, buzzed over impeaching President Clinton for lying about his sex life; the country was awash in the details of the stain on Monica Lewinsky's now-famous blue dress. Roth cites the story of Vanessa Williams and her dethroning as Miss America; she was deemed morally unfit to represent the nation because of one controversial early-career decision. With these examples and others, Roth makes clear that the term "conventional wisdom" is an oxymoron. He calls this keenness to identify loudly the errant acts of others "America's oldest communal passion, historically perhaps its most treacherous and subversive pleasure: the ecstasy of sanctimony" (2). This recalls the Puritan elders surrounding Hester on the scaffold as *The Scarlet Letter* opens (Hawthorne 2) as well as the townspeople's piercing glances and hurled asides when Hester attends Dimmesdale's Election sermon (246).

Certainly the community around and within Athena College exhibits the persecuting spirit with Coleman as the target.[3] The charges of racism arising from the "spooks" incident and public disdain for Coleman's relationship with Faunia effectively poison his life. Roth gives Coleman's lawyer, Nelson Primus, the role of community mouthpiece; when Coleman asks Primus for legal advice about thwarting Lester Farley's harassment, Primus reveals an even worse enemy: the small town's "malevolent Puritanism" (*Stain* 76). Primus warns that the town is full of "[n]arrow-minded churchgoers, sticklers for propriety, all sorts of retrograde folks eager to expose and punish guys like you" (77). Coleman exercises his significant self-restraint in the face of Primus's maddening condescension, telling himself, "don't put him down . . . There are no compassionate chinks in his armor? Fine with me" (77). Coleman hardly deserves a lecture on sexual mores from this 32-year-old; by extension, the community has no right to "expose and punish" or even to evaluate a private relationship between two consenting adults. Zuckerman notes that the enraged Coleman's face looks "bruised and ruined like a piece of fruit . . . kicked to and fro along the ground by the passing shoppers" (12). In other words, he is pummeled by the small-minded ordinary citizens of the community. Similarly, Hawthorne remarks upon the malice of popular opinion in *The Scarlet Letter*. "The public," he declares, "is despotic in its temper; it is capable of denying common justice when too strenuously demanded" (Hawthorne 162). Indeed, the colonists stare and sneer at Hester. Hawthorne and Roth are both commenting on the tyranny of public opinion, or, more precisely, the community's tyranny over the individual.

Hester deliberately stays in the community that torments her for seven long years. When there is no restraint on her leaving, why does she feel obliged not to run, but instead to resist her accusers by remaining in their presence? And why does Coleman feel compelled to remain in opposition to his tormentors? He does not simply scoff at the stupidity of the community's misguided claims against him, although he articulates to Zuckerman the lucid argument that quashes them. Rather, he seethes after enduring five months of "punishing immersion in meetings, hearings, and interviews . . . laborious, repetitious explanations . . . and always, perpetually, the pervasive sense of unreality" (*Stain* 12). Moreover, Coleman even believes that his wife, Iris, died as a direct result of the community's persecution of him: "they meant to kill me," he tells Zuckerman, "and they got her instead" (13). Coleman cannot believe this nightmare is happening to him. "[C]ompletely unhinged," he storms into a stranger's house and "all but order[s]" Zuckerman to write the story of his ordeal, exclaiming, "These people *murdered* Iris!" (11–12). Still, if Coleman will not reveal his secret, one must wonder (as with Hester), why not leave the scene with Faunia and let their connection be his salvation? Having positioned himself as an oppressed adversary against the community he despises for its stupidity, he nevertheless remains within that community, allowing himself to suffer its rejection. Why is that opposition so important to him, and why is it so important to Hester?

The "corroding indignation" of Remarkable Individuals

Coleman and Hester oppose their communities because they both feel the intense anger that results when a remarkable individual is constrained by society. For Coleman, the constraint—and the source of his "corroding indignation"—is American racism against blacks (63). Early in the novel, Roth foreshadows the idea of motivating anger when he has Primus think that Coleman seems compelled to find trouble in order to justify an immense grudge: he seems "in crazy pursuit of . . . an ultimate injustice that would validate his aggrievement forever" (79–80).

In America, blackness was, and perhaps still is, a scarlet letter: it carries with it others' prejudices which restrict human potential, both of the prejudiced and the judged. Bigotry against blacks results in Coleman's fury and thus his zealous resistance: his "great heroic struggle against their we . . . The passionate struggle for precious singularity, his revolt of one against the Negro fate," arise from his indignation (183). He will never forgive society for grossly underestimating his worth—based solely on his race. Coleman experiences "real disgrace" for the first time while serving in the Navy—he's beaten and humiliated as a direct result of a community's rigid racial rules (182). In turn, Hester's anger stems from her lower social status as a woman; she is held back by rigid societal rules and expectations. As one example of her thinking, Hester views Pearl as "the germ and blossom of womanhood, to be . . . developed amid a host of difficulties. Every thing was against her. The world was hostile" simply because she was born female (Hawthorne 165). This, too, leads to a palpable sense of disgrace: Hester is psychologically wounded, just as Coleman is, by the inflexibility of a strict—a hostile—community. This wounding is a genuine "human stain" which causes Coleman and Hester to defy their communities. The stain rubs both ways, for the community commits a "sin" (intolerance) just as surely as does the protagonist (defiance) in each novel. Coleman and Hester rebel against societal limitations primarily because they see themselves in similar ways: that is, they consider themselves remarkable individuals.

Hester and Coleman are exceptionally attractive and capable, and both are self-aware enough to recognize their exceptionality. Hester, for instance, emerges from jail with "a glance that would not be abashed," although the entire community is present to witness her humiliating punishment on the pillory (53). The onlookers notice "how her beauty shone out, and made a halo of the ignominy in which she was enveloped" (53). Besides being attractive, Hester is a talented seamstress: in fact, "her handiwork became . . . the fashion" in the colony and "was seen on the ruff of the Governor" (82–3). She has intellectual ambitions that go far beyond the entrepreneurial, for "earlier in life, [she] had vainly imagined that she herself might be the destined prophetess" who would "establish the whole relationship between man and woman on a surer ground of mutual happiness" (263). Perhaps the best illustration of Hester's heightened self-regard is the way she emboldens the scarlet letter itself, the emblem of shame that she embroiders in "fantastic flourishes of gold," with a "gorgeous luxuriance of fancy" (53). Yet in spite of her boldness, generations of readers have agreed that Hester is justified in possessing, through her "vivid self-perception," a strong sense of her own excellence, concurring that yes, on her, the A could stand for Admirable (84).

Roth conveys Coleman Silk's sense of self-worth thrillingly. Our initial image of young Silky Silk is of him bounding "up the street, in exuberant delight ... crying aloud, 'My two weakest subjects—which are those?'"; his delight stems from the certain knowledge that he *hasn't* a weak subject in school (*Stain* 87). His family's rejection of a cash offer to induce Coleman to step aside so that another student can be first in their class is but "[a]nother triumph," he thinks, "for the great, the incomparable, the one and only Silky Silk!" (88). Coleman's hyperbolic self-assessment is also accurate: he's the class valedictorian, a track champion, an undefeated boxer. In one exultant moment, he experiences

> a frenzy of love not only for himself but for all that was visible, as if everything in nature were a manifestation of his own life—the sun, the sky, the mountains, the river, the trees, just Coleman Brutus "Silky" Silk carried to the millionth degree. (101)

He possesses "tremendous advantages of intellect and of appearance" which his father knew "would launch him into the topmost ranks of Negro society, make of him someone people would forever look up to" (102). Coleman's mother also recognizes his exceptionality, for Coleman is "wrapped like a gift in every ameliorating dream Gladys Silk had ever had, and the handsomer he became and the smarter he became, the more difficult it was for her to distinguish the child from the dreams" (94). Coleman relishes "the raw I with all its agility"; he wants to be "[f]ree to go ahead and be stupendous" (108–9). Coleman's assertion of self pulses with energy—he is quintessentially American, striving to break with any entity that may hinder his trajectory upward and outward into the world: "He [is] Coleman, the greatest of the great *pioneers* of the I" (108). He is raised to be a golden child, but, Roth writes with ominous foreshadowing, "The larger picture he didn't get yet" (88).

That larger picture within which Coleman must operate is the ubiquitous and limiting racism of mid-twentieth-century America. Indeed, Coleman and Hester both recognize the restrictions their communities rigidly impose: a black man must behave in particular and proscribed ways, women must follow puritanical and prescribed rules. These societal shackles infuriate spirited people like Coleman and Hester. American readers understand this fury, and thus they admire these characters' efforts to create a life commensurate with their conception of themselves. In deciding to "color himself just as he chose," Coleman has "take[n] the future into his own hands rather than ... leave it to an unenlightened society to determine his fate" (109, 120). He recognizes and rejects the position of blacks in the American caste system, in which "there existed ... rigid distinctions between classes and races sanctified by the church and legitimized by the schools" (122). This institutionalized system dictated that a top black student like Coleman must go to Howard University, where suddenly his cherished "raw I was part of a we . . ., and he didn't want anything to do with it or with the next oppressive we that came along either" (108). For Coleman, "slipping the punch" of American racism by creating a new racial (and ethnic) identity allows him, he thinks, to live a less restricted life (75). But this transformation necessitates concealment of the most troublesome kind—he has to hide his true self and bury his past to achieve freedom. Still, he sees the move as essential, for

> [a]ll he'd ever wanted . . . was to be free: not black, not even white—just on his own and free . . . The objective was for his fate to be determined not by the ignorant, hate-filled intentions of a hostile world but . . . by his own resolve. Why accept a life on any other terms? (120–1)

Similarly, when Hester ponders the "whole race of womanhood," she asks herself a "dark question": "was existence worth accepting, even to the happiest among them? As concerned her own individual existence, she had long ago decided in the negative" (Hawthorne 165). As a woman, her fate depended upon meeting and marrying a suitable man—*not* upon her own agency. Reflecting upon Chillingworth, Hester "marvell[s] how she could ever have been wrought upon to marry him!" (176). Coleman and Hester both are "wrought upon" by the constraints of society: they burn with rage at the ease with which their communities overlook their excellence and impede their autonomy. Both seek nothing more than what Coleman believes is the "basic human right" of "disregarding prescriptive society's more restrictive demarcations and asserting independently a free personal choice" (*Stain* 155). This is *the* sacred American ideal, encompassing as it does the holy trinity of independence, individuality, and unfettered freedom. Yet, as compelling as this vision of freedom seems, seeking absolute autonomy is costly. Coleman's and Hester's insistence upon asserting personal choice while masking their true selves will eventually thwart—and in Coleman's case, destroy—them.

The "camouflage and the covering and the concealment"

In both novels, the drive to live freely causes the protagonist to keep a secret; the secret then becomes essential to living a life commensurate with her or his self-conception. For Coleman and Hester, what Zuckerman calls "the camouflage and the covering and the concealment" (84) gives them strength and energy, the inner excitement of the outlaw. Secrecy is an act of withholding, and withholding is a powerful form of resistance, especially against a community that would control you and your choices. The potency of secrecy is immense: Zuckerman speculates that for Coleman, the "power and the pleasure were to be found . . . in being counterconfessional" (100). He relishes the "secret of nobody's knowing what was going on in your head, thinking whatever you wanted to think with no way of anybody's knowing" (100). Coleman amplifies secrecy and employs it as leverage against others, all the while trusting no one—not even his wife Iris. Thus, both Coleman and Hester "pass" in their communities with relative ease, believing that they can only be free by not being known. Indeed, they practice active concealment—a fabulous paradox.

Secrecy becomes an inseparable part of Coleman's and Hester's identities, a source of their power, and a reinforcement of their expansive self-concepts. Coleman's secret becomes *the* animating force of his life—indeed, without the active concealment, his power would be diminished. With Ellie, who knows Coleman's secret, "some dimension is missing," and their affair, because he is undisguised, "fails to feed that conception of himself that's been driving him all his life" (135). He scorns other men in the Village who are passing, thinking that they achieve secrecy in "petty ways: they simply lie all the time" (135) rather than keeping secrets "in the grand and elaborate way" that he does (135). Why is his way so "grand"? Perhaps Coleman considers his concealment superior because he believes he has transformed himself utterly, and thus prides himself upon walking freely among the "oppressors" in their own territory. As long as Coleman has "got the elixir of the secret," he can propel himself "on the trajectory outward," and he can live "his life on the scale he wants to live it" (135–6). His secret enlivens and emboldens him.

Likewise, Hester Prynne's secret becomes an animating force of her existence. By keeping her inner life secret, Hester liberates herself; ironically, the punishment that was supposed to suppress her rebellious energies instead releases them into a forbidden realm. As Hawthorne puts it, "the tendency of her fate and fortunes had been to set her free. The scarlet letter was her passport into regions where other women dared not tread" (Hawthorne 199). Not only is she free to be entrepreneurial, to use her talents to earn money and to help persons in need with her "woman's strength" (161), but also, and far more significantly, her "life had turned . . . from passion and feeling, to thought"—an intellectual daring forbidden by the Puritan elders (164). Additionally, and shockingly, Hester sees herself and Dimmesdale united by "the iron link of mutual crime, which neither he nor she could break" (160). She and Dimmesdale alone hold the secret of their adultery, and thus, contradictory to every tenet of Puritan belief, she feels as if they alone are "inhabiting a mutual world" (240). Even more powerfully, she keeps from Dimmesdale the secret that Chillingworth, the asp at his very bosom, is her husband, until he is so severely broken that only Hester's energy and resolve can rescue him.

In a thrilling and unprecedented way, her womanhood flowers. Holding all these secrets, she "assume[s] a freedom of speculation," a wild inner realm of being that strengthens her until "she fe[els] herself no longer so inadequate to cope with Roger Chillingworth" (164, 167). Having broken their old association and its particular form of imprisonment, she will not allow the husband who wrought upon her in the past to do so any longer. It is a remarkable transformation, and this drive to create oneself anew—to invent a self that severs one's past and somehow fulfills an expansive self-concept known only by the conceiver—is an American archetype. The idea that an individual can abandon all foundational ties—origins, community, rules—in order to live freely and according to his or her nature is *the* great American myth, articulated by writers such as Emerson and Thoreau, and embodied in a character like Jay Gatsby—all of whom inhabit a great American literary continuity with Coleman and Hester.

Yet even as we admire these characters and their fierce opposition to constricting convention, we are forced to recognize the destruction caused by their choices, for deception and cruelty are correlatives to secrecy in these novels. Coleman's deceit permeates his entire life: he allows the community to live with a conception of him that is wrong; he resigns from Athena without setting the record straight. His losses—career, reputation, privacy, wife—might well have been avoided by his disclosure that he is black. Grasp the absurdity of Coleman Silk, charged with racism against black students, complaining to Zuckerman that he has been "[t]hrown out of Athena . . . for being a white Jew of the sort those ignorant bastards call the enemy" (*Stain* 16). His adherence to keeping the secret of his ethnicity is breathtaking; his self-discipline is both admirable and disturbing. He rails against his accusers, knowing their claims are baseless, yet while holding the fact that would prove their buffoonery, he will not reveal it. This rejection recalls Coleman's earlier refusal to box a good show, when he tells Solly, " 'I don't carry no nigger.' " "That's how obstinate he was," Roth writes, "that's how secretive he was" (117). Similarly, Hester deceives her community by feigning penitence and humility where there is none: Hawthorne famously tells us of Hester that "[t]he scarlet letter had not done its office" (Hawthorne 166). Hester's original defiance of Puritan law should have been transformed into a "genuine and stedfast penitence" (84), but "the effect of the symbol . . . on [her] mind was . . . peculiar" (163) and undesirable.

Wearing the letter leads not to contrition, but to Hester's "outlaw . . . wander[ings] in a moral wilderness" (199). Outwardly, though, "she never battle[s] with the public"; she permits, even encourages, the community to hold a false impression of her (160).

Even more disturbing than their deceit is Coleman's and Hester's cruelty. When Coleman informs his mother that he has chosen to live as if his parents were dead and his siblings nonexistent, he knows he is "murdering her" (*Stain* 138). He recognizes this betrayal as "the most brutal thing he had ever done," but justifies it by thinking that "only through this test can he be the man he has chosen to be, unalterably separated from what he was handed at birth, free to struggle at being free like any human being would wish to be free" (138–9). Her dignified response cannot hide her pain as she reflects upon his earliest rejections of her: "You've been giving fair warning almost from the day you got here. You were seriously disinclined even to take the breast" (139). Ruthlessly, and yet calmly, as if this encounter were just another boxing match, he enacts his plan to "[t]hrow the punch, do the damage, and forever lock the door" (139). Similarly, Hester is cruel to Dimmesdale, the man who, after seven long years, she "still so passionately loved" (Hawthorne 193). In spite of her promise otherwise, she could have— and should have—revealed to him the identity of her husband, for she has witnessed that "the continual presence of Roger Chillingworth—the secret poison of his malignity . . . had been turned to a cruel purpose" (193). Turned by whom? Certainly by Chillingworth, but also by Hester, since she allows Dimmesdale to suffer horribly for seven years. A word from her would have removed Chillingworth's malign influence, and yet she keeps the secret in service of her own need for power and freedom—perhaps even for revenge. In both novels, we are forced to reckon the price paid for "precious singularity" (*Stain* 183).

A "design of justice and retribution"

As exhilarating as it is to experience these intense struggles for autonomy, neither Roth nor Hawthorne will allow unfettered freedom to triumph. Forces in both novels work upon the transgressors, as if these stories were parables whose characters act out predefined roles to illustrate a moral lesson. Thus the cuckolded Chillingworth in *The Scarlet Letter* undertakes his own revenge upon Dimmesdale and, by extension, upon Hester. But he also, in another sense, symbolically enacts the culture's retribution for the deceit they have practiced. In *The Human Stain*, Coleman's role as a classics professor enables Roth to make multiple references to Greek tragedy, which call to mind ideas of fate, retribution, hubris—all ingredients in Coleman's own story.

He reflects at one point upon "how accidentally a fate is made . . . or how accidental it all may seem when it is inescapable" (127). After his first brush with "real disgrace," broken and bleeding, Coleman hears his father's voice "speaking back to him—the old admonishing authority rumbling up" against the "tragic, reckless thing that [he's] done" (182–3). His white uniform marred with a real human stain of "caking blood," Coleman feels that "this is what came of failing to fulfill his father's ideals . . . of deserting his dead father altogether" through renouncing his race and family (182).

Family ties have a crucial place in both novels, for Coleman and Hester are parents of children who, they fear, perceive their secrets. Mark's and Pearl's inquiries force readers to ponder the cost of the concealment and cruelty practiced by their parents. Mark questions his father about their origins; he "wanted the knowledge of who they were and where they came from," and he is "never satisfied" (176) with the invented narrative Coleman provides. He writes "interminable poems about how David had wronged his son Absalom and how Isaac had wronged his son Esau" that reflect "his unshakable enmity for his father" (61). Still, he cannot breach his father's inner fortress, for while Coleman considers whether Mark might intuit his deceit, "irrational as it might be to associate Markie's brooding anger with his own secret," he never relents (176). Similarly, Pearl engages in recurring questioning of her mother about the origin and meaning of the scarlet letter: on several occasions, she beseeches Hester to "Tell me! Tell me . . . It is thou that must tell me!" (Hawthorne 98). Once, in a fit of exasperation, when Hester plays turnabout and asks Pearl why she wears the letter, Pearl pipes up, "It is for the same reason that the minister keeps his hand over his heart!" (179). Thus wounded by her daughter, Hester "never felt a moment's safety" with Pearl; she "often fancied that Providence had a design of justice and retribution in endowing the child with this marked propensity" for knowing the meaning behind the letter (180). But she, too, never relents. Clearly, neither Coleman nor Hester keeps their secrets painlessly. The children's role is to unnerve their parents, to keep conscience afflicted.

If Mark is a Pearl figure, then Les is a Chillingworth one, pursuing his prey. What is the source of his malevolence as opposed to Chillingworth's? He is obviously anti-Semitic, but he may also, in his derangement, sense Coleman's hypocrisy, just as Chillingworth intuits Dimmesdale's. Like Chillingworth, Les can be read as an extension of the community, or perhaps a symbolic hand of fate—rooting out that which might be considered an undesirable element. If Hawthorne assigns Chillingworth the role of "evil"—he violates "in cold blood" the "sanctity of the human heart"—in order to satisfy the demand of his nineteenth-century narrative, then what role does Roth envision for Les in his end-of-the-twentieth-century one? Consider the endings of both novels: Chillingworth is foiled at the conclusion of *The Scarlet Letter* as Dimmesdale and Hester climb the scaffold together, but in *The Human Stain* there is no triumph over Les. In fact, Les is more coherent, and arguably more malevolent, than ever at the end of the novel. Not only is he the surviving character, but his voice is also steady and steely as he flaunts his control, toying with the nervous Zuckerman at the lake. For Les, it is as if Coleman's and Faunia's deaths create a sense of his own rightness—and we are horrified along with Zuckerman, who realizes there is nothing to do but run away, to head down the mountain. Fully 150 years after Hawthorne promulgated a future in which we would eventually get it right in America, we have not succeeded. Furthermore, Roth says, we will never succeed.

Reading the two novels side by side reinforces the idea that we are faced with a continuum of self-revelation; at one end lies an Emersonian openness of the individual to the world, and at the other lies vigilant concealment of the self from others. But both Hawthorne and Roth know that it is not possible to be fully revelatory; every human has secrets, though not necessarily guilty ones. For Roth, "our understanding of people must always be at best slightly wrong" (*Stain* 22). We are slightly wrong about our parents, our children, our lovers, and even ourselves—for Roth's line reads "our understanding of people," not "other people." By contrast, Delphine Roux expresses the mistaken and self-righteous sense of certainty that permeates the communal attitude in these novels: "Everyone knows" (39). But as we discover in *The Scarlet Letter*, nobody knows anything about the true Hester and Dimmesdale love relationship. Nobody really knows anything about Hester, even though the townspeople believe they do (thinking the A stands not for "Adultery" but "Able" [160]). And nobody knows anything about Dimmesdale, either—even when he symbolically "reveals" himself to the community. What, finally, does anybody know about Coleman? Roth provides instances of what characters both intuit and conclude about Coleman, such as Primus's condescension. It comes to this: "Nobody knows"—for Roth, this is final. The misunderstanding is inevitable; the mess and confusion comprise all.

The "fantasy of purity is appalling"

Indeed, both novels illustrate the inherent messiness of life. Roth deftly advances this idea when Coleman finds himself in "a hideous, raucous dive," hiding, after being ejected from a whites-only Norfolk brothel where he was badly beaten for being black, in a bathroom, in which the "seatless bowl was coated with shit, the soggy plank floor awash with piss, the sink . . . was . . . a swillish trough of sputum and puke" (181). Coleman is mired in a crisis of race, and yet he is also sunk in the same larger material circumstances in which his attackers and the whores and the Shore Patrol are rooted: blood and excrement and sweat are raceless fluids, simply part of the larger mess of being human. Delphine Roux, in a rare moment of clarity, calls herself "a mess of uncertainty" (276); this is apt, considering her anonymous note, her misdirected e-mail, and her frantic, fraudulent call to campus security. But Delphine is not alone: we all, Roth suggests, are natural-born bunglers of communication and wreckers of situations.

Hawthorne acknowledges the mess through Hester's perception that "the outward guise of purity was but a lie, and that, if the truth were everywhere to be shown, a scarlet letter would blaze forth on many a bosom besides" her own (Hawthorne 86). The letter is itself a stain of sorts: imposed from without, it is but a mirror of the internal, which is why Hester sees it everywhere. The inevitable messiness of human endeavor renders the main goal of Hester's Puritan community—to create "a land where iniquity is searched out, and punished in the sight of rulers and people"—doomed not only in seventeenth-century Salem but as well in any century on any continent, for the human stain cannot be erased (62). What Hawthorne merely insinuates, Roth clearly states: "The fantasy of purity is appalling. It's insane. What is the quest to purify, if not *more* impurity?" (*Stain* 242).

The ultimate hypocrisy, perhaps, resides in persons who presume to identify in others the impurity that resides in each of us. Roth is right to point out that we are all "inevitably stained creatures," but this state of being has "[n]othing to do with disobedience," for it is a "stain that *precedes* disobedience": "[i]mpurity, cruelty, abuse, error, excrement, semen—there's no other way to be here" (242). Thus, *The Human Stain* implicates those who, in the America of the 1990s, made fashionable sport of searching out iniquity. Roth quotes William F. Buckley characterizing Clinton's "incontinent carnality" (3) as rampant, uncontrolled, and filthy—as unredeemably messy. As if, Roth sneers, Buckley himself had somehow remained a pristine human being. Roth derides such high-handedness, and he, like Hawthorne, uses the word "stain" as a metonym for the inherent disorder humans create. Governor Bellingham deems Hester an unfit mother "because of the stain which that letter indicates" (Hawthorne 111). Faunia observes that her favorite crow's nature has been ruined by human meddling: "That's what comes of hanging around . . . with people like us. The human stain" (*Stain* 242).

But since there is no way to be human other than to be impure, we might as well stop lying about it.

This is what Hawthorne means when he admonishes readers, "Be true! Be true! Be true! Show freely to the world, if not your worst, yet some trait whereby the worst may be inferred!" (Hawthorne 260). We should be true—that is, faithful—not to Hawthorne's "multitude," and not to our own desires and ambitions, which may corrupt our true natures as they did Coleman's and Hester's. According to Hawthorne, "he who shows himself in a false light becomes a shadow or, indeed, ceases to exist" (145). Hester never recognizes that penance without penitence is meaningless; she never shows her rejection of the community's condemnation. In Hawthorne's world, the individual cannot and must not triumph over the community, and yet he creates a heroine so strong, so captivating, so promisingly American, that we struggle with the implication of his meaning. But Hester will never triumph if she never openly declares her beliefs—if she never reveals her true self "freely to the world" (though admittedly, such an act would have been punished, perhaps by death). Hester's real transgression is, finally, the same as Dimmesdale's and Chillingworth's: all three show themselves in a false light, and all three are doomed because of it. Hester's defiance should be bold and open; Dimmesdale should take full, not symbolic, responsibility for his actions; Chillingworth should wear his cuckoldry. If this doesn't sound much like triumph, that's because there is none to be had: only actions and consequences, choices and their costs.

Ultimately, Roth is more critical of Coleman than Hawthorne is of Hester. Like Hester, Coleman will not capitulate; readers are torn between admiration for his staunchness and scorn for his folly. Coleman, whose secret crime has far more serious implications than his outward acts, is once again like Hester, who is punished for adultery when ultimately her secret sin of rebelliousness poses a far greater threat. Readers never see Hester atone for her actions, unless her return to Salem years later indicates atonement rather than merely extending her defiance. Likewise, we never see Coleman admit that keeping his secret exacted too great a cost. Certainly, many Athena residents wrongly perceive the deaths themselves as expiation of the spooks incident and even of the alleged transgression of his sexual relationship with Faunia. But for Roth, this public shift in attitude toward Coleman is as false and unsupportable as were the claims against him. There is no expiation of the *real* transgressions Coleman committed: the concealment of his true identity and the breach of his obligation to his ancestors and his progeny. He owed it to his ancestors to live as himself—as a forceful, virile, intelligent, remarkable black American man. He owed it to his children to reveal his and their full heritage, and to teach them how to live well in spite of—or, even better, to spite—the constraints of a puerile society. That is why Roth gives us such a rich account of Coleman's Lawnside and Gouldtown ancestors, whose work ethic, attention to detail, and resourcefulness cannot fail to remind us of Coleman himself. His ancestor "[w]ay, way back," a slave who "from dawn to dark didn't stop doing what needed to be done" (*Stain* 141), helped endow Coleman with the resolve to "[hold] . . . his own against whatever the task" (60). Ironically, and painfully, though, Coleman's choice ensures that he has "lost himself to all his people," both ancestors and descendants (144). He can never fulfill their promise. In an exultant moment, a young Coleman basks in his singularity, in the "sliding relationship with everything." He believes in "Self-knowledge but *concealed*. What is as powerful as that?" (108). His story shows it to be extremely powerful, and very alluring to Americans—but self-knowledge *revealed* would have been more powerful still. Both Hawthorne and Roth stress revelation, but in regard to Hawthorne's Romantic intuition that the word bears transcendent meaning, Roth separates himself from his predecessor. In the end, Roth has nothing to reveal.

Hawthorne and Roth agree that the only way to live freely is to be undisguised. Hawthorne, believing in something (history, the future), presents the possibility of a time to come in which those like Hester would be free to be stupendous: "at some brighter period, when the world should have grown ripe for it . . . a new truth would be revealed, in order to establish the whole relation between man and woman on a surer ground of mutual happiness" (Hawthorne 263). The final image of *The Scarlet Letter* is thus, fittingly, one of unity: "on a field, sable, the letter A, gules"—red on black, acceptance, accord. Roth, however, is far more cynical than Hawthorne; he can neither see nor predict a future in which nonconformists—in which Colemans and Hesters—experience the lives they expect and deserve.

Hawthorne, Roth, and "the pointless meaningfulness of living"

Hawthorne would not have written "the pointless meaningfulness of living" because whatever darkness is present in *The Scarlet Letter*, it is not the darkness of meaninglessness. There are structures in Hawthorne's world, and in his fiction—like the "law" that Dimmesdale evokes when he tells Hester why they can't leave Salem together—that give order and meaning to social and political arrangements. Hester may be foiled in her attempts at independence and transcendence over the persecuting spirit of Puritan society, but she herself acknowledges that she was too flawed ("stained") to reach such an exalted state. She even looks forward to the future when a woman more able and less burdened than she could lead a revolution in thought, especially concerning women's role in society—the figure that she could not be. That "looking forward" is powerful in Hawthorne because history matters, and thus so does the future. The end of the novel tells you as much—Hester's and Dimmesdale's lives are accorded significance; they mattered, if for no other reason than they teach us about human yearning and inadequacy, about strength and weakness, about possibility and limitation. Someday, in some future generation, humankind may overcome inadequacy, weakness, limitation, and self-deception—the stain—and reach its full potential.

There is no future in Roth. And without a future, there can only be "*pointless* meaningfulness," because there is nothing to be learned, not even fragments to be shored up for the future against the ruins of today. The "meaningfulness" consists in the intensity of living—"to *live*, to go on taking, giving, feeding, milking, [all the while] acknowledging wholeheartedly, as the enigma that it is, the pointless meaningfulness of living." The only real choice we have is to live fully now, which Roth acknowledges in the next line when Zuckerman says, "The sensory fullness, the copiousness, the abundant—superabundant—detail of life, which is the rhapsody." There is nothing more than this. That's why Roth ends that section with the enigmatic lines: "Nothing lasts, and yet nothing passes, either. And nothing passes just because nothing lasts" (52). You must savor every passionate detail because nothing lasts. You can't, in any meaningful sense, bequeath anything to the future, because the future never learns anything from the past. It just is—no better, no worse.

The ending of the novel reinforces this Rothian idea when Zuckerman comes upon Les at the lake. In the New England setting, where we have already been immersed in Hawthorne country, Roth now evokes the great futurist, Thoreau, to thoroughly darken the vision. Thoreau went to Walden to find a future and declared it was very much there, because the meaning of *Walden* (1854) centers on the belief in rebirth ("Walden was dead and is alive again" [Thoreau 208], the beetle climbs out of the dead wood at the end, etc.). And what is rebirth, after all, if not the assertion of a meaningful future? What we have at the end of *The Human Stain* is a self-deceived homicidal maniac in place of the great proponent of self-revelation, and in the very place where he declared his achievement, only now the water is dark and icy, not clear and smooth. ("It's dark down underneath the ice" [*Stain* 358], where Walden was transparent.) Les is calm, though it is a menacing, threatening calm, which is yet another deception—of nature, of human nature. Les has triumphed once again—as he did over Coleman and Faunia, who have not escaped his maniacal grasp the way Hester and Dimmesdale averted Chillingworth's. All Zuckerman can do is flee down the mountain. To where? Into his next project, more pages, more text—this very novel. He alters or *improves* (a good Thoreauvian word) nothing. Moreover, the complicated irony of the last sentence is as chilling as that icy lake: a "pure and peaceful" vision of terror (361).

Part III

The Plot Against America

Introduction

A pleasing symmetry exists in Roth's sequence of American novels, especially if one stretches the American trilogy into a tetralogy, completed by *The Plot Against America*. *American Pastoral* begins when, recalling Swede Levov as a "magical name" (*Pastoral* 3) in the neighborhood when Nathan Zuckerman was a schoolchild, Zuckerman attends his forty-fifth high school class reunion. Bracketing the series, the beginning of *The Plot Against America* returns Roth to his 1940s Weequahic neighborhood to invent a biography and historical context for the young "Philip Roth." Yet this New Jersey Eden of Roth's memory and imagination is torn asunder by the same Hawthornian "persecuting spirit," expressed in a "purity binge" (*Stain* 2), that Seeley and Rubin-Dorsky find in Coleman Silk's 1990s America, 50 years later.

The word "Fear" begins *The Plot Against America*. Fear dominates the counterfactual narrative, as Roth moves the arc of mid-century history toward a fascistic version of the United States. In Roth's dystopia, the newly elected president Charles Lindbergh warms to the Nazi regime and looses anti-Semitic oppression on American soil. Philip, an uncomprehending and childishly self-centered Jewish boy, resembles the Swede, dedicated to the promise of American security and prosperity and unable to see beyond his own desires. Like the Swede's, Philip's consciousness is prelapsarian, especially in his blind faith that he can escape history. As in *American Pastoral*, too, Roth organizes *The Plot Against America* according to the archetypal narrative of the Fall. Fear, like the irruption of the uncanny that Glaser identifies in *American Pastoral*, is the emotion of recognition in *The Plot Against America*; fear recognizes that the Promised Land that was America is a myth.

Philip's fall is from myth into history. Roth frames this *bildungsroman* with two complementary tropes, whose near-rhyme seems bleakly coincidental: the stamps and the stump. In its colorful portraits of presidents, states, and national treasures, Philip's prized stamp collection figures the innocent dream of America. His dream vanishes twice—once figuratively, in the nightmare that covers each stamp in his 1934 National Parks set with a swastika; and again, literally, when the album disappears one night as Philip tries to run away from the home that no longer seems safe—"I wanted nothing to do with history" (*Plot* 233). If his stamps are the ideal, Philip's cousin Alvin's amputated stump, the result of his defiant entry into World War II, is the real. The stump connotes inevitable suffering, mortality, and Alvin's participation within the public sphere—it is the wound of history. Philip's fear of the stump, mixing fascination and revulsion, signals his fall from innocence into an America that, in Roth's imagination, might have been and may yet become, because it is not substantially displaced from the America that has been so far.

Roth has written about himself, or versions of himself, many times before—most obviously in *Operation Shylock* and the autobiographical works, but also, arguably, at arm's-length in the Nathan Zuckerman books. Critics have thus been drawn to contemplate his play in *The Plot Against America* with genre, especially the memoir form, which enables his speculative narrative to gain immediacy and plausibility and to disguise the tensions among realism, documentary history, fantasy, and satire (see Brauner; Cooper; Graham; Hedin; Morley, "Memories"; and Schweber). Unsurprisingly, some readers have attended to Roth's imaginative deployment not just of his own biography, but also of his family's, noting his glowing revivification of his father's dignity and his mother's compassion (see Wirth-Nesher). Indeed, critics have shown considerable interest in Roth's counterhistorical invention in the novel. Since *The Plot Against America* was published in 2004, some readers were quick to see it as a roman à clef about the previous few years in American history, namely, the terrorist attacks of September 11, 2001 and the administration of President George W. Bush (see Kellman; Lewis; and Shiffman), even though Roth has denied the connection ("Story" C11). Others, finding the allegory of the present unconvincing, have concentrated instead on Roth's deliberate engagement with the past (see Brauner; Neelakantan, "Nostalgia"; and Rothberg). As in considering *American Pastoral* and *The Human Stain*, critics have noted how *The Plot Against America* inquires into the racialized discourses embedded in American culture, especially the relationships among Americanness, Jewishness, and blackness (see Michaels and Wirth-Nesher).

The chapters on *The Plot Against America* that follow constitute a dialogue about all of these matters. Brett Ashley Kaplan zeroes in on a trope of doubleness that infuses Roth's historical imagination; she locates the source of the novel's traumatic vision in Roth's exposure of a hidden truth underlying the apparent conditions and expressed ideological positions in the United States. Connecting this doubled vision with what Roth presents in *American Pastoral* and *The Human Stain*, Kaplan sees the novel uncovering two histories at once, the past and the present. Like Glaser and Franco, she focuses on Roth's critique of the American self-image that represses grotesque truths in relation to racial and ethnic differences. Racism and anti-Semitism in *The Plot Against America* are thus stains upon the nation. Yet in arguing that Roth conveys a sentimental longing for the culture's potentialities, however postponed by the actualities of American history, Kaplan describes Roth's view as notably lacking in cynicism regarding whether such potential exists in America.

Kaplan's analysis dovetails with that of Elaine Kauvar, who also explores the trope of doubling, but in relation to configurations of Roth's characters rather than the ideological network that *The Plot Against America* reproduces. Whereas Kaplan examines the novel's details of real and invented public history, Kauvar looks intimately at how Roth capitalizes on the imaginative possibilities inherent in his family, especially in revisiting the father/son relationship that has often appeared in his fiction. With reference to Roth's two autobiographical works, *The Facts* and *Patrimony*, Kauvar considers that, in returning to his earlier play with the fact/fiction dichotomy, Roth is able both to show vividly how the outside world can make the home a battlefield and also to resurrect his own parents in loving portraits, thereby turning his fiction into a version of history.

Timothy Parrish shares similar insights but from a different angle. Like Kauvar, he sees that Roth reinvents the past to engage his family history, but Parrish finds irony in such nostalgia. Like Kaplan, he looks at the wider context of American history to frame Roth's representation of ethnic identity and self-invention in the United States. Parrish, however, cites Roth's early story "The Conversion of the Jews" as well as other writers, American and European, to elucidate his argument that Roth unfailingly idealizes America. Parrish concludes that in *The Plot Against America*, Roth negates his own premise of a dystopic counterhistory, unable in the end truly to imagine an American catastrophe. The chapter both complements and reverses Kaplan's reading of Roth's vision of a traumatic American history, suggesting at last that it *can't* happen here. Parrish's chapter thereby brings the volume full circle, back to Brauner's inquiry into the historiographic implications of *American Pastoral*. Clearly Roth's historical fictions are open to diverse readings, his imagined possibilities for the American self as rich, contradictory, and revealing as the history of the nation itself. This is Roth's America.

CHAPTER 8

Just Folks Homesteading: Roth's Doubled Plots Against America

Brett Ashley Kaplan

The Plot Against America (2004) puts into play a traumatic vision of a violently anti-Semitic United States that Philip Roth depicts with a level of detail so as to make it utterly "believable." In fact he suggests that the Holocaust can and could have happened here, and Roth's lifelong love of America is severely tested but ultimately salvaged through the curious plot twists he creates. For Roth loves America, which does not mean he is not one of its keenest critics. Indeed, he is sometimes corny in his approach to the American dream but that sensibility only serves to highlight the stark juxtapositions between the (always false, never attainable) ideal and the (always corrupted, doubled, shadowed) reality. In *American Pastoral*, for example, he brilliantly details the needless and ultimately self-destructive ruination of Newark during riots that rocked the Eastern Seaboard. In *The Human Stain*, to take another example, Roth exposes both the possibility for self-transformation that is the core of the American dream as well as its painful underside. The same dual analysis—the love letter colored by its realist, aching double— characterizes *The Plot Against America*.[1]

Three photographs together tell a story of glamour and promise sullied by fascist associations and capture the doubling that Roth achieves in *The Plot Against America*.[2] The first features two dapper young men, attired elegantly in tuxes, tall, handsome, goyish; it appeared in *The New York Times* with the caption "The two most popular young men in the world."[3] Taken on June 12, 1927, the photograph depicts Charles Lindbergh, who had just made monumental history by crossing the Atlantic in the world's first solo flight on May 21, 1927, and the then Prince of Wales, who was going to become the shortest-reigning British

King, Edward VIII, before abdicating in 1936 in order to marry the American divorcée Wallis Simpson. A few days after his flight, Lindbergh made the acquaintance of the Prince of Wales, and their shared, handsome, high-profile bachelorhood prompted the association between them.

The other two photographs, taken roughly ten years later, feature each of these dapper young men, now a little older, now both married, now both having undergone a great deal of stress, but nonetheless in both photos beaming while offering a firm handshake to or standing in support of a Nazi leader. One depicts Lindbergh shaking hands with a sturdy older man wearing a Swastika and the other portrays the Duke of Windsor (as he became after his abdication) smiling while his wife shakes hands with Hitler. The sentiment Roth expresses so forcefully in *The Plot Against America*, that the whole ruse of the Just Folks movement is a thin veneer that hides the violent anti-Semitism beneath the surface of the American myth of equality, finds an echo in the disjunction among these three photographs. The first photograph represents a mythical Nordic ease, the second and third reveal the violent underside of that masculine bravado. In the ten years between the first and the two later photographs, Lindbergh explored the world multiple times via plane, married Anne Morrow, and suffered the horrific loss of his first-born child; Edward became King only to abdicate to assuage a supposedly fussy citizenry who would wrinkle their noses at his marriage to a divorcée. From American and British perspectives these formerly "most popular" eligible young bachelors would become enamored of Nazism as a supposed bulwark against the onslaught of the "Jewish" Communist world threat.[4]

Philip Roth, with his endless fascination with the traumatic hidden truth behind the glowing mask of the American dream, would have found in Charles Lindbergh the perfect model for the double image of the American hero; on the one hand, the Nordic god, "America's Prince" (as Scott Berg, who wrote the most comprehensive and recent Lindbergh biography, reports the press often dubbed him), the promoter of aviation and the sufferer of the "greatest crime of the century," but on the other hand, a Nazi sympathizer and an anti-Semite. For Roth, racism, anti-Semitism, and other hatreds are the stains that discolor the happier possibilities of the human project. What Roth can never get right, of course, is how sexism and misogyny figure in this mix. Indeed, part of the "corny" aspects of Roth's portraits of America stem from this seemingly willful blindness to the more complex, less traditional, less sexist, possibilities for gender transformations offered to all Americans, especially in the wake of the social transformations encapsulated by 1960s style "liberation." But for a young American boy such as Philip Roth in the 1930s there was no model more compelling than Charles Lindbergh, and thus no model more compelling to explode completely than the all-American goyish Prince as a fascist president.

Mission Accomplished

When *The Plot Against America* appeared it was instantly surrounded by a great deal of excitement about the similarities Roth drew between America's then president, George W. Bush, and Roth's fictional president, Charles Lindbergh.[5] I suspect that many readers would agree with Ralph Goldstein's assessment that "many, maybe even most of the 58 million who voted for Bush in November would have voted for Lindbergh had they been of age in 1940" (1). Despite denials and refusals from Roth, who claimed that, "[s]ome readers are going to want to take this book as a roman à clef to the present moment in America. That would be a mistake," the resonances are plentiful. This disavowal is lessened as Roth also claims that "George W. Bush [is] a man unfit to run a hardware store let alone a nation like this one" ("Story" C10). Thus while I of course want to take seriously Roth's insistence that *The Plot Against America* is not about the Bush years, I think it is safe to say that there are undeniable echoes that allow for legitimate and fruitful comparisons.[6] For example, consider that, in *The Plot Against America*, during one of his speeches Lindbergh swoops down from his plane and speaks "without removing his leather headgear or flight goggles" (30), a deft publicity stunt clearly reminiscent of Bush's "mission accomplished" speech on the USS *Abraham Lincoln* on May 2, 2003 after the invasion of Iraq. Here not only are the two presidents, real and fictional, echoing each other, but Bush may well have been intentionally or unintentionally mimicking the historical Lindbergh. Another similarity between the fictional and historical presidents is the power that the little-seen but highly influential vice president in Roth's novel holds. The media's representation of then Vice President Dick Cheney as the man pulling the strings, especially marked at the beginning of the Bush presidency, is scarily borne out at the end of *The Plot Against America*. It is thus, as are most of Roth's novels, a very real-world fiction, but one in which the border between what is, what has recently or historically been, and what could have been is ephemeral to a striking degree.

In what follows I demonstrate how *The Plot Against America* portrays precisely what the American myth of infinite freedom forbids: an imagination of what *the Holocaust in America* would look like. Here is the myth Roth debunks in this novel: that America saved the world's Jews, that, because freedom prevails in the United States, the level of violent anti-Semitism that was the condition of possibility for genocide in Europe does not apply in America, that President Franklin Delano Roosevelt (FDR) did all he could to save the Jews of Europe. This powerful and widely circulated myth to some degree accurately reflects Roosevelt and American heroism, yet, as Roth's novel demonstrates, everyday anti-Semitism in America may well have erupted into violence had the political alchemies been differently aligned. Roosevelt, legitimately a hero in many respects, failed to act strategically at key times on behalf of European Jewry.[7] But what is fascinating about *The Plot Against America* is that Roth's exposé of the anti-Semitism that could have been is thickened by the racism that Roth explores somewhat obliquely here. Readers familiar with *The Human Stain*, though, will know what a keen observer, if from a distance, Roth is of racism in America. In *The Plot Against America* the Ku Klux Klan (KKK) rears its ugly head, there are comparisons to the genocide of Native Americans, and perhaps most interestingly, Roth includes a tangent about Leo Frank, the Jewish man who was lynched for a supposed liaison with a Gentile factory girl. Thus Roth is able to shadow his discussion of actual and imagined American anti-Semitism with its implicit comparison to actual American racism. The choice of Lindbergh as the fascist president allows both of these to unfold because, in Roth's assessment, Lindbergh stands in for that doubled American—the winning smile that hides an anti-Semitic, racist core.

Lindy for President

At the end of *The Plot Against America*, one of the wild stories circulating is that Lindbergh had his hands thoroughly tied; what appeared to the world as his fascist sympathies are revealed as nothing more than his being held hostage by Nazi Germany because it was they who had his son captive, alive, and thriving as a model Hitler Youth. But this story is quickly discredited and in fact Roth refuses to resolve the plot against America—to determine what actually happened—whether President Lindbergh was indeed a rabid anti-Semite whose seemingly innocent "Just Folks" movement actually masked the Holocaust in America or whether, because the Nazis had kidnapped his son, he was in fact the "'American Gauleiter'" (i.e., regional Nazi leader, *Plot* 323) whose speeches were written by the Nazi elite and whose every move was designed by Hitler. In keeping with one of Roth's favorite devices, he violently tears away the look of innocence of the American dream, the American family, the American hero.

The historical Lindbergh had in fact been a vocal member of the isolationist America First movement, and there was talk of him running for president, but he declined even though when he gave speeches the large crowds often shouted "Lindy for President." In a speech delivered in Des Moines, on September 11, 1941, Lindbergh claimed that while he understood why German Jews wanted to overthrow Hitler, American Jews should realize that "[t]heir greatest danger to this country lies in their large ownership and influence in our motion pictures, our press, our radio and our government" (*Plot* 387; Berg 427). While an entry in an encyclopedia of anti-Semitism claims that Lindbergh was not in fact anti-Semitic, his remarks were often understood to be so, even though he did not frequently expound on Jews, and even though some of his best friends, most notably the Guggenheim family, were Jewish (see Levy 423–4). After reading Scott Berg's magisterial biography, *Lindbergh*, it becomes clear that Lindbergh was anti-Semitic; I agree with Roth's assessment that "Lindbergh as a social force was distinguished not only by his isolationism but by his racist attitude toward Jews . . . He was at heart a white supremacist" ("Story" C10). Indeed, Lindbergh shared with Hitler a belief that international Jewry rampantly agitated for war. (Just as, in speech after repetitive speech, Hitler vehemently and strangely charged Jews with war mongering; see Kershaw). The historical and fictional Lindberghs both ardently admired Hitler. After attending the 1936 Berlin Olympics, the historical Lindbergh wrote "He [Hitler] is undoubtedly a great man, and I believe has done much for the German people" (qtd. in *Plot* 369). Granted, in 1936, the Holocaust had not yet happened and Germany was, indeed, much better off economically than it had been in the earlier interwar years; nonetheless, Hitler had by this time incarcerated thousands of communists and antifascists, and anti-Jewish legislation had been instituted. Roth's Lindbergh is depicted as a clever anti-Semite who incorporates prominent Jewish Americans within his ranks; these include the powerful (fictional) Rabbi Bengelsdorf, who becomes the narrator's uncle via marriage. Lindbergh concocts and begins to enact "Homestead 42," which deports Jews not to concentration camps but to the American Midwest where they are supposedly indoctrinated with Gentile values. "Homestead 42" clearly echoes the Department of Homeland Security, organized in response to the attacks on September 11, 2001.

By choosing Lindbergh, the darling of aviation-loving boys (and many others too) around the world, Roth is able to scrape the underside of the American hero—and he does this by drawing out the isolationism and anti-Semitism practiced by the historical Lindbergh. Roth wonders what "if Lindbergh had run? With that boyish manly aura of his? With all that glamour and celebrity, with his being virtually the first great American hero to delight America's emerging entertainment society" ("Story" C10), what would have happened? Berg's biography is full of the adoration Lindbergh instilled in children—particularly young boys who supposedly dreamed of adventures such as those enjoyed by the aviator. From Swedish stock, Lindbergh represented the perfect goyish hero; from what we know of Roth's general take on "shiksas" it is not such a stretch to see how that vivid imagination about Gentile "girls" would translate into an obsession with the epitome of a goyish boy. ("Shiksas" are non-Jewish girls; for the quintessential representation of them in the Rothian universe see *Portnoy's Complaint.*) Lindbergh offers Roth the perfect model for a fascist president not only because of his own, historically accurate, proclivities toward Nazi Germany but more importantly for Roth because the flip side of America's golden boy as fascist supports Roth's general trope of exposing the undesirable double behind the happy façade.

In the case of the historical Lindbergh, while the world adored its first solo trans-Atlantic flyer, this pilot had been from a typical American family—that is to say, a deeply unhappy, scandal-laden, and fragmented family. *Not* from the typical American family of the American dream but from the kind of background many—if not most—people actually experience. Berg notes that "Charles Augustus Lindbergh seemed the perfect antidote to toxic times" (112), which is exactly why he is the perfect model for Roth—he *seemed* a perfect antidote and yet he was toxicity itself. Anne and Charles Lindbergh (in the columnist Will Rogers's words, "our Prince and our President combined" [qtd. in Berg 143]) visited Reichsmarschall and Luftwaffe head Hermann Göring several times. Thus while debunking the myth of the unconditionally "good" America opposing the unconditionally "bad" Germany, Roth also debunks the widely held myth that America (and Britain to boot) was without exception universally condemnatory of the German dictator from his rise to power in 1933 onwards. Hidden in plain sight, in every newspaper and historical record, in contrast, is the fact that many in America and Britain supported the Hitler regime as a bulwark against what they saw as the rising threat of international communism.

The Fascist United States

Narrated by a young character called "Philip Roth," *The Plot Against America* does indeed make us feel the chill of what could have been had fascism come to America. The novel's beginning captures the tone:

> Fear presides over these memories, a perpetual fear. Of course no childhood is without its terrors, yet I wonder if I would have been a less frightened boy if Lindbergh hadn't been president or if I hadn't been the offspring of Jews. (1)

Underscoring and echoing these opening words, the final chapter of *The Plot Against America* is titled "Perpetual Fear," and throughout the course of the novel Roth charts the subtle changes that irrevocably transformed the seven- to nine-year-old narrator's Jewish-American family (the novel spans two years). Like many highly assimilated German, French, or other Jews in areas of the world taken over by or collaborating with the Hitler regime, the characters in the fictional Roth family did not distinguish between their Jewishness and their Americanness. Indeed they were deeply patriotic. For many Jewish Americans such as this fictionalized version of the author Roth's family, patriotism was (and is) a way of asserting an alliance with a homeland outside Israel (see Kaplan, "Contested"). Just as was the case in Nazi Germany, change came incrementally, so that whereas many see the violent anti-Semitism of Germany from the post-Holocaust perspective, what is harder to grasp fully is the way in which small pieces of legislation were issued one by one—that the prohibition against Jewish people swimming in public pools, for instance, should have ended in genocide was no more visible to German Jews than the violent outcome of the concentration of Jewish families in the Midwest was to the Roth family in *The Plot Against America*. Through a fictional setting, then, Roth helps us to envision the sort of concrete changes that would have—and indeed could have—taken place had history looked different. But what I want in particular to argue here is that this sort of doubling is a repeated trope in Roth's universe: the underside, the hidden story, the changed mask or face, the trauma behind the exterior of the American dream house, like the one in *The Plot Against America* that sits on "a tree-lined street of frame wooden houses with red-brick stoops, each stoop topped with a gable roof and fronted by a tiny yard boxed in with a low-cut hedge" (2). As Alan Cooper phrases it, in *The Plot Against America*, "readers are drawn into terrors that can lurk behind the most friendly apple-pie-American smiles" (252).

In *The Plot Against America*, it is a fascist president who forces the skeletons out of the happy American family closet; but this same doubling appears in *American Pastoral* through the terrorist daughter of the perfect masculine model of Swede and the tiny perfect wife, all three doubled with a traumatic secret. This doubling also appears in *The Human Stain* where the happy Jewish-American family hides a secret of passing and a traumatic rejection of loving parents and siblings. It is part of what makes Roth an incisive portrayer of the transformations in American life from the 1950s until the early 2000s—that he exposes the trick behind the mirage of the tree-lined American street with its whitewashed fences and tidy hedges. Benjamin Hedin notes of *The Plot*

Against America that "Roth has conjured this alternate past to revive the shock of the present, the blindness that crowds each moment of life only to be blunted by memory and hindsight" (96).

This doubling is perfectly conjured up through a vision that is so enduring it ended up being forged into the cover of *The Plot Against America*, when the young narrator dreams about how the fascist takeover of America has colored these whitewashed fences:

> It was when I looked next at the [stamp] album's facing page to see what, if anything, had happened to my 1934 National Parks set of ten that I fell out of the bed and woke up on the floor, this time screaming. Yosemite in California, Grand Canyon in Arizona, Mesa Verde in Colorado, Crater Lake in Oregon, Acadia in Maine, Mount Rainier in Washington, Yellowstone in Wyoming, Zion in Utah, Glacier in Montana, the Great Smoky Mountains in Tennessee—and across the face of each, across the cliffs, the woods, the rivers, the peaks, the geyser, the gorges, the granite coastline, across the deep blue water and the high waterfalls, across everything in America that was the bluest and the greenest and the whitest and to be preserved forever in these pristine reservations, was printed a black swastika. (43)

From the perspective of the narrator, the child who is in love with America, with its freedom and its beauty, the whole country is overlaid with the ultimate symbol of the violent anti-Semitism he and his family and friends have suffered. Roth here exhibits an at times almost corny adoration of America but it is (thankfully) colored with a good dose of America's ironies, pitfalls, treachery, and comedy. This is part of the doubling that Roth achieves. At the time he wins a surprise presidential victory, Lindbergh had been the darling of the stamp-collecting Philip and his older brother Sandy, so from the child's eye view it becomes difficult for the boys to fathom the dismay of the Jewish adults in their lives at the rise of a fascist president in America. Things go from confusing to worse as Philip and Sandy are traumatized by the burgeoning anti-Semitism of the Lindbergh era.

Indeed, because the Roth family of the novel is so patriotic, they had planned, long before Lindbergh was elected, to drive "three hundred miles to Washington, D.C., to visit the historic sites and the famous government buildings." The family had been saving, since "FDR was a second-term president and the Democrats controlled both Houses" (44) in, ironically enough, a "Christmas Club" account for the trip. The fictional Roth's father adored America and had been looking forward, during the two years of saving, to showing his sons the monumental sights of the city. As they approach Washington, the Roths take a wrong turn and find themselves face to face with "the biggest white thing I had ever seen" (57). Upon seeing the Capitol for the first time, Bess, Roth's mother, begins to cry and Sandy, his older brother, falls into a "patriotic stupor" (58). This fervent patriotism is quickly checked by three anti-Semitic events that follow rapidly upon one another and that function to let the family know beyond a shadow of a doubt that Lindbergh's America is a racist, unwelcoming, transformed place.

The first incident happens at the Lincoln Memorial. As the Roth family stands before the colossal statue, overcome with patriotic fervor, another group forms nearby. In the overhearing and bravado that results from Herman Roth's remarking aloud that Lincoln's assassination was a tragedy, two members of the other group hiss "'loudmouth Jew,'" quickly followed by the response: "'I'd give anything to slap his face.'" It is not lost on Philip's father, Herman, that this anti-Semitism is uttered literally in the shadow of the engraved words "All men are created equal." In an effort to placate Herman, Mr. Taylor, their quiet but knowledgeable guide to the sites of the capital city, attempts to steer Mr. Roth's attention toward a mural: "'See there? An angel of truth is freeing a slave'" (65).[8] By so closely associating anti-Semitism with racism here, Roth makes an implicit analogy between them. Indeed, the second anti-Semitic incident that befalls the fictional Roth family is a scene that would most likely have been very familiar to black Americans. Tired from their emotional and trying time at the Lincoln Memorial, the family decides to retire to their hotel for a brief nap before imbibing more of Washington's sights. However, when they return to their hotel their belongings have been packed up and the manager explains that they are not welcome. No reason is given by the manager but Philip whispers to Sandy "'What happened?' 'Anti-Semitism,' he whispered back" (69). So the reason for their unfair expulsion is given only by Sandy, never by the manager nor by the policemen who come to sort the matter out—and who entirely support the anti-Semitic decision of the manager.

After the first anti-Semitic incident at the Lincoln Memorial, Philip reports that "it was impossible any longer to feel the raptures of patriotism turning me inside out" (66). Immediately after the second incident, the roar of a plane overhead elicits the Roths' attention and it is Sandy, who could "recognize just about anything flying from its silhouette" (71), who shouts out that it is the "'Lockheed Interceptor!'" (71). Mr. Taylor then explains that President Lindbergh enjoys taking the plane for a little spin every afternoon and the people enjoy the spectacle. "We all watched along with Sandy, who was unable to conceal his enchantment with the very Interceptor that the president had flown to and from Iceland for his meeting with Hitler" (72). Here again Roth doubles the historical intertext by reminding us at every turn that this spectacular presidency is stained by fascism. In Philip's words: "It was the most beautiful panorama I'd ever seen, a patriotic paradise, the American Garden of Eden spread before us, and we stood huddled together there, the family expelled" (66). After its expulsion, the American family retires to a café for a snack only to be yet again beset with anti-Semitism. This time a walruslike man accosts Herman, charging him again with being a "'loudmouth Jew'" (78)—indeed the chapter in which these incidents occur is aptly named "Loudmouth Jew." Roth is careful to demonstrate how these anti-Semitisms accrue in young Philip's soul, as he began "envisioning all our humiliation sticking to the skin like a coat of thick filth that you could never get off" (79).

I have lingered over these scenes because they expose the careful doubling of Roth's vision of America: anti-Semitism in the very place where the end of slavery is most monumentally celebrated; the neat, well-scrubbed white American family being evicted from a hotel for no other offense than being Jewish; the president flying the same plane he used for a visit to Hitler. In each case the traumatic double of the apparently ordinary is exposed. Roth demonstrates this doubling brilliantly. But what is harder to untangle—and what several scholars of his work have grappled with uneasily—is the corny side of this doubling, the Edenic image of America before it was shattered, as we saw with the postcard nature of the swastika over pristine America. For many leftists, for example, there has never been an Eden precisely because America had always already shattered its own Edenic hopes, from the genocide of Native Americans to the enslavement of millions of Africans, to segregation, to the internment of Japanese-Americans after Pearl Harbor, to the very fact of Roosevelt turning away Jewish refugees during World War II, and on and on. There is, in other words, no cynicism in Roth's dystopic novel. There is instead a love letter to American potentiality tempered by the acute awareness of the under-side of American hatred.[9]

This tension between a sharp critique of American potentiality for the worst racism and the schmaltzy promise of American greatness that Roth has his characters express can be explained in part by the fact that the narrator is an idealistic child and that it is actually a kitschy Nazi aesthetic that Roth exposes through his depiction of the Just Folks movement. But more than this, the sentimental depiction of American idealism serves ultimately in Roth's oeuvre to deepen the sense of traumatic devastation virtually all his major characters feel when the mask is inevitably torn away. Developed by the fictional Lindbergh regime, Just Folks was designed to relocate urban Jewish boys to rural settings where they would work as "field hands and day laborers with farm families hundreds of miles from their homes" (85). While the explicit aim of Just Folks was to assimilate Jewish difference and thus smooth out the American population into ever more sameness, Roth's words here resonate with the experience of slaves who worked as "field hands" and were also relocated to distant spaces as children. Like the invocation of slavery in the scene in the Lincoln Memorial, slavery here functions as the repressed background to the myth of American freedom. To heighten this analogy between the Jewish boys removed from their homes and the legacy of slavery, Sandy, after returning from his Just Folks experience in Kentucky with a rural Christian family, whispers to Philip that "[w]e'd work with the hired hands, and there were some Negroes, day laborers" (99). Herman, of course, is not at all misty-eyed about Just Folks and, after refusing to let Sandy dine with Hitler's Minister of Foreign Affairs Joachim von Ribbentrop at the White House, he explains the underlying force of the "movement": "The only purpose of this so-called Just Folks is to make Jewish children into a fifth column and turn them against their parents" (192).

The wholesome and Lindbergh-adoring Sandy is sharply contrasted in the novel with Alvin, Philip's cousin who, seeing through it all from the beginning, gave up on America and fought with the Canadian army against the German army. The cost for his prescience was his left leg. Thus while Sandy returns in beefed-up, macho, shapely, tanned form from his American version of a Hitler Youth experience, Alvin returns disturbed and unheroically disabled—revolting to Philip, who declares "'No! Alvin can't stay here—he has only one leg!'" (109). The juxtaposition of Alvin and Sandy allows Roth to present, on the one hand, the naïve idealism encouraged by the simple optimism of Just Folks and the fact that Sandy refuses to see what is before him in the increasingly anti-Semitic America, and, on the other, the portent of what it looks like to fight Hitler: to be disabled with a "colossal freakishness" (127), which Roth does not shy away from describing in detail. Indeed, an entire chapter is titled "The Stump." Alvin's stump is at first concealed from Philip, but after the child leaps out of bed from a nightmare, the stump is revealed to him:

> What I saw extending down from his knee joint was something five or six inches long that resembled the elongated head of a featureless animal, something on which Sandy, with just a few well-placed strokes, could have crayoned eyes, a nose, a mouth, teeth, and ears, and turned it into the likeness of a rat. (136)

It is no accident that Roth places Sandy here, in the intimate scene between Philip, who becomes Alvin's valet, caretaker, and stump wrapper, and Alvin. And in this imagined role Sandy makes a mockery—a cartoon—out of Alvin's stump. By representing the disjunction between these two boys, Roth complicates the bravery of the antifascist in opposing Alvin to the wholesomeness of the profascist (Sandy).

Sandy is portrayed throughout the novel as an excellent artist and it is Sandy's well-executed but ideologically grotesque portraits of Lindbergh that Alvin discovers—even though Sandy had promised he had destroyed them. Roth includes yet another example of the hidden grotesquery—the gracefully executed portrait of Lindbergh takes on Dorian Grayesque transformations in the minds of Alvin and Philip. Alvin, with his disability, represents the undoubled; he curses, he masturbates, he tells it like it is; and above all he hates Lindbergh. Sandy, in marked contrast, is a typically doubled Roth character whose façade is eventually exposed but whose front is so convincing as to be seductive to even the most cynical observers. But despite his stubborn hatred of Lindbergh, Alvin, who had become something of a petty thief before going to Canada to fight Hitler, "blatantly repudiat[es] all the ideals that had made him a cripple" (163) by turning a blind eye to politics when he returns to the Roths to convalesce.

Like Alvin, Walter Winchell tells it like it is. Winchell, the columnist radio personality whose rants against the American fascist regime Herman, and most of America's other Jewish people, listen to with great admiration, loses his position on a Hearst paper and decides to run for the presidency. On September 8, 1942, Winchell campaigns on the

> Upper West Side, where he was welcomed as their savior by the Roosevelt Jews, and eventually north to Harlem, where, in the crowd of several hundred Negroes who gathered at dusk to hear him speak at the corner of Lenox Avenue and 125th Street, a few laughed and a handful applauded but most remained respectfully dissatisfied. (260–1)

In Roth's book-length muckrake of what a fascist America would look like, there is relatively little discussion of what the fascist presidency feels about the large black population of the country. In Germany, Italy, and Japan, for obvious reasons, the issue of black populations hardly came into the racist discussions, but in South Africa, especially after the forgers of apartheid had learned Aryan racial ideas from German universities, there was an intimate link between racist legislation and the myth of Aryan supremacy (see Kaplan, *Landscapes*).

Soldiering on, Winchell takes his campaign north to Boston where "somebody brandishing a burning cross rushed toward the soapbox to set him aflame." There is no mistaking, of course, the connection between the burning cross and the horrific racist exploits of the KKK, whose signature burning crosses besmirched the South for years. But then,

> thugs with clubs surged forward screaming "Kill him!" and, two weeks from its inception in New York's five boroughs, the Winchell campaign, as Winchell had imagined it, was under way. He had at last brought the Lindbergh grotesquery to the surface, the underside of Lindbergh's affable blandness, raw and undisguised. (262)

In this moment Roth describes his own process of uncovering the "undersides" as he does here in *The Plot Against America*, in *The Human Stain*, in *American Pastoral*, and elsewhere. Winchell's campaign is precisely to make the mask fall away and for Roth's fictional 1940s America to bare its fascist, racist, anti-Semitic soul. As Winchell continues his campaign, walking with a cane because one of his legs had been set on fire by the burning cross, "American history had recorded its first large-scale pogrom, one clearly modeled on the 'spontaneous demonstrations' against Germany's Jews known as *Kristallnacht*" (266). This series of pogroms had included "kerosene-soaked crosses . . . ignited on the lawns" of many Jewish residents (265). Winchell's brief campaign for president ends abruptly with his assassination in Louisville, Kentucky, the same state to which Sandy went as one of the Just Folks adherents.

After Winchell's assassination a crowd of 30,000 mourners gathers in New York to view Winchell's coffin. The mayor of New York, Fiorello H. La Guardia, a Republican, is

> alone among the members of his party in displaying his contempt for Lindbergh and for the Nazi dogma of Aryan superiority that he (himself the son of an unobservant Jewish mother from Austrian Trieste and a freethinker Italian father who came to America as a ship's musician) has identified as the precept at the heart of Lindbergh's credo and of the huge American cult that worships the president. (303)

In his speech, La Guardia describes Winchell as a "'muckraker who hates everything hidden'" (303). As was the case with the narrator's description of the underside of American anti-Semitism—and of course let's remember that the narrator's name is "Philip Roth"—the muckraker who roots out the hidden applies equally well to the impulse in much of Roth's work. La Guardia goes on to argue that, loud and not always decorous, not always as composed as the fascist Lindbergh, "Walter's vulgarity is something great, and Lindbergh's decorum is hideous" (305). Roth's La Guardia, then, argues for uncovering the dangerous repression necessary for decorum to prevail.

It would be too simple to place a loud Jewish muckraking sensibility against a quiet goyish tendency toward decorum but that is exactly what erupts at other places in the novel. The tidy living room Bess Roth labored, scrimped, and saved to forge into the American dream house, for example, is covered in the blood of the warring Alvin and Herman when Alvin goes several steps too far and spits in the face of his Uncle Herman just as he had, immediately before losing his leg, spit in the face of a dead German soldier during the war. La Guardia concludes his speech by echoing what many actual, postwar American Jews have felt or uttered: "It can't happen here? My friends, it *is* happening here—and where is Lindbergh?" (305). It can't happen here is of course exactly what Roth challenges throughout the novel. Could it? Would it have with a few tweaks of the historical record? Could it in future? While many acts of anti-Semitism still plague America, what is of course more urgent is the institutionalized racism that segregates schools and populates prisons. This is another "underside" of American consciousness that Roth addresses most obviously in *The Human Stain*, but that also haunts *The Plot Against America* to some degree.

It is significantly less scary to write about *The Plot Against America* today (spring of 2009) than it was when Roth published it five years ago. Indeed, in the fall before the 2008 presidential election, when I was asked to contribute to this volume, I almost immediately penned a late-night, fevered reflection on how prescient, how scary, Roth's depiction had become in light of the prospect of hailing Republican vice presidential candidate Sarah Palin as our (the "our" of America) VP. As the *New York Times* columnist Frank Rich noted, Palin quoted Westbrook Pegler in her nomination acceptance speech; Pegler was nostalgic for the Third Reich and used distasteful anti-Semitic language that I do not want to reprint here (google Westbrook Pegler and it is easy to find; in "Story" Roth mentions Pegler in a long list of anti-Semites, and he appears briefly in the novel, 327; see Rich, "Ticket"). Similarly, former Republican presidential candidate John McCain actively sought and received the endorsement of John Hagee, an evangelical leader who had argued that the "Nazis had operated on God's behalf to chase the Jews from Europe" (see Stein). While a McCain-Palin ticket was unlikely to have the same inverse power ratio of the Bush-Cheney presidency or Roth's fictional Lindbergh-Wheeler presidency, where it is the shadowy vice president who pulls the presidential puppet strings, Palin's appearance on the national stage could not fail to resonate, for those of us who had read, taught, thought about, or worked on *The Plot Against America*, with the image of the populist Lindbergh in the White House. One could not fail to notice the shared naïve populism and bravado between the pilot and the Alaskan governor. That said, as I write, President Obama resides in the White House, struggling to correct the severe economic downturn caused by years of deregulated financial mayhem. The specter of a White House peopled by those who received at rallies shouts of "lynch him" in reference to their rival, Obama, has not become reality. A fictional text could well be written about what kinds of racism and anti-Semitism might have flowered had that ticket won national support.

CHAPTER 9

My Life as a Boy:
The Plot Against America

Elaine M. Kauvar

For over two decades, Philip Roth has brooded over the relationship between facts and fiction, sometimes casting doubt on their separability, sometimes purposely intertwining them. At the beginning of *The Facts: A Novelist's Autobiography*, Roth tells his character Zuckerman, "the facts have always been notebook jottings, my way of springing into fiction" (1). Until *The Facts*, Roth maintains, he had used the "past as the basis for transformation, for, among other things, a kind of intricate explanation to myself of my world" (4). Yet facts take on a different significance in *Operation Shylock* and *The Plot Against America*, both of which have notes to the reader at the end of the book. They each proclaim the respective novel a "work of fiction"; and in the postscript to *The Plot Against America* Roth even offers "a reference for readers interested in tracking where historical fact ends and historical imagining begins" (364). Told from the perspective of an older man reflecting on his childhood—from the point of view of an "adult looking back 60-odd years at the experience"—*The Plot Against America* belongs to the group of books now called by the publisher the "Roth books," a category that includes *The Facts*, *Patrimony*, and *Operation Shylock* ("Story" C11). Together the four works provide "different worlds, and different instruments of understanding" (Wood).

What kind of world and what instrument of understanding does *The Plot Against America* afford? Philip Roth in his "Story behind *The Plot Against America*" reveals the matrix of his idea to have come from Arthur Schlesinger's autobiography, *A Life in the Twentieth Century: Innocent Beginnings, 1917–1950*, where the novelist saw a likeness between how historical events impinged on the historian's life and his memory of how they had impinged on his own. Roth sought to take a reference to the Republican desire to run Lindbergh for president and to imagine him president while maintaining as many of the facts as he could. Out of Roth's account of the novel's origin arises the question: what kind of historical fiction is *The Plot Against America*? When the novel was published in 2004, reviewers compared it to Sinclair Lewis's *It Can't Happen Here* (1935), a dystopian tale about totalitarianism appearing in a small New England town, an admonitory story depicting the terrible world of fascism. Roth himself calls his imagined world in *The Plot Against America* an "uchronia," a period of time difficult to determine, a period utterly suitable for exploring a plot against America ("Story" C10).

Roth's uchronia belongs to the battle between fact and fiction he entertains throughout the "Roth books." He states his task precisely in "The Story behind *The Plot Against America*":

> To tell the story of Lindbergh's presidency from the point of view of my own family . . . To alter the historical reality by making Lindbergh America's 33rd president while keeping everything else as close to factual as I could. ("Story" C10)

On the one hand, the novelist sought to portray the members of his family as though he were "writing nonfiction" ("Story" C10). On the other hand, he wanted to reimagine the historical past, to write a fiction that incorporated facts into an imaginative structure. Why this interest in the importance of factual events?

The answer lies in where authentic truth can be found. Historians and psychoanalysts as well as novelists agree that reality cannot be discovered from historical facts alone but in the process of writing fiction where psychical reality is recounted accurately. The reality in Schlesinger's book—an "authentically American" reality—attracted Roth because he believes that the "unpredictability that is history" ambushes even Americans ("Story" C10, C12). Powerfully drawn to the autobiographical, Roth envisions the turmoil engendered in the Roth family by unpredictable historical events. The young Philip, for example, grows profoundly disillusioned with his father in the course of the novel; and that feeling becomes, among other things, a kind of symbol of the larger loss of confidence in the American promise as the novel represents it.

Lindbergh as President

That *The Plot Against America* draws on the idea that Lewis's title expresses—a robust American conviction—signals the direction Roth's novel will take. Roth underscores the idea's persistence in the scene at the murdered Walter Winchell's funeral when Mayor LaGuardia declares, "It can't happen here? My friends, it *is* happening here" (*Plot* 305). What might have happened after the presidential election of 1940 had Charles A. Lindbergh won rather than Franklin D. Roosevelt captures Roth's fancy. Taking the germ of the story from Schlesinger's statement that Lindbergh was wanted as a candidate for president in 1940, Roth constructs his novel. That Lindbergh might qualify for so important a position stems from the fact that he became an international hero when, at 25, he made the world's first nonstop solo flight from New York to Paris. In 1932 when his first child was kidnapped and murdered, Lindbergh became a martyr. After going to Germany in 1935 and witnessing the promulgation of the racial laws, Lindbergh called Hitler a "great man" (369). Returning to America in 1939, Lindbergh began to give speeches blaming Jews, declaring them a matter of serious concern, deeming them foreigners albeit American citizens (see Berg).

In the novel, his victory a decisive one, Lindbergh signs non-aggression treaties, one with Hitler's Germany and another with Japan. He favors America staying out of a war that is not its concern. To champion the Nazi conviction of Aryan superiority and to weaken the Jews' solidarity, the new president creates the Office of American Absorption (OAA). Its program "Just Folks" has urban Jewish children spending a summer on farms where they not only learn about farm life but are fed unkosher foods, food prohibited by Jewish law. What will surprise none of Roth's readers is that a rabbi, Rabbi Lionel Bengelsdorf, becomes Lindbergh's staunch collaborator; for the rabbi sees nothing wrong in encouraging Jewish children to eat unkosher food, or in stripping themselves of their last vestige of Jewishness, for that matter. Worse: Bengelsdorf is blind to the similarities between Lindbergh's decisions and those of Hitler. Here is Bengelsdorf on the goals of OAA:

> The Nuremberg Laws deprived Jews of their civil rights and did everything to exclude them from membership in their nation. What I have encouraged President Lindbergh to do is to initiate programs inviting Jews to enter as far into the national life as they like—a national life that I'm sure you would agree is no less ours to enjoy than anyone else's. (*Plot* 111)

To enter far into the national life, the mainstream, is to promote the disappearance of Jewish life into the surrounding Gentile culture and to become just folks. That impulse, Roth suggests, may itself "constitute a form of anti-Semitism" (Parrish, "Review Essay" 95).

Indeed, when Philip's brother Sandy is invited by his Aunt Evelyn and Rabbi Bengelsdorf to be the "nationwide representative of Just Folks," his father Herman protests:

> But here the Nazis pretend to invite the Jews *in*. And why? To lull them to sleep. To lull them to sleep with the ridiculous dream that everything in America is hunky-dory. But *this*? . . . *This*? Inviting them to shake the blood-stained hand of a Nazi criminal? Unbelievable! Their lying and their scheming do not stop for a minute! . . . No! They have mocked us enough with what they are doing to Sandy! He is not going anywhere! They have already stolen my country—they are not stealing my son! (*Plot* 186)

Herman's outcry reflects what Schlesinger observes in his memoir, "but none so tore apart families and friendships as the great debate of 1940–41 . . . justice has not been done to the searing personal impact in those angry days" (241). It is just this observation that *The Plot Against America* explores, for at the nub of this "exercise in historical imagination" lies the searing personal impact that history has on the Roth family ("Story" C11). In his "Story behind *The Plot Against America*," Roth explains that his "every imaginative effort" is "directed toward making the effect of that reality as strong as [he] could and not so much to illuminate the present through the past but illuminate the past through the past" ("Story" C11). It is not, then, as historical imagining that the novel makes its mark, for after all, Lindbergh's supposed presidency lasts only two years; and moreover, the history is untrue. Instead, *The Plot Against America* belongs to Roth's own memoirs, glimpses his childhood, illustrates what the narrator comes to learn about history:

> Turned wrong way round, the relentless unforeseen was what we schoolchildren studied as "History," harmless history, where everything unexpected in its own time is chronicled on the page as inevitable. The terror of the unforeseen is what the science of history hides, turning a disaster into an epic. (*Plot* 113–14)

Plain Narrative versus Significant Narrative, or Fact versus Fiction

In that explanation, Roth suggests he regards the truth that we associate with history as less true than the kind that fictional narrative can impart. The novelist's tetralogy of autobiographies are interrelated; facts give way to fantasy as the novelist struggles to arrive at the authenticity of his experiences. A distinction the philosopher of history W. H. Walsh employs seems relevant here. For Walsh, historians who write a "straightforward statement of what occurred" have written a "plain" narrative, a narrative that should be distinguished from "significant" narratives that seek not only to relate what happened but also to explain why it happened (480). Not content simply to spell out the events as they occurred in *The Facts*, Roth engages Zuckerman, his fictional and opposing self, to comment on the sincerity of his autobiography. Resisting his creator, Zuckerman impugns the novelist for the plain narrative he has constructed:

> Why is it that when they talk about the facts they feel they're on more solid ground than when they talk about the fiction? The truth is that the facts are much more refractory and unmanageable and inconclusive, and can actually kill the very sort of inquiry that imagination opens up. (*Facts* 166)

Zuckerman thus protests the novelist's plain narrative and praises instead the significant narrative that fiction yields.

An illustration of Roth's use of plain narrative as opposed to significant narrative becomes evident when the opening paragraphs of *The Facts* and *The Plot Against America* are compared. In the first section of *The Facts*, which Roth titles "Safe at Home," he describes "the greatest menace" coming from the Germans and the Japanese and his "terror as a nine-year-old" (20). But the danger was not limited to the Germans and the Japanese; there were threats at home as well. The greatest of those "came from the Americans who opposed or resisted us—or condescended to us or rigorously excluded us—because we were Jews" (20). As Zuckerman observes, however, Roth makes a "fictional world that is far more exciting than the world it comes out of" (162).

Consider the beginning of *The Plot Against America*, for example. There Roth immediately captures the feelings aroused by the menace:

> Fear presides over these memories, a perpetual fear. Of course no childhood is without its terrors, yet I wonder if I would have been a less frightened boy if Lindbergh hadn't been president or if I hadn't been the offspring of Jews. (1)

The boy is 7, a stamp collector, a patriotic third-grader modeling his hobby after President Roosevelt's. In both the memoir and the novel, the child is threatened by anti-Semitism; but the fear in *The Plot Against America* is not only palpable, it suffuses the novel. Nonetheless, Roth pronounces his family a happy one in 1940, living in a neighborhood where "All were Jews," which fuels the family's illusion of invisible assimilation (2). His was a world dominated by Jewish Americans, a place where no one looks like a Jew: "Nobody in the neighborhood had a beard or dressed in the antiquated Old World style or wore a skull-cap either outdoors or in [their] houses" (3). Until the Republican nomination of Charles Lindbergh, the Roth family's "homeland was America" (5).

What happens to that homeland and how it affects the Roth family dominates *The Plot Against America*. The family, Roth writes, gave him as a child "that huge endowment of personal security that [he] had taken for granted as an American child . . . in an American city in an America at peace with the world" (7). The passage recalls one in *The Facts* where Roth describes his "intensely secure and protected childhood" fueled by the conviction, "the first commandment," that "*the family is God, the family is One*" (14). Roth deftly replaces the Sh'ma, the Hebrew prayer that affirms belief and trust in the One God, with his own version. Memories of his parents, the desire to bring them back "from the grave and restore them to what they were at the height of their powers," and the narrative demand to make the imagined Lindbergh presidency believable are interwoven in the fabric of this "child's first cohesive mythology" ("Story" C10; *Plot* 5).

It begins to unravel when a speech Rabbi Bengelsdorf gives on behalf of Lindbergh renders his father unable to speak, "divested for perhaps the first time in his life of that relentless passion he brought to the struggle against set-back and disappointment" (40). As if to heighten the fear with which the first chapter begins, it ends with Philip's nightmare about his stamp collection in which his 1932 Washington Bicentennials, each with a portrait of Washington, "were now the same and no longer of Washington but of Hitler" (43). More frightening yet are the black swastikas all over his set of 1934 National Parks stamps. At the end of chapter one, Herman Roth's speechlessness and his son's transformed stamp collection intimate the roil about to overtake the Roth family.

The nightmare emerging from the depths of unconscious life incorporates a truth that facts are unable to predict. In Washington on a trip, the family is denied the hotel room reserved months ago. Puzzled by the manager's return of their deposit, Philip asks his brother to explain. One whispered word suffices: "Anti-Semitism" (69). The Gettysburg Address and its proclamation "All men are created equal" notwithstanding, the family is "expelled" (66). Patriotism ebbs in such moments; and the young Philip, suddenly aware of his mother's panic, begins to lose some of his unworldly sense of safety. He feels "that it had fallen to [him] to hold her together, to become all at once a courageous new creature" (66). Aware of the taunts—his father twice labeled a "Loudmouth Jew"—Philip envisions "humiliation sticking to the skin like a coat of thick filth that you could never get off" (79), but the reader senses that the humiliation unglues his naiveté. It is as if the child awoke and found his nightmare true.

Our sense of him turning into a new creature becomes more apparent as the seven-year-old develops. As Lindbergh continues to espouse isolationism, Philip asks his father, just as in Washington he had questioned his brother, what Lindbergh means; for in growing up, he "was more and more asking what everything meant" (84). And along with Philip's increasing maturity comes Sandy's decreasing adherence to his father's wishes. Just Folks, which aims "to erode the solidarity of the Jewish family," has with the efforts of Aunt Evelyn begun what Herman Roth fears—the separation of Jewish children from their parents (86). The return of his wounded cousin Alvin, who had lost both parents by age 13 and whom Herman Roth was dedicated to saving, demonstrates at once the meaning of the first commandment and the pain that historical events bring to the Roth family. The father's reaction to the news of Alvin's lost leg—he had fled the safety of the family to fight in the Canadian forces against Hitler—results in a "childhood milestone, when another's tears are more unbearable than one's own" (113). Witnessing his "father fall apart" and knowing he "would never return to the same childhood," Philip embarks on a "new life" (113) and alerts the reader to what *The Plot Against America* focuses on—his coming-of-age, a period ineluctably accompanied by the vicissitudes of the father and son relationship. Philip's "stamp mentor" Earl Axman also teaches him to learn the "liberties a boy from an exemplary household could take when he stopped working to please everyone with his juvenile purity and discovered the guilty enjoyment of secretly acting on his own" (114).

What those liberties entail are stealing from his parents, following Christian men as they wend their way homeward, and pretending to be a "lost boy" in flight from the Nazis. His "great new aim [is] unearthed for [his] eight-year-old life: to escape it" (117). But he cannot escape the next phase of his life, which commences with Alvin's arrival and which generates its "own chaos of feelings" (127). Alvin, Sandy, Seldon Wishnow, Philip—these four boys appear in the novel and they are all present in "The Stump," a crucial chapter. The sharp differences among the boys, with all of whom Philip has a relationship, help distinguish his evolution from theirs. Whereas Sandy works for Lindbergh in full rebellion against Herman, his younger brother Philip determines "to make everything turn out right by being the best little boy imaginable, much, much better than Sandy and better even than myself" (132). Part of that involves him sharing a room with Alvin because, unlike Sandy, who worked for Lindbergh, Alvin lost his leg going to war against the Nazis whom Lindbergh revered. Philip's relationship with Alvin and the stump that remains of his leg crystallizes his sense of being the best little boy, quite the opposite of Sandy. Worshiping Alvin, Philip wants "to run away, and not merely from the stump" (136). It is this desire to run away, to attain new liberties, to become independent, that clashes with his desire to please everyone and to make everything right.

The Best Little Boy

But being the best little boy involves Philip in more than he bargained for. Learning to take care of Alvin's stump—"a small animal . . . one whose head had to be muzzled extra carefully to prevent it from sinking its razor-sharp teeth into the hand of its captor"—Philip discovers a scab broken off from the stump and runs to the cellar where he vomits (137). The cellar becomes his underworld, his River Styx, and it is there that he imagines "manning the furnace all alone" and where he thinks about "the inevitability of dying," a tormenting subject for a nine-year-old (139). His realization that Alvin is "semihelpless" augments the boy's adulation of his older cousin, but Philip's growing awareness brings with it the sense that "what there was to pity was a little less impossible to bear" (144). What Alvin offers in return is his Canadian medal.

Philip has become Alvin's "personal valet," his "mascot," and Alvin his surrogate brother (145, 162). In his "great supporting role," Philip elicits "sublime recognition" and surprises his real brother Sandy, who is startled to realize that what Philip understands are "the waning years of [his] long career as his little brother" (146). That he remains a child, however, is manifest in his misinterpretation of Alvin's masturbation and his thought that the ejaculate "was something terrible" that appears when a man "was completely consumed by grief" (148). It is not grief that consumes Alvin when his Uncle Monty accuses him of being a "professional misfit" (151), but it is Philip's grasp of what takes place in the aftermath of bullying that prompts him to crack, "alone later in the one place . . . where [he] knew [he] could go to be apart from the living and all that they cannot not do" (152). The two reports—the child's perspective and the adult's concern—record the same event as it occurred and as it is remembered. For the child, such unhappy feelings will dissipate, but the adult's understanding of the inevitable suffering in life abides. And the coalescence of those experiences becomes the significant narrative for the reader.

What Alvin cannot do is keep his worshiper, for Philip's recent perception of Alvin as bereft of "every decent habit inculcated in him when he was living as my parents' ward," coupled with his loss of "interest in the fight against fascism," sparks another insight—that "Alvin didn't care one bit. No longer was he burdened by concern for anyone's suffering other than his own" (157, 158). Philip's idol, the "maimed and suffering American pariah who had come to loom larger for [him] than any man [he'd] ever known, including [his] father," is a petty gambler; and the horrified Philip thinks, "I'd never before had to grow up at a pace like this" (157, 172). Alvin's mascot has become Alvin's Momus, the Greek god of mockery and censure.

Alvin's critic, Philip is also Seldon Wishnow's "secret sharer" (Posnock, *Rude Truth* 30). The nine-year-old Philip has a "shadow" who is omnipresent and to whom he feels contracted (221). "About the same size," the two boys reflect the diverging fates born of the anti-Semitic Lindbergh administration (222). His double's loneliness, his sorrow, his brains—these Philip finds repellent, for Seldon "is the responsibility you can't get rid of" ("Story" C10). When Philip attempts to do so, however, he effects a tragedy for Seldon and spawns guilt in himself. At her nephew's request, Aunt Evelyn arranges for Mrs. Wishnow's and Seldon's move to Kentucky, where Mrs. Wishnow is murdered because she is a Jew and where Seldon "suffers something like the European Jewish experience," becoming the boy "whose child-hood is destroyed" and the boy whom Philip fears to be ("Story" C11). Sharing his double's fate, he is driven to tell the tale.

Though he avoids the destiny of "Solitary Seldon," Philip imagines himself in his shoes. Like Herman Roth, Mr. Wishnow was an insurance agent with the Metropolitan; but unlike the robust Herman Roth, Mr. Wishnow coughs uncontrollably from his cancer. His son discovers his father "hanging face down on the closet floor" (168). The magical thinking belonging to a juvenile prompts the guilt-ridden Philip to think, "because I was relieved he was dead, he would go out of his way to haunt me for the rest of my life" (168). In Philip's mind, Mr. Wishnow's ghost is transformed into a replica of his own father, whom he imagines as the suicide, not because of a terminal illness but because of Lindbergh's presidency. That his father is "vividly alive" has no effect on his young son, for he clings to his fearful notion that the figure under the sheet on the stretcher will turn out to be Herman Roth after all.

The fantasy of his father's death, coupled with Philip's perception of him as a protector, signals a further stage of his maturation—the beginnings of his rebellion against his father, along with the parricidal impulses Philip Roth unfolds in *Patrimony*. And those impulses bring in their wake the guilty feelings responsible for Philip's six-day illness, "that not uncommon childhood ailment called why-can't-it-be-the-way-it-was" (172). His affliction recalls those manifest in Victorian novels like Charles Dickens's, for example, where rising from their sick beds the characters have not only atoned but are prepared to begin anew and to see afresh. Part of that renewed vision involves Philip's consciousness that his brother Sandy "was leading a double existence" as a "Lindbergh loyalist" (183, 184). His brother's example and Seldon's "omnipresence" accelerate his "urge to rebel" and his desire "to be an orphan"—like Seldon (221, 233). Certain an unavoidable disaster is about to overtake his family and friends, Philip runs away from home dressed in Seldon's clothes. His collision with a horse lands him in the hospital where he discovers that Seldon Wishnow has saved his life but that he has lost his treasured stamp collection. The irretrievable and "irreplaceable" stamp collection foreshadows another loss, the end of his "incomparable American childhood" (235, 301).

Perhaps the most difficult task of all and one vital to maturation, Freud conjectures, is an individual's necessary separation from the parent. Everywhere on the pages of Philip Roth's work is the figure of the father; for, as Roth remarks in *The Facts* about some fatherless boys in his acquaintance, "they too struck me as scary and a little taboo" (13–14). Like the small "repertoire" and the "vernacular expressiveness" possessed by Herman Roth, Philip Roth's "talent isn't for imagining events on the grand scale [but on] something small, really small enough to be credible" (*Facts* 16; *Plot* 220; "Story" C10). With this announcement, Roth aligns himself with Herman Roth, underscoring the problematic nature of the son's dividing himself from his father.

The apprehension the narrator has in *The Plot Against America*, however, is telling. Beset by his wife's pleas to go to Canada and "in the prime of his manhood," Herman Roth nonetheless sees himself with "mortifying clarity: a devoted father of titanic energy no more capable of protecting his family from harm than was Mr. Wishnow hanging dead in the closet" (*Plot* 226). But it is the older narrator who remembers the event and interprets it, and the young boy who witnesses the "abrupt decline in [his] father's vocational status" when he quits his job rather than be transferred to Kentucky (238). Shocked by his father's decline, the son recognizes in his father's transformation the diminishment of a parent's powers.

There is more. The return of Alvin and the "battle royal" that ensues between him and Herman bring a further but equally grim conclusion: "I'd had no idea my father was so well suited for wreaking havoc or equipped to make that lightning-quick transformation from sanity to lunacy that is indispensable in enacting the unbridled urge to destroy" (293). That urge forces the son, who envisions his father as a protector, to realize that he never considered his father's capacity to beat "somebody up—let alone battering bloody his beloved older brother's fatherless son" (294). The reassuring safety at home, "traditionally the staging area for the collective effort to hold the line *against* the intrusions of a hostile world," has become the battlefield on which the hallowed family takes "up the cudgels and hysterically" destroy themselves unaided by the anti-Semites they have been fleeing (295). The historical events surrounding them intrude on the family dynamics: fleeing the anti-Semitism provoked by the Lindbergh administration, the family members turn on each other and experience the hatred characteristic of anti-Semites. History thus encroaches on the Roth family.

The Transforming Power of History

In the aftermath of the fight, in the "airless, gag-inducing slaughter-house smell," the narrator comes to acknowledge another of his father's failings, his inability "to understand that Alvin's nature was never really reformable," as his cousin's spitting into Herman's face the "way he'd spit into the face of that dead German soldier" who destroyed his leg surely indicates (296, 297). Looking back, the narrator reflects on the impact history has had on the conflict. Alvin, he concludes, wants to fight "Because there is a war going on" and he is "historically trapped" (298). Because of the times, Alvin becomes "like the very fathers he wants to be rid of" (298). Philip, the witness to the heartbreaking violence, collapses "from uncontrollable fear" to be "carried off" in his father's arms (298). Though the battle royal ceases, the Roth family has been "overpowered" by the historical forces Lindbergh has unleashed against the Jews, and they force Herman Roth to make the decision to leave his beloved country and emigrate to Canada.

Just as history appears to have changed the family's status as Americans, Lindbergh disappears and with him the OAA and the nightmare concluding the first chapter of *The Plot Against America*. The frightening dream dissipated, the family remains safe once more. But historical events mar and ultimately vanquish the "unfazed sense of security first fostered in a little child by a big, protective republic and his ferociously responsible parents" (301). Through the disastrous events imagined by Philip Roth, the child enters the disillusioning travail demanded by adulthood.

Allegedly a memoir—its subtitle declaring the book a "True Story"— and published in 1991, 13 years before *The Plot Against America*, *Patrimony* makes plain the outcome of that travail; for it is with death and loss that it attempts to come to grips (see Kauvar, "Doubly Reflected"). Like the dream in *The Plot Against America*, the dreams in *Patrimony* shed further light on the history of the dreamer; for Roth's dream, "a portrait of the aftermath of a disaster," contains "all the family history" (*Patrimony* 235, 236). The death of his father, the feeling of being a "fatherless evacuee," is countered by a contrary message delivered up in another dream six weeks later (237). In the second dream with which Roth concludes *Patrimony*, Herman Roth reproaches his son for burying him in the wrong clothes. A competing feeling—that the father will remain alive as "*the* father, sitting in judgment" on whatever the son does—adds to the sadness of the loss experienced in the first dream (238). Memories of his father's failings coalesce with the guilt ignited by the sense of having nullified the father by seeing him not in his prime but in his decline. Though *Patrimony* is not fiction but a true story, its narrative effectively completes the one begun in *The Plot Against America*, albeit over a decade earlier. In revealing that he wished to bring his parents back in *The Plot Against America*, Roth discloses his unconscious desire to resurrect the father in whose arms he had been so safe and to conquer the guilt aroused by having outdistanced him.

His father's obedience to "fair play" accords with the depth of his mother's compassion (*Plot* 255). Together they "form the novel's moral center" (Posnock, *Rude Truth* 29). After Mrs. Wishnow is "dead . . . beaten and robbed" (*Plot* 331) in Kentucky and Bess Roth accepts and makes long distance calls to Seldon, her son thinks, "Never would she seem more remarkable to me than she did that night" (334). As he had identified the dead Mr. Wishnow with his father, so now he links Mrs. Wishnow to his mother, feeling responsible for "the orphaning of her son" (349). Bess's son, however, experiences his strong tie to his mother when his "whole idea of her underwent a startling change: my mother was a fellow creature. I was shocked by the revelation, and too young to comprehend that there was the strongest attachment of all" (340). Haunted by guilt "for the death of Mrs. Wishnow," he determines to run away again and signs a letter of application for a job with Seldon's name, for Philip "couldn't for the life of me think of another name" (349).

He has become one with his double, a "[m]otherless and fatherless" boy "vulnerable to manipulation, to influences . . . rootless and . . . vulnerable to everything" (358). But it is Seldon who needs a "rescuer" and since "orphans [are] his specialty," Herman Roth brings Seldon home the way Alvin had been brought home (358). Having cared for Alvin's stump, Philip now becomes responsible for Seldon who "himself was the stump" (362). If the orphan is the stump, his secret sharer is the "prosthesis" (362), the replacement for all that Seldon has lost. The "romance of [his] childhood gone," Philip enters the "relentless unforeseen" territory of adulthood and Philip Roth ends the novel's narrative (*Facts* 168; *Plot* 113–14).

If the guiding interest of the novel is a boy's coming-of-age, *The Plot Against America* pays homage to Roth's parents just as it denigrates anti-Semitism. Although Lindbergh's presidency is not real and the fictional plot against America lasts only two years, the anti-Semitism is all too real and turns Philip "from a Jewish American into an American Jew, or in the eyes of his enemies just a Jew in America" (Coetzee, *Inner Workings* 240). Continually denying his real self as a presence in any of his novels and introducing an opposing self to challenge a so-to-speak factual self, the novelist calls the narrator of *The Plot Against America* "Philip Roth" and gives him the same birthday and the same parents as his own. He not only narrates the child's story six decades later but he writes it as well: in that sense, then, we are reading "the story of the real, historical Philip Roth" (Coetzee 234).

Fact versus Fiction Revisited

But his habit of distinguishing fact from fiction evinces itself in the postscript he attaches to *The Plot Against America*, the "Note to the Reader" that contains "A True Chronology of the Major Figures, Other Historical Figures in the Work, and Some Documentation." There in the first line he states, "*The Plot Against America* is a work of fiction. This postscript is intended as a reference for readers interested in tracking where historical fact ends and historical imagining begins" (364). In a similar fashion, the novelist calls *Operation Shylock* "a confession" and names Moishe Pipik his "shadow" (*Operation Shylock* 378). And having designated the novel a "confession," Roth avows in the novel's preface, as he does in *The Facts*, his allegiance to fact: "I've drawn *Operation Shylock* from notebook journals. The book is as accurate an account as I am able to give of actual occurrences that I lived through during my middle fifties and that culminated, early in 1988, in my agreeing to undertake an intelligence-gathering operation for Israel's foreign intelligence service, the Mossad" (*Operation Shylock* 13). Enjoining him to suppress the last chapter "as a Jew" (388) and to proclaim the book a series of "Hallucinatory projections" (389), a fiction, the spy Smilesburger in *Operation Shylock* serves Roth the way Zuckerman does in *The Facts*—as a critic keen to disclose the novelist's defective depiction of objective reality. Just as he does in the note to the reader in *The Plot Against America*, Roth denies the truthfulness of his confession in his note to the reader of *Operation Shylock*:

> This book is a work of fiction . . . the verbatim minutes of the January 27, 1988, morning session of the trial of John Demjanjuk in Jerusalem District Court provided the courtroom exchanges quoted in chapter 9. Otherwise the names, characters, places, and incidents either are products of the author's imagination or are

used fictitiously. Any resemblance to actual events or locales or persons, living or dead, is entirely coincidental. This confession is false. (399)

If a confession shaped by narrative invention and an historical tale formed by imagining reality are declared false, then "the bare bones, the structure of a life without the fiction," an autobiography, should best be able to measure the truth of the self (*Facts* 6). But Zuckerman in *The Facts* argues a brief against the falsity and fluidity of autobiography as opposed to the credibility and stability of fiction, a conviction Roth twice denies. Where does such an aporia—an impasse—leave the reader? What events should be deemed formative? Which experiences should be pronounced decisive? In other words, how does *The Plot Against America*, an historical imagining, furnish the truth? It conveys the impact on the Roth family of imaginary historical events and arrives at emotional actuality through circuitous means, along the tangled trail of fantasy.

For Philip Roth genuine experience cannot be depicted without the transforming power of narrative. Embedding his history "in a context of meaning and relevance" and pursuing the hidden paths that go from the child to the adult, he affirms a central tenet of psychoanalytic thought (Meissner 287). Each of the four "Roth books" follows a different road and each achieves a disparate vision of the self, leaving us "with a self which is a tissue of contingencies rather than an at least potentially well-ordered system of faculties" (Rorty 32). But the self is not shaped in isolation, as the portrait of the Roth family testifies. It is in the "evocation of the strength of parental love and family loyalty" (Posnock, *Rude Truth* 23) so apparent in *The Plot Against America* that the reader apprehends the rendering of the self's origins and a "defining preoccupation of [Roth's] oeuvre," what a character in another novel calls "the eternal power of attachment" (23). Fore-grounded in *The Plot Against America* are the "close attachments to other people . . . the fundamental role of trust in the constitution of selfhood and community" (Chodat 710).

Subjectivity, Roth implies, is achieved by constructing a meaning out of individual experience and family life. In *The Plot Against America*, as in the other three volumes of his tetralogy, there are two kinds of truth, "historical truth" and "narrative truth," which are akin to Walsh's designation of plain and significant narratives (Spence 279–97). Fearing that he will forever dwell in the "house of Ambiguity," Roth indicates what is fundamental to his fiction, that it is dialogic (*Operation Shylock* 307). The narrative and historical truth, then, of *The Plot Against America* and the other Roth books remain dialogic: his work is "shaped by a constellation of voices, structured not by rules and imperatives but by contexts and habits," by the varying worlds and diverging instruments of understanding (Chodat 714). Whether through autobiographical formulation or narrative invention, one truth is explored and then overturned by a second, to reach what Hans Loewald calls a "*conscire*, a knowing together" (Loewald 410). With the four Roth volumes, the writer has created a series of books that confirms the self's multiplicity, evident now in unadorned fact, now in narrative invention, or finally in the intertwining of facts with imagination, in the historical imagining supplied by *The Plot Against America*.

CHAPTER 10

Autobiography and History in Roth's *The Plot Against America,* or What Happened When Hitler Came to New Jersey

Timothy Parrish

In Philip Roth's *The Plot Against America*, the specter of Adolph Hitler's Nazi hordes, unleashed by Charles Lindbergh, invades New Jersey and disrupts the otherwise happy home of young Philip Roth. Before we can see how the Roth clan heroically withstands the Nazi menace, though, we need to establish how *The Plot Against America* fits within the Roth canon and in particular Roth's understanding of history and its relation to individual identity. With the possible exception of Ralph Ellison, no major American novelist since World War II has been as avowedly "American" in his public self-presentation as Philip Roth. Roth's late-career American trilogy, beginning in 1997 with *American Pastoral* and culminating in 2000 with *The Human Stain*, was widely praised for its achievement in retelling the second half of the American twentieth century as a single, compelling saga. Arguably, *The Human Stain*'s Coleman Silk was the definitive Roth protagonist: one who enacts a version of one ethnicity (Jewish) while being born of another ethnicity (African American), yet whose identity, no matter how conflicted, comes from being "American." Perhaps paradoxically, Roth's method for expressing his characters' affiliation with the meaning of America has often taken the form of opposing what is sometimes called one's ethnic identity, one's not necessarily "American" cultural heritage, in an antagonistic and, ultimately, mutually constitutive relationship with what may be called, for lack of a better phrase, one's Americanness. Thus, to imagine one's identity to be threatened by history, as Roth does in *The Plot*

Against America, is a significant event in Roth's fiction. However, in introducing a menacing history to his American shores, Roth is in fact—and quite contrarily—reinforcing an idealized view of America as the last, best place in which one may pursue the seemingly endless opportunities for self-reinvention and renewal.

Happy History, American History

In Roth's other works, exploring one's American freedom has generally meant constructing, or performing, versions of a Jewish identity that are animated by Roth's belief that America allows one to pursue, even to the point of annihilation, the historical and psychological possibilities one inherits as a consequence of having a self. As he remarked for a television interview in 1997, "If I'm not an American, I'm nothing . . . That epithet American Jewish writer has no meaning. Jew is just another way of being American. There's no separation, not in America, not for me, not for my generation" (Shostak 236). For Roth, the promise of being an American is a kind of state of grace in which one is allowed to perform the most compelling version of self that one's imagination allows. Thus, for Roth, the promise afforded one by being born American equates to the possibilities allowed one who chooses to write: the opportunity and even the necessity to create yourself in whatever form you can best imagine.

In an early story, "The Conversion of the Jews," a character, Ozzie, expresses this point of view provocatively. Questioning the belief that he is "chosen" because he was born a Jew rather than being born an American—although he was born both—the child asks "how Rabbi Binder could call the Jews 'The Chosen People' if the Declaration of Independence claimed all men to be created equal" (*Goodbye* 153). Arguably, Ozzie's question merges a sacred (Jewish or biblical) sense of being chosen with a secular sense of being chosen that is consistent with the sense of historical destiny put forward first by the Puritans and then later by the Founding Fathers. Where the Puritans in coming to America understood themselves to be following the destiny God appointed them by giving them the chance to build, in John Winthrop's famous words, "a city on a hill," the Founding Fathers justified their separation from England and subsequent dominion over a land already peopled by others in terms of a right they attributed to the Creator in their own name. The Puritans' power to rule derived from God and the early Americans' power to rule derived from a self-identified status afforded to them by the Creator, or destiny. In either case, the sacred and the secular are conjoined and then confirmed by the facts of the claimants' material and political success. By this logic, the creation and continuity of the nation known as the United States is living proof of the justice of the nation's having been founded in the first place.

In Ozzie's case, however, the question is how to resolve the contradictory claims he is presumably hearing from his secular schoolteachers and religious mentors. The answer that Roth's fiction gives is that Jews may have become "the chosen people" by coming to America where the freedom to become American makes it possible for Jews to be Jews without being persecuted or murdered. Roth's work never denies that Jews in America have been persecuted for being Jewish, but Roth's heroes are more likely to be persecuted either by their own individual neuroses or, indeed, by other Jews. Thus, "The Conversion of the Jews" reaches its climax when Ozzie, in part to counteract the trauma he has experienced on account of his religious instruction as a Jew, holds his family and community hostage by threatening to jump off a building unless they agree, in his presence, to mouth the words that they accept Jesus Christ as their personal savior. Ozzie becomes a kind of renegade rabbi or priest as he orchestrates a ritual whereby the Jews at last become Christians. He symbolically obliterates their identity as Jews. Were the story set in the Tsars' Russia, Hitler's Germany, or the Catholic Inquisitors' Spain, the story might be understood to enact a type of cultural genocide. In Roth's story, though, there is of course no sense that the Jewish adults are doing anything other than mollifying a wayward and potentially dangerous child. The comedy comes from what is not happening. Thus, the story invokes the historic practice of pogroms past but only to render them ancient, ludicrous, and comic. That familiar and terrifying dimension of Jewish history that goes back to the Pharaohs disappears once the Jews have been displaced to the promised land of America.

At the outset of his 1988 autobiography, *The Facts*, Roth announces that "[t]he greatest menace while I was growing up came from abroad, from the Germans and Japanese, our enemies because we were American" (20). The young Philip could not know about the death camps that history was preparing for European Jews because he was, happily, safe in the cocoon that his Jewish family provided him. "In our lore," Roth says,

the Jewish family was an inviolate haven against every form of menace, from personal isolation to gentile hostility. Regardless of internal friction and strife, it was assumed to be an indissoluble consolidation. *Hear, O Israel, the family is God, the family is One.* (14)

Hitler's ominous shadow could threaten but not touch Philip so safe within his Jewish family's fortress.

Thus, while history in the figure of Hitler was preparing European Jews for slaughter, recently Americanized Jews such as the Roths were relatively free to pursue the comparative innocence of a bourgeois American existence. What sustained Philip's safe zone was not only the love of his mother and father, which he says was abundant, but the America that gave equal security to all of its believers. "In our apartment a framed replica of the Declaration of Independence hung above the telephone table on the hallway wall—it had been awarded by the Metropolitan to the men of my father's district for a successful year" (*Facts* 21). Roth's father was employed by the giant insurance firm. Roth notes that the social contract implied by the Declaration, and its "venerated champions of equality," at times seemed to have been issued, as it were, by his family's other "benefactors, the corporate fathers at Number One Madison Avenue, where the reigning president was, fortuitously, a Mr. Lincoln" (21–2). Roth does convey something potentially ominous about this union between the Founding Fathers and the Corporate Fathers of Metropolitan Life since Roth knows that "these awesomely named gentiles . . . conspired to prevent more than a few token Jews from assuming positions of anything approaching importance within the largest financial institution in the world" (22). The subdued—when compared to Nazi Germany—suppression of Jews in corporate America is reinforced by the occasional "race riots" that young Roth finds anomalous, "since we were all supposed to be pulling together to beat the Axis Powers" (24). Roth is even provoked to wonder "why" anyone would "make a bloody pulp of a Jewish child's face?" (25).

The power of the question, though, accrues from the reader's knowledge that both random acts of violence and concerted corporate quotas against Jews still do not make the question answerable except in the context of European history. Roth's fiction prior to *The Plot Against America* continually expresses the view that American history insofar as it concerns Jews provides no analogue to the horror that Philip's childish question would, were it to be read in the diary of Anne Frank. World War II confirmed young Roth's sense of place; it did not shatter it. Indeed, in a subtle way Roth is raising the question to highlight the exceptionally blessed condition of being born Jewish in America. Thus, Roth emphasizes not the riots but the camaraderie he felt growing up among Jews. Describing the Friday night wanderings he enjoyed with his friends, Roth does not speak of preparing for the ritual of the impending Sabbath but of how "[s]tretched on our backs in the open night air," satiated from eating "warm bagels" baked by "the Watson

Bagel Company on Clinton Place" in the era "before the bagel became a breakfast staple at Burger King," he and his Jewish friends luxuriated in the sense that "we were as carefree as any kids anywhere in postwar America, and certainly we felt ourselves no less American" (*Facts* 31).

Thus, "[a]bout being Jewish there was nothing more to say than there was about having two arms and two legs" (31). What was remarkable was not simply that they were Jews together, but that they were Americans. "Simultaneously," Roth emphasizes, "this intense adolescent camaraderie was the primary means by which we were deepening our Americanness" (31). Moreover, their sense of being American, even more remarkably, was deepened by their casual acceptance of being Jewish. Like Ozzie, though without his sense of conflict, Roth is protected by the history proclaimed by the Declaration of Independence and it is appropriate that it should be framed and hung in a prominent place of their home as other generations of Jews might have affixed a mezuzah in their doorframe.

History Hurts

No Declaration of Independence protected Isaac Babel, a Russian Jew, from being killed by Stalin or Bruno Schulz, a Polish Jew, from being killed by Hitler. I mention these two great Jewish writers whose voices were silenced by history, because their fates are almost unimaginable when seen from Roth's comfortable American vantage point. Roth, as an American, has to imagine his relationship to a history that he did not have to suffer; it is more complicated to imagine what the dead might make of Roth's position as a Jewish writer whose relationship to the Holocaust is wholly invented. Lest this seem a needlessly anachronistic perspective to bring to bear on Roth, one must stress that Roth's works themselves are often predicated on such anachronistic possibilities. "The Conversion of the Jews" gets its comic kick from the Holocaust, while a major work such as *The Ghost Writer* alludes to Babel and pretends to resurrect Anne Frank as an American college student in order to clarify the protagonist's place as a Jewish-American writer. Moreover, as we shall see, *The Plot Against America* imagines how the Roth family responds once they realize that the United States has become allied with Hitler.

The "history" that *The Ghost Writer* or *The Plot Against America* summons is almost entirely imagined. Anne Frank was killed in the camps; she did not come to America. Hitler was never an ally of the U.S. government. The historical plots of these novels exist only as a kind of playful fiction that may or may not do aesthetic or moral justice to the terrible and known history that serves as the novels' point of departure. Yet, insofar as Roth's work has a developed historicism, it is apparent only in the contrast he draws between the experience of American Jews and that of non-American Jews. In *The Ghost Writer*, the historical moral may be that in the face of the awesome destruction that the Holocaust enacted, a concerted and sympathetic silence is the only appropriate witness that one can bear. On the other hand, when compared to works by Jewish survivors such as Aharon Appelfeld, Primo Levi, or Natalia Ginzburg, Roth's sense of history is often merely the stage for his characters' narcissistic, if always engaging, theatrics of the self. The Declaration of Independence that hangs on the wall of the Roth household sanctions Philip Roth's pleasure to imagine himself, or his protagonists, doing anything that they can imagine doing, precisely because they are unconstrained by the kind of history that has afflicted Jews since Moses.

To the extent that Roth's fiction betrays the sense that history determines who you are and what you can be, Roth has suggested that it comes from being Jewish rather than American. Even so, Roth's historic sense often strikes one as being wholly contingent, and utterly re-writable. In *The Counterlife*, Nathan Zuckerman, Roth's fictional alter ego, announces that even though he is not a religious believer, he would nonetheless insist that any son he might have should be circumcised because such an act would symbolize the child's initiation into history. Zuckerman reflects,

> Circumcision makes it clear as can be that you are here and not there, that you are out and not in—also that you're mine and not theirs. There is no way around it: you enter history through my history and me. (323)

You cannot escape the mark or its meaning, Roth suggests, because the mark designates for you the fact that there is no origin for yourself prior to the historical-psychological context in which you first know yourself. Yet, in this example, the mark is a choice. One could presumably evade the implications that Roth ascribes to Zuckerman as well. Thus, if Roth wishes to acknowledge that his work is necessarily embedded within history, he still inevitably understands history in relation to the power of his own inventions. Aharon Appelfeld, a Polish Jewish writer who survived the aftermath of the Holocaust to settle in Israel, identifies the fragile thread that connects Roth's "American" work to the Holocaust or Israel. Appelfeld puts Roth's work in the broader world-historical context that some of Roth's fiction courts, which is, paradoxically, in terms of the very history that Roth as an American Jew escaped. Appelfeld says that Roth's characters are "the descendants of the Eastern

European Jewish tribe who in the beginning of the century were threatened by evil forces, both from within and without, that dispersed them to the four corners of the world. Some came to America" (14).

Some came to America. This terse, eloquent sentence describes Roth's focus as a writer and also helps us to understand the limited historical context that shapes his fiction. When Roth is not contrasting his characters' Jewish fates with that of Jews whose history lies beyond America, he generally portrays the astonishing opportunities his heroes have to invent themselves. Moreover, in dramatizing the freedom of a Portnoy, Kepesh, or Zuckerman to test their fantasies against what the world will allow, Roth's characters can only account for their blessed state of endless self-exploration by the logic that young Ozzie supplies in "The Conversion of the Jews." As Americans, they are born not so much into history as into a state of almost innocent freedom that they can perhaps ruin but not destroy.

Previous Jewish-American writers such as Abraham Cahan, Henry Roth, and Delmore Schwartz, for instance, portrayed the historical agony of "becoming American"— they captured the difficult transformation that immigrant European Jews underwent as a consequence of being displaced from Europe to America. Their characters carried their history as a weight and their encounter with America enforced upon them a kind of tragic recognition of the past that they could not slough off. Roth's characters, despite Zuckerman's elegant definition of circumcision as a kind of synecdoche for historical consciousness, do not suffer the type of recognition that the protagonist of Schwartz's "In Dreams Begin Responsibilities" (1938) endures when he futilely shouts "no" at the image of his parents' union and thus his own birth. The fact of being born into his history confers no curse but something like a blessing on Roth's characters. Two of Roth's Jewish-American contemporaries, Saul Bellow and Bernard Malamud, also set their characters within an evolving history that looked back to the Jewish immigrant experience as a context for their characters' actions and dilemmas. Roth's historical context, however, is set explicitly in the post-World War II period when Jews were rising to the highest levels of American society, and the historical context that shapes their acts is usually the one that they try to create for themselves. They invent not only themselves, but the history that allows their self-invention.

Roth is often characterized as a postmodern author, but it is important to understand that for Roth the question of history is less important than the question of self. Roth's sense of identity is recognizably postmodern. Indeed, Roth's aesthetic indifference to the historical process by which Jews became Americans is why the critic Irving Howe, in a famous essay, dismissed him as not a serious writer. As Zuckerman suggests in *The Counterlife*, if there is "an irreducible self, it is rather small, . . . and may even be the root of all impersonation—the natural being may be the skill itself, the innate capacity to impersonate" (320). In *The Facts*, Roth presents his life also as a kind of impersonation. To emphasize this point, he begins his book with a letter to Zuckerman, his fictional invention, and concludes it with Zuckerman's reply. To Zuckerman, Roth explains that he wrote "the facts" of his life in order "to transform myself into *myself*" (5). That is, the "real" Philip Roth, like the "real" Nathan Zuckerman, is a narrative supposition before he can be known as a historical entity.

As Linda Hutcheon and Hayden White have argued, postmodern novelists generally treat "history" as a narrative art, or practice. The "facts" of history matter only insofar as they are arranged in a narrative that controls and manipulates their meaning. No historical "facts" can be known independent of a narrative that puts them to interpretive work. As Hutcheon remarks, for postmodern novelists "history does not exist except as text" (5). Hutcheon speaks of "historiographic metafiction" in which "the narrativization of past events is not hidden" and thus "the events no longer speak for themselves" but are the invention, or reinvention, of the people speaking and attending to the story of these events (63). Roth, by contrast, seems to accept history as Tolstoy presented it in *War and Peace*: events that happen because they could not have happened otherwise. For Roth, no amount of narrativizing can change either the Holocaust or Roth's exemption from it. One cannot invent a story that can truly resurrect Anne Frank just as one cannot invent a story that will truly transform Philip Roth into history's victim. As we shall see, *The Plot Against America* challenges this logic only to confirm it by novel's end.

Pretend History

In *The Plot Against America*, Roth reimagines the events of World War II in order to reinvent himself and to confirm history's implacable inevitability. In Roth's novel, Franklin Delano Roosevelt did not win the presidency in 1940 and America instead is under the rule of the casually anti-Semitic Charles Lindbergh and his more openly fascist vice president, Burton Wheeler. The reader is told that "the first shock came in June of 1940" when Lindbergh received the Republican nomination for president (1). An American hero who argued against joining World War II, Lindbergh quickly captures the imagination of the nation and becomes president. Under the Lindbergh administration, Nazis are welcome and soon America plans to remake its Jewish populations by sending them to internment camps.

The novel never explains how America could be transformed so quickly into a scary, anti-Semitic place. Part of the appeal of the novel is how uncanny and how typically "American" Lindbergh's ascension at first seems. In "The Story behind *The Plot Against America*" Roth explains that Lindbergh "was at heart a white supremacist" and his attitude toward Jews had a sanctioned public voice in Henry Ford, who financed anti-Semitic newspapers and promulgated the vicious Protocol of the Elders of Zion myth ("Story" C10). Combined with his isolationism, Lindbergh's white Supremacist stance would have logically dictated an appeasement strategy with Hitler. And one could further note that Neville Chamberlain, the architect of Britain's appeasement strategy, never had the honor, as Lindbergh had, of being awarded an Iron Cross from Hitler's government. Not only did much of America at that time fear the prospect of Roosevelt bringing the country to a war, but for many Americans Roosevelt was a dangerous figure because he wanted to extend his rule to an unprecedented third term. From a historical perspective, Roth is not wrong to declare, "I don't think it's far-fetched to imagine the election outcome as I do in the book, to imagine Lindbergh's depriving Roosevelt of a third term" ("Story" C10). If you combine this anti-Roosevelt fear with the national anxiety caused by an economic depression, then the prospect of a populist American hero sweeping into office to save a country that was definitely in trouble is not far-fetched at all.

Given such a startling and powerful premise, some readers may be surprised to discover that Roth restricts the Lindbergh presidency to two years, after which Roosevelt takes over and history resumes its known course. While *Plot*'s events are sometimes harrowing and have prompted some to praise the book's capacity to create dread in the reader, the novel's conclusion is upbeat and effectively negates its originating premise. The book you read, the one that so powerfully causes you to submit to the proposition that Americans might just as well have elected a president sympathetic or at least indifferent to many of Hitler's aims, turns out not to be interested in that premise after all. Rather than portraying America's tendency to confirm the tyrannous will of the majority, Roth's novel is in fact reinventing American history so that Roth can engage his own Roth family history. As Roth explains, his historical premise "gave me the opportunity to bring my parents back from the grave and restore them to what they were at the height of their powers in their late 30's" ("Story" C10). The appeal of writing the book for Roth was allowing himself "to imagine how they might have conducted themselves under the enormous pressure of a Jewish crisis such as they never really had to encounter as native born Jerseyans" ("Story" C10).

Whereas in *The Facts* Roth recalls his boyhood under the rubric, "Safe at Home," here his fictional memoir begins with this ominous description: "Fear presides over these memories, perpetual fear" (*Plot* 1). The power of the book comes not from imagining a Nazi America but from Roth's ability to convey how quickly events occurring outside of a family's control can terrify its members. As in *The Facts*, the child Roth seeks comfort from his parents and extended family, but in this case the family's actions take on more palpably the dimension of the heroic. Thus, Roth's shrewd portrayal of the fear and paranoia experienced by his parents on account of Lindbergh's rise to power is ultimately surpassed by his depiction of his parents' courage in meeting the challenges that confront them. Throughout the ordeal, Herman Roth, Philip's father, insists that Roosevelt and his allies will not allow the country to betray its ideals of equality. As it turns out, Roth's father is right and Roth's novel is intent on portraying his parents as earning the bounty that history will bestow upon them in the form of victorious Americans after the war. The most powerful sections are the ones that explore how the national conflict affects Philip's perception of his family. In a chapter titled, "Loudmouth Jew," Roth's father speaks out against the anti-Semitic practices that have suddenly become sanctioned by the government. While visiting the patriotic national landmarks in Washington, D.C., the family is asked to vacate a hotel where they have reservations. When, at a nearby restaurant, Herman expresses his concern that Lindbergh has reached an accommodation with Hitler about America's Jews, he is labeled a "loudmouth Jew" by another patron. But the novel grants Herman the gift of historical prophecy. "'They live in a dream,'" Herman Roth tells friends of his experience among the goyim in Washington, "'and we live in a nightmare'" (76). The "nightmare" the father foresees becomes the fictional history that the son writes. Thus, Roth's brother, Sandy, as the poster boy for Lindbergh's novel "Just Folks" program, is sent to Kentucky among Christians to learn how to farm. Working under the auspices of the Office of American Absorption, the Just Folks program aims to eradicate the Jews as a distinctive and minority culture. Among his new friends, Sandy's life is not threatened but his sense of identification with his Jewish family is. One could interpret this episode to be an ironic commentary on the costs for Jews of assimilating to a Gentile American culture, yet Roth never allows the anti-Semitism the novel portrays to reach a critical mass that would allow readers to see the novel as a condemnation of American racism. Thus, Sandy eventually returns to the family fold as they band together to survive the temporary, if terrifying, aberration that "history" has sent to challenge the Roths.

The novel consistently reduces "history" to the conflicts experienced by the Roth family. The novel's most exciting—and perplexing—conflict is not between Lindbergh and Roosevelt, or American Jews and American Christians, but between Philip's cousin, Alvin, and Philip's father, Herman. In rebelling against the novel's father, Alvin plays the role of rebellious son that Roth has often assigned to Nathan Zuckerman. Initially, Alvin seems amenable to Herman's nurturing influence. Upon the election of Lindbergh and with it the country's declared neutrality toward a Germany that seems headed for European domination, Alvin enlists with the Canadian Army in order to fight Hitler. Alvin quickly loses a leg in battle and returns home a bitter veteran of a war that no one in America cares about. In a Freudian twist typical for Roth, Alvin's status as a war hero is undermined through family analysis. Rather than earning honor for fighting Hitler, Alvin is accused by one family member as a coward whose war injury was in fact an instance of self-maiming. Fighting Hitler, by this logic, provided the pretext for self-mutilation, and history merely a stage for each individual to enact his or her own subjective psychological conflict. Alvin confirms this interpretation when he confronts Herman concerning his damaged life. Alvin charges that in fighting Hitler, he was actually the victim of Herman's defenseless and misplaced courage in the face of the danger Lindbergh seemed to pose. " 'The *Jews?*' " Alvin screams at Herman. " 'I wrecked my *life* for the Jews! I lost my fuckin' *leg* for the Jews! I lost my fuckin' leg for *you!*' " (297). Thus, Alvin's heroic gesture is denied a significance that is not specifically familial. Moreover, insofar as Alvin is right, his physical and psychological mutilation condemns Herman's heroism as misplaced. Roth tries to resolve the possible aesthetic conflict posed by heroic Herman's rejection of the family's only flesh-and-blood-warrior-against-Hitler by having the young Philip nurse Alvin even as he reveres his father's courage. Regardless of how one chooses to interpret this conflict, its existence suggests the extent to which the novel is conflating history's possibilities with author Philip's personal Roth family drama.

The novel's premise accounts for why Lindbergh's followers do not hail Alvin but it is less clear why his Jewish family members do not praise his heroism in fighting Hitler. Roth suggests in his *New York Times* essay that what matters "isn't what [Lindbergh] does (which is very little once he's signed a non-aggression pact with Hitler . . .) but what American Jews suspect, rightly or wrongly, that he might be capable of doing, given his public utterances" ("Story" C10). Is the novel's aim not to interrogate the assumptions of American history but to imagine how American Jews would have responded to the threat of the Holocaust in their homeland? Some Jews flourish under the new regime, including the Jewish Mafia that employs Alvin. There is never the sense that *The Plot Against America*'s American Jews will suffer the fate that European Jews did, despite Philip's parents' heroism, and even if some Jews are depicted as possibly being traitorous to other Jews. Philip's Aunt Evelyn and her paramour, Rabbi Bengelsdorf, achieve positions of power through the Lindbergh Administration, but even they do not turn out to be villains. Rabbi Bengelsdorf, the confidante of Anne Morrow Lindbergh, becomes part of the plot that eventually unseats President Lindbergh, while Aunt Evelyn, after betraying the Roth family, hides in their basement and inspires young Philip's unconditional love. Aunt Evelyn suffers the same fear that Philip and his family experience and through this fear is in a sense reunited, as a Jew, with her Jewish family.

As was true in *The Facts* and, in fact, in American history, the Holocaust in *The Plot Against America* occurs offstage, largely limited to the Wishnow family. Philip contrasts his own fate with that of classmate Seldon Wishnow, whose family is made to live out every fear that young Philip suffers. First, Seldon's father dies; next his mother agrees to be moved to Kentucky and eventually is killed in an anti-Semitic riot. Philip bears the guilt of this tragedy since he was responsible (through his Aunt Evelyn) for having had Seldon's family moved to Kentucky. Arguably, the book's aesthetic high point occurs when Philip's mother speaks to Seldon on the phone, tries to assure the terrified child that his mother is not dead, and endeavors to get him to fix himself something to eat. The pathos of the scene is almost unbearable. Eventually, Herman risks his life to drive to Kentucky to rescue Seldon and bring him back to the Newark he never should have left, having endured a fate that Philip was spared. Seldon's family, not Roth's, is destroyed. At the novel's close the figure of Seldon remains in Philip's bedroom, in the same space where cousin Alvin had recuperated from his war wounds, as the embodiment of the potential truth of Philip's worst fears—fears that, in the end, were only fictional.

As Roth points out, "Seldon, that nice, lonely little kid in your class whom you run away from when you're yourself a kid because he demands to be befriended by you in ways that another child cannot stand," is in his novel "the responsibility that you can't get rid of." What the novel's Philip learns is that "the more you want to get rid of him, the less you can, and the less you can, the more you want to get rid of him. And that the little Roth child wants to get rid of him is what leads to the tragedy of the book" ("Story" C11). The terror of what happens to the Wishnows derives from the fact that they are ordinary people who did nothing to bring upon themselves the fate that they suffered.

The terror for Philip is that he was the unwitting tool of history who hastened the Wishnows' destruction. But if Seldon provides the thematic key to the novel, what insight does this key open? What does it mean that the Wishnows are made to stand in for the Roths and what precisely is the tragedy that they represent?

Their fate is terrifying but not "tragic" in the sense defined by Aristotle, since the Wishnows are not endowed with any of the traits of the hero. As it happens, Roth's parents are the ingenious, heroic actors in this drama. Moreover, in this historical drama that is also a novel, it may be difficult for the reader to suspend disbelief so that the Wishnows' fate may be endowed with the full significance that Roth wishes to attribute to them, simply because the novel everywhere insists that what happened in Europe did not and could not happen in the United States. As Roth asserts, the Holocaust "didn't happen here. Though a lot of things that didn't happen here did happen elsewhere" ("Story" C11).

In *The Ghost Writer* Roth portrayed Zuckerman's fascination with Anne Frank's story as way of engaging "what didn't happen here" from the freedom of perspective that comes from having been born "here," in America. In that novel Roth was unable to imagine a relationship with Anne Frank's story that was not literary. In *The Facts* Roth argues that "[i]t isn't that you subordinate your ideas to the force of facts in autobiography but that you construct a sequence of stories to bind up the facts with a persuasive *hypothesis* that unravels your history's meaning" (8). But in *The Plot Against America* he unravels his "true" story to bind up the facts of history's meaning. Just as Zuckerman could not take responsibility for Anne Frank's fate, neither can Philip Roth take responsibility for Seldon's fate except as a fiction. Even in the imagination, Zuckerman cannot turn himself into Anne Frank. The reason that Zuckerman cannot add to Anne Frank's story, or that Seldon lacks true tragic significance, is the grace bestowed upon Roth by being born an American descended from Jewish immigrants. Like *The Ghost Writer*, *The Plot Against America* portrays how the stories of European and American Jews, though perhaps related, are finally not the same.

Despite the Wishnows' fate, then, the book that begins in an atmosphere of abject fear ends with a sense of relief and even celebration. "Why it didn't happen is another book," Roth says, "one about how lucky we Americans are" ("Story" C11). The fact about the Wishnows, then, is that they are presented as victims of a history that Roth even as a novelist could not fully imagine. Moreover, as the book acknowledges, what happened to the Wishnows did happen elsewhere and the terrible facts of the murder of millions cannot be changed either. The Wishnows represent an opportunity for Roth to engage a historical event that may turn out to be as far from him as the fall of Rome. Explaining the accomplishment of his novel, Roth says, "I can only repeat that in the 30's there were many of the seeds for its happening here, but it didn't. And the Jews here became what they became because it didn't" (11). Insofar as Seldon is a double for a character named Philip Roth, *The Plot Against America* perhaps tries to identify Roth more concretely with the Holocaust than any of his other works. That it fails to do so, though, only means that for Roth history is something that has already been written by the actions of men and women and that he has inherited as the subject matter for his literary inventions.

Thus, with *The Plot Against America*'s conclusion Roth surrenders his fantasy to the facts of history he cannot unmake. He confesses, "I present 27 pages of the documentary evidence that underpins a historical unreality of 362 pages in the hope of establishing the book as something other than fabulous" ("Story" C12). But what point is there to a novel other than the presentation of the fabulous? Comparing his work to Orwell's *1984* or Kafka's *The Trial* (1925), Roth notes that it was a misuse of Kafka to say that his works told us anything about the future. Yet, Kafka's work helped the future make sense of what had happened. Roth's book, by contrast, seems calculated to encourage his contemporary Americans to understand how fortunate they are. History for Roth is not, as it was for Joyce, a nightmare from which he is trying awake but a nightmare that he is trying to invent as an artist. Likewise, it may be a misuse of this book to think that it tells anything important about history other than the hard fact that it cannot be changed.

In *The Facts* Roth made the construction of his "real" self the emblem of his postmodern narrative strategies. In *The Plot Against America*, he shows how the facts of history allowed him to invent the self he wanted to become. The novel does not so much allow Roth to pretend he was a near-Holocaust victim as allow him to perform as a novelist: to reinvent himself yet again through his fiction. To show how far *The Plot Against America* is from challenging an exceptionalist understanding of American history, one might compare the novel's approach to World War II with that of Nicholson Baker's *Human Smoke* (2008). Baker's book is not a historiographic metafiction so much as an authentic postmodern history. Baker's narrative is composed entirely of actual, documented voices. The imaginative act he performs is to select and order snippets of commentary from people who lived before and during World War II. Reading Baker's artful arrangement of "the facts"—hundreds of historical documents culled from letters, journals, and news reports— the reader experiences a version of World War II very unlike the one Roth assumes as the background to his novel. *Human Smoke* makes you doubt, for instance, that Roosevelt heroically worked to save the Jews or that Churchill heroically battled Hitler. What comes across is the uneasy sense that history as most American have known it—as Roth understands it—is as much a fiction as the invented history that *The Plot Against America* presents.

In the end *The Plot Against America* refuses such an interpretation. Nor does it portray catastrophe (as Baker does) because it cannot imagine it as a possibility of American history. The novel never reaches the terrifying dimensions of *1984* or Ray Bradbury's *Fahrenheit 451* (1953) and it denies the logic of its obvious precursor, Sinclair Lewis's *It Can't Happen Here* (1935). Roth explicitly signals the connection during Fiorella La Guardia's heroic funeral address for Walter Winchell. Addressing the threat of fascism raised by Lindbergh's regime, La Guardia thunders, "It can't happen here? My friends, it *is* happening here" (305). Lewis's novel, though, provokes the reader to imagine the imminent triumph of fascism in America as a real possibility. When *The Plot Against America* first appeared, Frank Rich, writing in the *New York Times*, attributed the book's initial popularity to readers' perception that the novel's "perpetual fear" defined American life under the second President Bush. Yet, insofar as the book celebrates American history as the haven where bad things cannot happen, the reading is unpersuasive. As bad as things seem to get in *The Plot Against America*, they will be repaired. Acknowledging that some readers will want to see a historical roman à clef, Roth likewise counsels against such readings. Noting that Kafka's novels were turned by subsequent readers into parables about the terrors of totalitarian regimes, Roth suggests that it is important to remember that they were not written by Kafka with such readings in mind. The future, as it were, had conferred upon Kafka's work a meaning that the author could not name.

Roth is right to suggest that *The Plot Against America* cannot be read as one would *The Trial*. Kafka's hero is doomed even without projecting his story onto history's scaffolding. Yet, as Roth acknowledges, a truly powerful novel sometimes has the gift of prophecy since it provides a framework by which future readers can orient themselves within their contemporary experience and its relationship to the past. If Roth's book has a discernible message for future Americans, it is his view that past Americans made of their situation something worth preserving. In so doing, Roth's book continually backs away from the potentially unsettling implications of its premises and surrenders its imaginative will to history as he understood it had to have been. For Roth, history is something that is known, and in America what is known is good. Thus, despite his counterfactual premises, Roth's *Plot Against America* in the end does not deny history (thought it does imply a particular interpretation of history). At most it denies that even the most gifted writer can ever change history. A gifted writer can change the future, maybe, but not the past. *The Plot Against America* recreates the past to sing what cannot be changed but must be made known: a novelist is free to invent whatever he can imagine within the possibilities already inherent in the history to which he has been born.

In *The Facts* Roth portrayed his undying devotion to his parents in terms of a enduring connective cord that is physical as well as psychological. He recalls "the colossal bond" that he felt "to my mother's flesh, whose metamorphosed incarnation was a sleek black sealskin coat into which I, the younger, the privileged, the pampered papoose, blissfully wormed myself" (18). Roth classifies himself as "the unnameable animal-me bearing her dead father's name, the protoplasm-me, boy-baby, and body-burrower-in-training, joined by every nerve ending to her smile and her sealskin coat" (18). He says there that "[t]o be at all is to be her Philip," while adding that "for the writer" that "I would become" his father's attributes became his model (19). *The Plot Against America*'s principal achievement is to reaffirm this self-understanding already presented in *The Facts*. Unlike Seldon's mother, Roth's mother survives her son's imagined Nazi threat, just as she was there in his real life to wrap young Philip in her coat when he was cold and needed succor. As Roth well knows, the camps at Auschwitz or Treblinka allowed no such scenes of comfort for cold and frightened Jews. It may be that *The Plot Against America* is best read as yet another attempt by the Jewish-American Roth to work himself and his characters into a history that he and they in fact escaped. From this perspective, the novel's failure to create a nightmare America equal to what European Jews experienced is a consequence of Roth's view that in America "history" has had a happy ending. To the reader, Roth's exceptionalist American history may render this particular novel a curious failure since by the novelist's own conception "the facts" are what matters and those facts render the novel's premise implausible. Orwell or Kafka (unknown to themselves) could imagine the future as a version of what it would become but Roth the novelist still sees the world as he did when he was a child: a wonderful place to be born Jewish and American in 1933.

Notes on Chapters

AMERICAN PASTORAL

4. America's Haunted House: The Racial and National Uncanny in *American Pastoral* by Jennifer Glaser

1. Roth's *American Pastoral* conforms to the central tenet of the Aristotelian tragedy: namely, that a tragedy depicts the fall of a "great man"—one whom the audience looks up to and seeks to emulate.
2. This preoccupation takes more overt form in the many works in which Roth addresses the question of diaspora and the place of Israel in the American Jewish imagination, most notably *Operation Shylock* and *The Counterlife*.
3. The Swede's Aryan appearance also emphasizes that this dialectic of sameness and difference is often corporealized and racialized.
4. Lorrie Moore takes Roth to task for this clichéd, and often misogynistic, depiction of the 1960s radical in her review of *The Human Stain*.

THE HUMAN STAIN

5. Race, Recognition, and Responsibility in *The Human Stain* by Dean Franco

1. See Sedgwick. Butler draws the link between closetedness and passing in *Bodies That Matter*, chapter four.
2. Of the many excellent works describing the rejection by Jewish institutions of group-based political recognition for African Americans, see Greenberg.

6. Possessed by the Past: History, Nostalgia, and Language in *The Human Stain* by Catherine Morley

1. This framing device characterizes both the other novels, *American Pastoral* (1997) and *I Married a Communist* (1998), in what Roth has termed his American trilogy. *American Pastoral* is addressed elsewhere in this volume. In *I Married a Communist*, Zuckerman encounters an old school teacher, Murray Ringold, who reveals the sad history of his brother Ira (a.k.a. Iron Rinn) who was once idolized by a young Zuckerman. In all three cases, these larger-than-life hero figures fall victim to the tides of history and their life stories are salvaged by the fiction writer. All of Roth's heroes throughout the trilogy bear godly associations: the Swede is a "household Apollo," Ringold is an "irate giant," and Athena-residing Coleman has the ability to make himself invisible. Furthermore, each is linked with an American president,

connecting the individual to a wider symbol of the nation—the Swede with Kennedy (*American Pastoral* 83), Ira Ringold with Abraham Lincoln (*I Married a Communist* 283), and Coleman with Bill Clinton. For a discussion of the novels' collective status as a trilogy see Royal ("Plotting" 114).

2. Roth has frequently commented upon the influence of Joyce upon his work. See especially *Reading Myself and Others* (1975) and *The Facts: A Novelist's Autobiography* (1988), in which Roth recalls reading his brother's copy of *A Portrait of the Artist as a Young Man*. A comic homage to Joyce appears at the conclusion of *Portnoy's Complaint* (1969) where the exiled artist is free to commence his life in pursuit of artistic truth and beauty. For an excellent treatment of Roth's engagement with Joyce see Charles Berryman; see also Morley, *Quest*.

3. Roth's insistence upon the implication of the self and the textures of real life in his fiction has, in much criticism, led to a confusion between Roth and his various narrators (Portnoy, Tarnopol, Kepesh and Zuckerman)—a confusion the author himself has exploited in his fictions. Nathan Zuckerman, too, is repeatedly mistaken for his fictional, Portnoy-based Carnovsky in the *Zuckerman Bound* novels (1979–83). According to Roth, this uncertainty, this confusion, makes the fiction more interesting. In *The Professor of Desire* (1977) he suggests, via his character/narrator David Kepesh, how to approach the fiction: "I hope that by reading these books you will come to learn something of value about life in one of its most puzzling and maddening aspects. I hope to learn something about myself" (183). For Roth, the self must be implicated in the text, must be within it. Thus, critical confusion between the writer and his fictions is perfectly understandable, especially with regard to "middle Roth" which purposely sets out to complicate various fictional and real-life versions of the self (one thinks, for instance, of the 1993 novel *Operation Shylock: A Confession*).

4. David Brauner has also written on "History and the Anti-Pastoral" in the American trilogy (148–85). Other treatments of the past, historical and literary, in the American trilogy include those of Posnock (*Rude Truth*), Safer ("Tragedy and Farce"), Shechner ("Roth's American"), Royal ("Plotting" and "Contesting"). Royal ("Plotting") and Shostak pay particular attention to the role of Zuckerman and his deliberate shaping of the events of the past in the mediation of Coleman's story.

5. Royal also observes the Gatsbyesque nature of Silk ("Plotting" 136). See also Lisa A. Kirby 151–61.

6. See Royal for an extended discussion of the epistemological gaps in Zuckerman's narrative ("Plotting" 118–20). See also Safer, "Tragedy and Farce."

7. The latter reference is to the 1998 battle between Sammy Sosa (Chicago Cubs) and Mark David McGwire (St. Louis Cardinals) to break the Roger Maris record for the number of home-runs hit in a single season.

8. Royal emphasizes this scene in the novel, linking the dance to Zuckerman's fascination with Coleman ("Pastoral Dreams" 124–6). Royal reads the dance as the novel's central metaphor. Just as Coleman dances Zuckerman "back into life," Zuckerman brings Silk onto the "dance floor" of the text and revives the dead man with the telling of his story.

9. The emphasis on Coleman's legs is interesting when one considers that it was an observation of Steena's legs that brought the couple together. In imagining the meeting of Steena and Coleman, Zuckerman refers to the postwar period as "the great American era of aphrodisiacal legs" (111).

10. Roth takes up this technique most overtly in *The Plot Against America*, with the rupture of history and the insertion therein of fictional, alternate, imagined historical landscapes. For an in-depth discussion of Roth's conjoining of history and fiction, see Brauner 186–217.

11. Morley offers a sustained discussion of the similarities between Ira Ringold and Paul Robeson (*Quest* 108–12).

12. See Parrish ("Ralph Ellison") for an excellent analysis of the affinities between Coleman Silk and Ralph Ellison. Also, although never confirmed by Roth, Coleman's tale may be derived from the life history of Anatole Broyard, a critic for the *New York Times*, who died in 1990 having spent most of his life "passing" as white. Broyard's story was recounted in Henry Louis Gates's *13 Ways of Looking at a Black Man*.

13. Morley offers a sustained discussion of the symbolism of the frozen lake (*Quest* 84–5). Royal also discusses the lake and the symbolic meaning of the "X" as a Derridean signifier ("Plotting" 135).

14. Zuckerman supposes that Delphine sends her messages in the height of passion and frenzy, thereby explaining the failure to conceal her identity and her erroneous sending of her lonely-hearts advertisement to her entire faculty. The Delphic oracles, from whom the name obviously derives, were said also to have uttered their prophecies and truths in a frantic state of fervor (often induced by the vaporous gases of Mount Parnassus).

15. For a sustained discussion of the impossibility of purity in the novel, see Posnock, *Rude Truth*.

16. In the earlier mentioned letter to Coleman, Steena Palsson describes him as "swooping" in upon her, thereby strengthening the affinities drawn between Coleman and Prince.

7. "The pointless meaningfulness of living": Illuminating *The Human Stain* through *The Scarlet Letter* by Gabrielle Seeley and Jeffrey Rubin-Dorsky

1. Ross Posnock, in "Purity and Danger," mentions Hawthorne in his discussion of *The Human Stain* (87) and briefly aligns Coleman with Hester and Dimmesdale as keepers of secrets (97). In *Philip Roth's Rude Truth*, Posnock mentions *The Scarlet Letter* (116–17) in a chapter titled "Ancestors and Relatives: The Game of Appropriation and the Sacrifice of Assimilation" and Hawthorne and Dimmesdale in his chapter on *The Human Stain* ("Being Game in *The Human Stain*"), but only minimally.

2. James Duban's article is an earlier, general essay on Roth and Hawthorne.

3. Elaine B. Safer, in *Mocking the Age*, mentions Hawthorne and *The Scarlet Letter* in regard to the "hypocrisy" of Coleman's Athena College colleagues being similar to that of the crowd of women outside the prison calling for a more severe punishment for Hester (122).

THE PLOT AGAINST AMERICA

8. Just Folks Homesteading: Roth's Doubled Plots Against America by Brett Ashley Kaplan

1. Many thanks are due to Anna Stenport for her extremely useful reading of a draft of this essay. I owe much gratitude to Debra Shostak for inviting me to join this volume and for her invaluable editorial changes; she brilliantly examines the doubling I discuss here via the idea of counterlives, demonstrating how Roth's work can "sketch out a host of counterlives" (3). On *The Human Stain* see my articles, "Anatole Broyard's Human Stain" and "Reading Race."

2. The photograph of Lindbergh can be found in the photo inset in Berg between pages 308 and 309; the image of the Windsors with Hitler has been widely reproduced and can be found in Allen in the photo inset that follows page 155.

3. Weinreich defines goyim as "gentiles, non-Jewish populace."

4. Peter Allen notes that "Edward has often been compared with the American aviator Charles Lindbergh: both were youthful heroes to a generation of a troubled and unheroic time, and they both had exceptional opportunities to form erroneous judgements. Although both believed in the phoenix-like power and might of the new Germany, neither recognized that eventually this would have to be fought, if necessary to the death" (55). In a letter, Wallis Simpson compared the situation that she and Edward suffered vis-à-vis the press with that endured by the Lindberghs: "One's countrymen ought to be loyal. I haven't found them so and therefore like the Lindberghs prefer to live elsewhere" (Bloch 212).

5. See, for example, J. M. Coetzee ("What Philip Knew") and Michael Wood; Elaine Safer notes that "[n]ot since *Portnoy's Complaint* has Roth created such a tumult" (*Mocking the Age* 160). For extremely interesting readings of *The Plot Against America* see Michaels and Rothberg.

6. Indeed, Roth's readers and critics sometimes take this comparison to the Bush years rather seriously. In his reflections on *The Plot Against America*, for example, Myles Weber argues that it is time "for America to ignore conventional wisdom and consider implementing a foreign policy even more unilateralist than the one George W. Bush has pursued, but of an appeasing, noninterventionist nature" (210).

7. This is of course a complicated and unresolved debate; for two texts that delve into the question of Roosevelt's relationship to the Nazi genocide see Newton and Rosen.

8. Here Taylor refers to the murals at the Lincoln Memorial painted by Jules Guerin (see his article on the dedication of the Lincoln Memorial).

9. Matthew S. Schweber, for example, finds it ironic that the frightened little Philip (character) became the famous, self-confident Philip Roth. Nick Hornby terms Roth's project an "essay," finding that "*The Plot Against America* is a brilliant, brilliantly argued, and chilling thesis about America in the twentieth century, but I'm not sure it works as a novel, simply because one is constantly reminded that it is a novel" (83). T. Austin Graham offers an analysis of Roth's novel as counterhistory, and Gavriel Rosenfeld, who includes a short section on *The Plot Against America* in his book, argues that "[a]lternate history is inherently presentist. It explores the past less for its own sake than to utilize it instrumentally to comment upon the state of the contemporary world" (10). William Lansing Brown, in considering *The Plot Against America* as alternative history, notes that Roth "gives us a vision of America contorted into something unthinkable, yet somehow hovering on the threshold of recognition" (108).

Works Cited

Abrams, M. H. *A Glossary of Literary Terms*, 5th ed. New York: Holt, Rinehart and Winston, 1988.

Allen, Peter. *The Windsor Secret: New Revelations of the Nazi Connection.* New York: Stein and Day, 1984.

Alter, Robert. "The Spritzer." Rev. of *Operation Shylock*, by Philip Roth. *New Republic* April 5, 1993: 31–4.

Appelfeld, Aharon. "The Artist as a Jewish Writer." *Reading Philip Roth.* Ed. Asher Milbauer and Donald G. Watson. New York: St. Martin's, 1988. 13–16.

Baker, Nicholson. *Human Smoke.* New York: Simon and Schuster, 2008.

Bakewell, Geoffrey W. "Philip Roth's Oedipal *Stain*." *Classical and Modern Literature* 24.2 (2004): 29–46.

Berg, A. Scott. *Lindbergh.* New York: Putnam, 1998.

Bergland, Renee L. *The National Uncanny: Indian Ghosts and American Subjects.* Hanover and London: UP of New England, 2000.

Bergner, Gwen. *Taboo Subjects: Race, Sex, and Psychoanalysis.* Minneapolis: U of Minnesota P, 2005.

Bernstein, Jay. "Melancholy as Form: Towards an Archaeology of Modernism." *The New Aestheticism.* Ed. John J. Joughin and Simon Malpas. Manchester: Manchester UP, 2003. 167–89.

Berryman, Charles. "Philip Roth and Nathan Zuckerman: A Portrait of the Artist as a Young Prometheus." *Contemporary Literature* 31.2 (1990): 177–90.

Bloch, Michael, ed. *Wallis and Edward, Letters 1931–1937: The Intimate Correspondence of the Duke and Duchess of Windsor.* New York: Summit Books, 1986.

Bloom, Claire. *Leaving a Doll's House.* New York: Little, Brown, 1996.

Boxwell, D. A. "*Kulturkampf*, Now and Then." *War, Literature, and the Arts: An International Journal of the Humanities* 12.1 (2000): 122–36.

Boyers, Robert. "The Indigenous Berserk." Rev. of *American Pastoral*, by Philip Roth. *The New Republic* July 7, 1997: 36–41.

Brauner, David. *Philip Roth.* Manchester: Manchester UP, 2007.

Brown, William Lansing. "Alternate Histories: Power, Politics, and Paranoia in Philip Roth's *The Plot Against America* and Philip K. Dick's *The Man in the High Castle*." *The Image of Power in Literature, Media, and Society.* Pueblo: Selected papers, Society for the Interdisciplinary Study of Social Imagery, 2006. 107–11.

Butler, Judith. *Bodies That Matter: On The Discursive Limits of Sex*. New York: Routledge, 1993.

——. "Giving an Account of Oneself." *Diacritics* 31.4 (2001): 22–40.

Carlos del Ama, José. "Everyone Knows: Public Opinion in Philip Roth's Contemporary Tragedy *The Human Stain*." *Philip Roth Studies* 5.1 (2009): 93–110.

Castle, Terry. *The Female Thermometer: Eighteenth Century Culture and the Invention of the Uncanny*. New York: Oxford UP, 1995.

Chodat, Robert. "Fictions Public and Private: On Philip Roth." *Contemporary Literature* 46.4 (2005): 689–719.

Coetzee, J. M. *Inner Workings: Literary Essays, 2000–2005*. New York: Vintage, 2007.

——. "What Philip Knew." *The New York Review of Books* November 18, 2004: 4–6.

Cooper, Alan. "It Can Happen Here, or All in the Family Values: Surviving *The Plot Against America*." *New Perspectives on an American Author*. Ed. Derek Parker Royal. Westport: Praeger, 2005. 241–53.

Duban, James. "Being Jewish in the Twentieth Century: The Synchronicity of Roth and Hawthorne." *Studies in American Jewish Literature* 21 (2002): 1–11.

Ellison, Ralph. *Invisible Man*. New York: Vintage, 1980.

Empson, William. *Some Versions of Pastoral*. London: Chatto and Windus, 1935.

Epstein, Joseph. "What Does Philip Roth Want?" *Commentary* 77.1 (January 1984): 62–7.

Fishman, Sylvia Barack. Rev. of *American Pastoral*, by Philip Roth. *America* August 30, 1997: 23–5.

Fitzgerald, F. Scott. *The Great Gatsby*. New York: Charles Scribner's Sons, 1925.

Franco, Dean. "Being Black, Being Jewish, and Knowing the Difference: Philip Roth's *The Human Stain*; or, It Depends on What the Meaning of 'Clinton' Is." *Studies in American Jewish Literature* 23 (2004): 88–103.

Freedman, Jonathan. *Klezmer America: Jewishness, Ethnicity, Modernity*. New York: Columbia UP, 2008.

Freud, Sigmund. "The Uncanny." *The Norton Anthology of Theory and Criticism*. Ed. Vincent B. Leitch. New York: Norton, 2001. 929–52.

Gates, Henry Louis. *13 Ways of Looking at a Black Man*. London: Vintage, 1998.

Gitlin, Todd. "Weather Girl." *Philip Roth*. Ed. Harold Bloom. Philadelphia: Chelsea House, 2003. 199–203.

Glaser, Jennifer. "The Jew in the Canon: Reading Race and Literary History in Philip Roth's *The Human Stain*." *PMLA* 123.5 (2008): 1465–78.

Goldstein, Eric. *The Price of Whiteness*. Princeton: Princeton UP, 2007.

Goldstein, Ralph. "The Great American Jewish Nightmare." *The Sinclair Lewis Society Newsletter* 13.2 (2005): 1, 4.

Graham, T. Austin. "On the Possibility of an American Holocaust: Philip Roth's *The Plot Against America*." *Arizona Quarterly* 63.3 (2007): 119–49.

Greenberg, Cheryl. *Troubling the Waters: Black-Jewish Relations in the American Century*. Princeton: Princeton UP, 2006.

Guerin, Jules. "On the Dedication of the Lincoln Memorial." *Art and Archaeology* 13.6 (1922): 247–68.

Hawthorne, Nathaniel. *The Scarlet Letter*. Columbus: Charles E. Merrill, 1969.

Hedin, Benjamin. "A History That Never Happened: Philip Roth's *The Plot Against America.*" *The Gettysburg Review* 18.1 (2005): 93–106.

Herberg, Will. *Protestant—Catholic—Jew: An Essay in Religious Sociology*. Chicago: U of Chicago P, 1983.

Hogan, Monika. "'Something so Visceral in with the Rhetorical': Race, Hypochondria, and the Un-Assimilated Body in *American Pastoral.*" *Studies in American Jewish Literature* 23 (2004): 1–14.

Hornby, Nick. "Stuff I've Been Reading: A Monthly Column." *The Believer* 3.1 (2001): 81–4.

Howe, Irving. "Philip Roth Reconsidered." *Commentary* 54.6 (1972): 69–77.

Hutcheon, Linda. *The Politics of Postmodernism*. New York: Routledge, 1989.

Iannone, Carol. "An American Tragedy." Rev. of *American Pastoral*, by Philip Roth. *Commentary* 104.2 (1997): 55–8.

Itzkovitz, Daniel. "Passing Like Me." *The South Atlantic Quarterly* 98.1/2 (1999): 35–57.

Johnson, Gary. "The Presence of Allegory: The Case of Philip Roth's *American Pastoral.*" *Narrative* 12.3 (2004): 233–48.

Joyce, James. *A Portrait of the Artist as a Young Man*. London: Penguin, 1965.

Kakutani, Michiko. "A Postwar Paradise Shattered From Within." Rev. of *American Pastoral*, by Philip Roth. *New York Times* April 15, 1997: C 11.

Kaplan, Brett Ashley. "Anatole Broyard's Human Stain: Performing Postracial Consciousness." *Philip Roth Studies* 1.2 (2005): 125–44.

——. "Contested, Constructed Home(lands): Diaspora, Postcolonial Studies, and Zionism." *Journal of Modern Jewish Studies* 6.1 (2007): 85–100.

——. *Landscapes of Holocaust Postmemory*. New York: Routledge, 2010.

——. "Reading Race and the Conundrums of Reconciliation in Philip Roth's *The Human Stain.*" *Turning Up the Flame: Philip Roth's Later Novels*. Ed. Jay L. Halio and Ben Siegel. Newark: U of Delaware P, 2005. 172–93.

Kauvar, Elaine M. "This Doubly Reflected Communication: Philip Roth's 'Autobiographies.'" *Contemporary Literature* 36.3 (1995): 412–46.

Kellman, Steven G. "It *Is* Happening Here: *The Plot Against America* and the Political Moment." *Philip Roth Studies* 4.2 (2008): 113–23.

Kemp, Peter. "Once Upon a Time in America." Rev. of *American Pastoral*, by Philip Roth. *Sunday Times* June 1, 1997: "Books" 13.

Kershaw, Ian. *Hitler*. 2 vols. New York: Norton, 1998 and 2000.

Kirby, Lisa A. "Shades of Passing: Teaching and Interrogating Identity in Roth's *The Human Stain* and Fitzgerald's *The Great Gatsby.*" *Philip Roth Studies* 2.2 (2006): 151–60.

Kral, Françoise. "F(r)ictions of Identity in *The Human Stain.*" *Philip Roth Studies* 2.1 (2006): 47–55.

Levy, Richard S., ed. *Antisemitism: A Historical Encyclopedia of Prejudice and Persecution*. Santa Barbara: ABC-Clio, 2005.

Lewis, Charles. "Real Planes and Imaginary Towers: Philip Roth's *The Plot Against America* as 9/11 Prosthetic Screen." *Literature after 9/11*. Ed.

Ann Keniston and Jeanne Follansbee Quinn. New York: Routledge, 2008. 246–60.

Lewis, R. W. B. *The American Adam: Innocence, Tragedy, and Tradition in the Nineteenth Century*. Chicago: U of Chicago P, 1955.

Locke, Alain. "The New Negro." *The New Negro: Voices of the Harlem Renaissance*. New York: Touchstone, 1999.

Loewald, Hans W. "The Experience of Time." *Papers on Psychoanalysis*. New Haven: Yale UP, 1980.

Lundegaard, Erik. "Roth's Back, with More Complaints." Rev. of *American Pastoral*, by Philip Roth. *Seattle Times* Book Section, May 11, 1997: M3.

Lyons, Bonnie. "Philip Roth's American Tragedies." *Turning Up the Flame: Philip Roth's Later Novels*. Ed. Jay L. Halio and Ben Seigel. Newark: U of Delaware P, 2005. 125–30.

MacArthur, Kathleen. "Shattering the American Pastoral: Philip Roth's Vision of Trauma and the American Dream." *Studies in American Jewish Literature* 23 (2004): 15–26.

Maslan, Mark. "The Faking of the Americans: Passing, Trauma, and National Identity in Philip Roth's *Human Stain*." *Modern Language Quarterly* 66.3 (2005): 365–89.

McDonald, Brian. "'The Real American Crazy Shit': On Adamism and Democratic Individuality in *American Pastoral*." *Studies in American Jewish Literature* 23 (2004): 27–40.

Medin, Daniel L. "Trials and Errors at the Turn of the Millennium: On *The Human Stain* and J. M. Coetzee's *Disgrace*." *Philip Roth Studies* 1.1 (2005): 82–92.

Meissner, W. W. "Subjectivity in Psychoanalysis." *Kierkegaard's Truth: The Disclosure of the Self*. Ed. Joseph H. Smith. New Haven: Yale UP, 1981. 267–311.

Michaels, Walter Benn. "Plots against America: Neoliberalism and Antiracism." *American Literary History* 18.2 (2006): 288–302.

Millard, Kenneth. *Contemporary American Fiction*. Oxford: Oxford UP, 2000.

Miller, Arthur. *Death of a Salesman*. *Arthur Miller's Collected Plays*. New York: Viking, 1957. 130–222.

Moore, Lorrie. "The Wrath of Athena." Rev. of *American Pastoral*, by Philip Roth. *New York Times*. Web. May 7, 2000.

Morley, Catherine. "Memories of the Lindbergh Administration: Plotting, Genre, and the Splitting of the Self in *The Plot Against America*." *Philip Roth Studies* 4.2 (2008): 137–52.

——. *The Quest for Epic in Contemporary American Fiction: John Updike, Philip Roth and Don DeLillo*. New York: Routledge, 2009.

Neelakantan, G. "Monster in Newark: Philip Roth's Apocalypse in *American Pastoral*." *Studies in American Jewish Literature* 23 (2004): 55–66.

——. "Philip Roth's Nostalgia for the *Yiddishkayt* and the New Deal Idealisms in *The Plot Against America*." *Philip Roth Studies* 4.2 (2008): 125–36.

Newton, Verne W., ed. *FDR and the Holocaust*. New York: St. Martin's, 1996.

Obenzinger, Hilton. "Naturalizing Cultural Pluralism, Americanizing Zionism: The Settler Colonial Basis to Early-Twentieth-Century Progressive Thought." *South Atlantic Quarterly* 107.4 (2008): 651–69.

Parrish, Timothy. "Becoming Black: Zuckerman's Bifurcating Self in *The Human Stain*." *Philip Roth: New Perspectives on an American Author*. Ed. Derek Parker Royal. Westport: Praeger, 2005. 209–23.

——. *The Cambridge Companion to Philip Roth*. Cambridge: Cambridge UP, 2007.

——. "The End of Identity: Philip Roth's *American Pastoral*." *Turning Up the Flame: Philip Roth's Later Novels*. Ed. Jay L. Halio and Ben Seigel. Newark: U of Delaware P, 2005. 131–50.

——. "Ralph Ellison: The Invisible Man in Philip Roth's *The Human Stain*." *Contemporary Literature* 45.3 (2004): 421–59.

——. "Review Essay: *The Plot Against America*." *Philip Roth Studies* 1.1 (2005): 93–101.

——. "Roth and Ethnic Identity." *The Cambridge Companion to Philip Roth*. Ed. Timothy Parrish. Cambridge: Cambridge UP, 2007. 127–41.

Podhoretz, Norman. "Bellow at 85, Roth at 67." *Commentary* 110.1 (2000): 35–43.

Posnock, Ross. *Philip Roth's Rude Truth: The Art of Immaturity*. Princeton: Princeton UP, 2006.

——. "Purity and Danger: On Philip Roth." *Raritan* 21.2 (2001): 85–101.

Powers, Elizabeth. Rev. of *American Pastoral*, by Philip Roth. *World Literature Today* 72.1 (1998): 136.

Rankine, Patrice D. "Passing as Tragedy: Philip Roth's *The Human Stain*, the Oedipus Myth, and the Self-Made Man." *Critique* 47.1 (2005): 101–12.

Remnick, David. "The Challenge of Fiction." *Sunday Telegraph* March 16, 2003, Culture sec.: 3.

Rich, Frank. "The Palin-Whatshisname Ticket." *New York Times* September 14, 2008, New York ed.: WK11.

——. "President Lindbergh in 2004." *New York Times* September 26, 2004, Sec. 2: 1+.

Rogin, Michael. *Black Face, White Noise*. Berkeley: U of California P, 1998.

Rorty, Richard. *Contingency, Irony, and Solidarity*. New York: Cambridge UP, 2008.

Rosen, Robert R. *Saving the Jews: Franklin D. Roosevelt and the Holocaust*. New York: Thunder's Mouth P, 2006.

Rosenfeld, Gavriel. *The World Hitler Never Made: Alternate History and the Memory of Nazism*. New York: Cambridge UP, 2005.

Roth, Philip. "After Eight Books." *Reading Myself and Others*. New York: Farrar, Straus and Giroux, 1977; Rev. ed., New York: Penguin, 1985. 99–113.

——. *American Pastoral*. Boston: Houghton Mifflin, 1997.

——. *The Anatomy Lesson*. New York: Farrar, Straus and Giroux, 1983. Reprinted in Roth, *Zuckerman Bound*. New York: Farrar, Straus and Giroux, 1985. 407–697.

——. *The Breast*. New York: Holt, Rinehart and Winston, 1972; New York: Vintage, 1994.

——. "Contains Notes & Original 1972 Version of *American Pastoral*, 'How the Other Half Lives.'" Philip Roth Collection, Library of Congress. Blue binder in Box 3 of 17, accession 21,771.

——. *The Counterlife*. New York: Farrar, Straus and Giroux, 1986.

——. *Deception*. New York: Simon and Schuster, 1990.

——. "Document Dated July 27, 1969." *Reading Myself and Others*. New York: Farrar, Straus and Giroux, 1977; Rev. ed., New York: Penguin, 1985. 23–31.

——. *The Dying Animal*. Boston: Houghton Mifflin, 2001.

——. *Everyman*. Boston: Houghton Mifflin, 2006.

——. *Exit Ghost*. Boston: Houghton Mifflin, 2007.

——. *The Facts: A Novelist's Autobiography*. New York: Farrar, Straus and Giroux, 1988.

——. *The Ghost Writer*. New York: Farrar, Straus and Giroux. Reprinted in Roth, *Zuckerman Bound*. New York: Farrar, Straus and Giroux, 1985. 1–180.

——. *Goodbye, Columbus and Five Short Stories*. Boston: Houghton Mifflin, 1959.

——. *The Great American Novel*. New York: Holt, Rinehart and Winston, 1973; New York: Penguin, 1986.

——. *The Human Stain*. Boston: Houghton Mifflin, 2000.

——. *The Humbling*. Boston: Houghton Mifflin, 2009.

——. *I Married a Communist*. Boston: Houghton Mifflin, 1998.

——. *Indignation*. Boston: Houghton Mifflin, 2008.

——. *Letting Go*. New York: Random House, 1962; New York: Simon and Schuster, 1991.

——. *My Life as a Man*. New York: Farrar, Straus and Giroux, 1974; New York: Vintage, 1993.

——. "On *The Great American Novel*." *Reading Myself and Others*. New York: Farrar, Straus and Giroux, 1977; Rev. ed., New York: Penguin, 1985. 75–92.

——. *Operation Shylock: A Confession*. New York: Simon and Schuster, 1993.

——. *Our Gang (Starring Tricky and His Friends)*. New York: Random, 1971.

——. *Patrimony: A True Story*. New York: Farrar, Straus and Giroux, 1991.

——. *The Plot Against America: A Novel*. Boston: Houghton Mifflin, 2004.

——. *Portnoy's Complaint*. New York: Random, 1969; New York: Fawcett Crest, 1985.

——. *The Prague Orgy*. In Roth, *Zuckerman Bound*. New York: Farrar, Straus and Giroux, 1985. 699–784.

——. *The Professor of Desire*. New York: Farrar, Straus and Giroux, 1977; New York: Penguin, 1985.

——. *Reading Myself and Others*. New York: Farrar, Straus and Giroux, 1977; Rev. ed., New York: Penguin, 1985.

——. *Sabbath's Theater*. New York: Houghton Mifflin, 1995.

——. *Shop Talk: A Writer and His Colleagues and Their Work*. Boston: Houghton Mifflin, 2001.

——. "The Story behind *The Plot Against America*." *New York Times Book Review* September 19, 2004: C10–12.

——. *When She Was Good*. New York: Random. 1967; New York: Vintage, 1995.

——. "Writing about Jews." *Reading Myself and Others*. New York: Farrar, Straus and Giroux, 1977; Rev. ed., New York: Penguin, 1985. 205–25.

——. "Writing American Fiction." *Reading Myself and Others*. New York: Farrar, Straus and Giroux, 1977; Rev. ed., New York: Penguin, 1985. 173–91.

——. *Zuckerman Bound*. New York: Farrar, Straus and Giroux, 1985.

——. *Zuckerman Unbound*. New York: Farrar, Straus and Giroux, 1981. Reprinted in Roth, *Zuckerman Bound*. New York: Farrar, Straus and Giroux, 1985. 181–405.

——. "Zuckerman's Alter Brain." Interview with Philip Roth, by Charles McGrath. *New York Times Book Review* May 7, 2000: 8.

Rothberg, Michael. "Against Zero-Sum Logic: A Response to Walter Benn Michaels." *American Literary History* 18.2 (Summer 2006): 303–11.

Royal, Derek Parker, "Contesting the Historical Pastoral in Philip Roth's American Trilogy." *American Fiction of the 1990s: Reflections of History and Culture*. Ed. Jay Prosser. London: Routledge, 2008. 120–33.

——. "Fictional Realms of Possibility: Reimagining the Ethnic Subject in Philip Roth's *American Pastoral*." *Studies in American Jewish Literature* 20 (2001): 1–16.

——. "Pastoral Dreams and National Identity in *American Pastoral* and *I Married a Communist*." *Philip Roth: New Perspectives on an American Author*. Ed. Derek Parker Royal. Westport: Praeger, 2005. 185–207.

——, ed. *Philip Roth: New Perspectives on an American Author*. Westport: Praeger, 2005.

——. "Plotting the Frames of Subjectivity: Identity, Death, and Narrative in Philip Roth's *The Human Stain*." *Contemporary Literature* 47.1 (2006): 114–40.

Rubin-Dorsky, Jeffrey. "Philip Roth and American Jewish Identity: The Question of Authenticity." *American Literary History* 13.1 (Spring 2001): 79–107.

Safer, Elaine. *Mocking the Age: The Later Novels of Philip Roth*. Albany: State U of New York P, 2006.

——. "Tragedy and Farce in Roth's *Human Stain*." *Critique* 43.3 (2002): 211–27.

Sánchez Canales, Gustavo. "The Classical World and Modern Academia in Philip Roth's *The Human Stain*." *Philip Roth Studies* 5.1 (2009): 111–28.

Schiller, Mayer. Rev. of *American Pastoral*, by Philip Roth. *National Review* June 16, 1997: 53–4.

Schlesinger, Arthur M. *A Life in the 20th Century: Innocent Beginnings, 1917–1950*. New York: Mariner, 2002.

Schur, Richard. "Dream or Nightmare? Roth, Morrison, and America." *Philip Roth Studies* 1.1 (2005): 19–36.

Schweber, Matthew S. "Philip Roth's Populist Nightmare." *Cross Currents* 54.4 (2005): 125–37.

Scott, A. O. "In Search of the Best." *New York Times Book Review* May 21, 2006: 1, 17–19.

Sedgwick, Eve. *The Epistemology of the Closet*. Los Angeles: U of California P, 2008.

Shechner, Mark. "Roth's American Trilogy." *The Cambridge Companion to Philip Roth*. Ed. Timothy Parrish. Cambridge: Cambridge UP, 2007. 142–57.

——. *Up Society's Ass, Copper: Rereading Philip Roth*. Madison: U of Wisconsin P, 2003.

Shiffman, Dan. "*The Plot Against America* and History Post-9/11." *Philip Roth Studies* 5.1 (2009): 61–73.

Shostak, Debra. *Philip Roth—Countertexts, Counterlives*. Columbia: U of South Carolina P, 2004.

Sollors, Werner. *Beyond Ethnicity: Consent and Descent in American Culture*. New York: Oxford UP, 1987.

Sophocles. *Oedipus the King*. Trans. David Grene. *Greek Tragedies*, vol. I. Ed. David Grene and Richmond Lattimore. Chicago: U of Chicago P, 1970. 107–76.

Spence, Donald P. *Narrative Truth and Historical Truth: Meaning and Interpretation in Psychoanalysis*. New York: Norton, 1982.

Stanley, Sandra Kumamoto. "Mourning the 'Greatest Generation': Myth and History in Philip Roth's *American Pastoral*." *Twentieth Century Literature* 51.1 (2005): 1–24.

Stein, Sam. *The Huffington Post*. Web. May 21, 2008.

Tanenbaum, Laura. "Reading Roth's Sixties." *Studies in American Jewish Literature* 23 (2004): 41–54.

Thoreau, Henry David. *Walden and Resistance to Civil Government*. Ed. William Rossi. 2nd ed. New York: Norton, 1992.

Varvogli, Aliki. "The Inscription of Terrorism: Philip Roth's *American Pastoral*." *Philip Roth Studies* 3.2 (2008): 101–13.

Vidler, Anthony. *The Architectural Uncanny*. Cambridge: MIT P, 1994.

Walsh, W. H. "'Plain' and 'Significant' Narrative in History." *Journal of Philosophy* 55.11 (1958): 479–84.

Weber, Myles. "Whose War is This?" *New England Review* 27.4 (2006): 206–11.

Weinreich, Uriel. *Modern English Yiddish, Yiddish-English Dictionary*. New York: Schocken Books, 1977.

West, Nathanael. *Miss Lonelyhearts*. New York: New Directions, 1969.

Williams, William Carlos. "At Kenneth Burke's Place." *The Collected Poems of William Carlos Williams, Vol. II: 1939-1962*. Ed. Christopher McGowan. New York: New Directions, 1991, 106–8.

Wirth-Nesher, Hana. "Roth's Autobiographical Writings." *Cambridge Companion to Philip Roth*. Ed. Timothy Parrish. Cambridge: Cambridge UP, 2007. 158–72.

Wood, Michael. "Just Folks." *London Review of Books* 26.21. Web. November 4, 2004: 3–6.

Further Reading

A considerable body of critical work is in print on Philip Roth, and the bibliography keeps growing as Roth enjoys sustained interest from scholars. The following references count among the most important and useful titles that have appeared in the past 25 years to address the full scope of Roth's oeuvre. Many of the books and collections listed here address the three novels under discussion alone or in relation to Roth's other work. Some examine Roth's other writing beginning in the late 1950s and are useful to readers interested in the broader context of his career. A scholarly journal, *Philip Roth Studies*, is entirely devoted to Roth's work, at times juxtaposed to that of other writers, and approaches to his fiction are often featured in the journal *Studies in American Jewish Literature*.

Books

Baumgarten, Murray, and Barbara Gottfried. *Understanding Philip Roth.* Columbia: U of South Carolina P, 1990.

Brauner, David. *Philip Roth.* Manchester: Manchester UP, 2007.

Cooper, Alan. *Philip Roth and the Jews.* Albany: SUNY P, 1996.

Halio, Jay. *Philip Roth Revisited.* New York: Twayne, 1992.

Milowitz, Steven. *Philip Roth Considered: The Concentrationary Universe of the American Writer.* New York: Garland, 2000.

Morley, Catherine. *The Quest for Epic in Contemporary American Fiction: John Updike, Philip Roth and Don DeLillo.* New York: Routledge, 2009.

Posnock, Ross. *Philip Roth's Rude Truth: The Art of Immaturity.* Princeton: Princeton UP, 2006.

Safer, Elaine. *Mocking the Age: The Later Novels of Philip Roth.* Albany: State U of New York P, 2006.

Shechner, Mark. *Up Society's Ass, Copper: Rereading Philip Roth.* Madison: U of Wisconsin P, 2003.

Shostak, Debra. *Philip Roth—Countertexts, Counterlives.* Columbia: U of South Carolina P, 2004.

Wade, Stephen. *Imagination in Transit: The Fiction of Philip Roth.* Sheffield: Sheffield Academic P, 1996.

Essay Collections and Collected Interviews

Bloom, Harold, ed. *Philip Roth*. Philadelphia: Chelsea House, 2003.

Halio, Jay L., and Ben Siegel, eds. *Turning Up the Flame: Philip Roth's Later Novels*. Newark: U of Delaware P, 2005.

Milbauer, Asher, and Donald G. Watson, eds. *Reading Philip Roth*. New York: St. Martin's, 1988.

Parrish, Timothy, ed. *The Cambridge Companion to Philip Roth*. Cambridge: Cambridge UP, 2007.

Roth, Philip. *Reading Myself and Others*. New York: Farrar, Straus and Giroux, 1977; Rev. ed., New York: Penguin, 1985.

Royal, Derek Parker, ed. *Philip Roth: New Perspectives on an American Author*. Westport: Praeger, 2005.

Searles, George J., ed. *Conversations with Philip Roth*. Jackson: UP of Mississippi, 1992.

Special Issues of Journals

Philip Roth Studies (all issues).

Shofar: An Interdisciplinary Journal of Jewish Studies 19.1 (2000). Ed. Jay L. Halio.

Studies in American Jewish Literature 23 (2004). Ed. Derek Parker Royal.

Website

http://rothsociety.org/ (Philip Roth Society: features links to excellent resources, including a biography, a bibliography of Roth's works, an extensive, frequently updated bibliography of scholarship on Roth, and upcoming events).

Journal Articles and Book Chapters

Selected Entries on *American Pastoral*

Gentry, Marshall Bruce. "Newark Maid Feminism in Philip Roth's *American Pastoral*." *Shofar* 19 (2000): 74–83.

Johnson, Gary. "The Presence of Allegory: The Case of Philip Roth's *American Pastoral*." *Narrative* 12.3 (2004): 233–48.

Millard, Kenneth. "Philip Roth: *American Pastoral*." *Contemporary American Fiction: An Introduction to American Fiction since 1970*. Oxford: Oxford UP, 2000. 239–48.

Parrish, Timothy L. "The End of Identity: Philip Roth's Jewish *American Pastoral*." *Turning Up the Flame: Philip Roth's Later Novels*. Ed. Jay L. Halio and Ben Siegel. Newark: U of Delaware P, 2005. 131–50.

Pozorski, Aimee. "*American Pastoral* and the Traumatic Ideals of Democracy." *Philip Roth Studies* 5.1 (2009): 75–92.

Royal, Derek Parker. "Fictional Realms of Possibility: Reimagining the Ethnic Subject in Philip Roth's *American Pastoral*." *Studies in American Jewish Literature* 20 (2001): 1–16.

Stanley, Sandra Kumamoto. "Mourning the 'Greatest Generation': Myth and History in Philip Roth's *American Pastoral*." *Twentieth-Century Literature* 51.1 (2005): 1–24.

Varvogli, Aliki. "The Inscription of Terrorism: Philip Roth's *American Pastoral*." *Philip Roth Studies* 3 (2007): 101–13.

See also the special issue of *Studies in American Jewish Literature* 23 (2004) for articles by David Brauner, Monika Hogan, Kathleen L. MacArthur, Brian McDonald, G. Neelakantan, and Laura Tanenbaum.

Selected Entries on *The Human Stain*

Bluefarb, Sam. "*The Human Stain*: A Satiric Tragedy of the Politically Incorrect." *Turning Up the Flame: Philip Roth's Later Novels*. Ed. Jay L. Halio and Ben Siegel. Newark: U of Delaware P, 2005. 222–8.

Green, Jeremy. "The Fall of the House of Silk." *Late Postmodernism: American Fiction at the Millennium*. New York: Palgrave Macmillan, 2005. 63–74.

Faisst, Julia. "'Delusionary Thinking, Whether White or Black or in Between': Fictions of Race in Philip Roth's *The Human Stain*." *Philip Roth Studies* 2 (2006): 121–37.

Franco, Dean J. "Being Black, Being Jewish, and Knowing the Difference: Philip Roth's *The Human Stain*; or, It Depends on What the Meaning of 'Clinton' Is." *Studies in American Jewish Literature* 23 (2004): 88–103.

Glaser, Jennifer. "The Jew in the Canon: Reading Race and Literary History in Philip Roth's *The Human Stain*." *PMLA* 123 (2008): 1465–78.

Kaplan, Brett Ashley. "Anatole Broyard's Human Stain: Performing Postracial Consciousness." *Philip Roth Studies* 1 (2005): 125–44.

——. "Reading Race and the Conundrums of Reconciliation in Philip Roth's *The Human Stain*." *Turning Up the Flame: Philip Roth's Later Novels*. Ed. Jay L. Halio and Ben Siegel. Newark: U of Delaware P, 2005. 172–93.

Kral, Françoise. "F(r)ictions of Identity in *The Human Stain*." *Philip Roth Studies* 2 (2006): 47–55.

Maslan, Mark. "The Faking of the Americans: Passing, Trauma, and National Identity in Philip Roth's *Human Stain*." *Modern Language Quarterly* 66.3 (2005): 365–89.

Neelakantan, G. "Secrecy and Self-Invention: Philip Roth's Postmodern Identity in *The Human Stain*." *International Fiction Review* 34 (2007): 27–39.

Omer-Sherman, Ranen. "'A Stranger in the House': Assimilation, Madness, and Passing in Roth's Picture of the Pariah Jew in *Sabbath's Theater* (1995), *American Pastoral* (1997), and *The Human Stain* (2000)." *Diaspora and Zionism in Jewish American Literature: Lazarus, Syrkin, Reznikoff, and Roth*. Hanover: Brandeis UP, 2002. 234–66.

Parrish, Timothy. "Ralph Ellison: *The Invisible Man* in Philip Roth's *The Human Stain*." *Contemporary Literature* 45 (2004): 421–59.

Royal, Derek Parker. "Plotting the Frames of Subjectivity: Identity, Death, and Narrative in Philip Roth's *The Human Stain*." *Contemporary Literature* 47 (2006): 114–40.

Safer, Elaine B. "Tragedy and Farce in Roth's *The Human Stain*." *Critique* 43 (2002): 211–27.

Selected Entries on *The Plot Against America*

Coetzee, J. M. "Philip Roth, *The Plot Against America.*" *Inner Workings: Literary Essays 2000–2005.* New York: Viking, 2007. 228–43.

Graham, T. Austin. "On the Possibility of an American Holocaust: Philip Roth's *The Plot Against America.*" *Arizona Quarterly* 63.3 (2007): 119–49.

Hedin, Benjamin. "A History That Never Happened: Philip Roth's *The Plot Against America.*" *Gettysburg Review* 18.1 (2005): 93–106.

Kellman, Steven G. "It *Is* Happening Here: *The Plot Against America* and the Political Moment." *Philip Roth Studies* 4.2 (2008): 113–23.

Morley, Catherine. "Memories of the Lindbergh Administration: Plotting, Genre, and the Splitting of the Self in *The Plot Against America.*" *Philip Roth Studies* 4.2 (2008): 137–52.

Parrish, Timothy. "Philip Roth, *The Plot Against America.*" *Philip Roth Studies* 1 (2005): 93–101.

Salzberg, Joel. "Imagining the Perverse: Bernard Malamud's *The Fixer* and Philip Roth's *The Plot Against America.*" *Philip Roth Studies* 4 (2008): 19–27.

Severs, Jeffrey. "'Get Your Map of America': Tempering Dystopia and Learning Topography in *The Plot Against America.*" *Studies in American Fiction* 35 (2007): 221–39.

Shiffman, Dan. "*The Plot Against America* and History Post-9/11." *Philip Roth Studies* 5.1 (2009): 61–73.

Sokoloff, Naomi. "Reading for the Plot? Philip Roth's *The Plot Against America.*" *AJS Review* [Association for Jewish Studies] 30.2 (2006): 305–12.

Other Sources

Following are suggestions for reading other Jewish-American fiction writers, both contemporary with Roth during his early career and recent, and for scholarly work on Jewish culture, identity, and literature. Items in the category of "Other Fiction" suggest a few titles but are not exhaustive.

Other Fiction to Explore

Auster, Paul. *The Book of Illusions* (2002).

——. *The Invention of Solitude* (1982).

——. *The New York Trilogy* (1990).

Bellow, Saul. *The Adventures of Augie March* (1953).

——. *Herzog* (1964).

——. *Mr. Sammler's Planet* (1969).

Chabon, Michael. *The Amazing Adventures of Kavalier & Clay* (2000).

——. *The Yiddish Policeman's Union* (2007).

Foer, Jonathan Safran. *Everything is Illuminated* (2002).

——. *Extremely Loud and Incredibly Close* (2006).

Heller, Joseph. *Catch-22* (1961).

——. *Good as Gold* (1979).

Mailer, Norman. *An American Dream* (1965).

——. *The Naked and the Dead* (1948).

Malamud, Bernard. *The Assistant* (1957).

——. *The Fixer* (1967).

——. *The Magic Barrel* (stories; 1958).

——. *The Natural* (1952).

Olsen, Tillie. *Tell Me a Riddle* (stories; 1962).

Ozick, Cynthia. *The Messiah of Stockholm* (1987).

——. *The Puttermesser Papers* (1997).

——. *The Shawl* (stories; 1989).

Paley, Grace. *Enormous Changes at the Last Minute* (stories; 1974).

——. *The Little Disturbances of Man* (stories; 1985).

Studies of Jewish Experience

Biale, David, Michael Galchinsky, and Susan Heschel, eds. *Insider/Outsider: American Jews and Multiculturalism*. Berkeley: U of California P, 1998.

Boyarin, Jonathan. *Thinking in Jewish*. Chicago: U of Chicago P, 1996.

——, and Daniel Boyarin, eds. *Jews and Other Differences: The New Jewish Cultural Studies*. Minneapolis: U of Minnesota P, 1997.

Finkielkraut, Alain. *The Imaginary Jew*. Trans. Kevin O'Heill and David Suchoff. Lincoln: U of Nebraska P, 1994.

Gilman, Sander. *Jewish Self-Hatred: Anti-Semitism and the Hidden Language of the Jews*. Baltimore: Johns Hopkins UP, 1986.

Goldberg, David Theo, and Michael Krausz, eds. *Jewish Identity*. Philadelphia: Temple UP, 1993.

Studies of American Jewish Writing

Aarons, Victoria. *A Measure of Memory: Storytelling and Identity in American Jewish Fiction*. Athens: U of Georgia P, 1996.

Brauner, David. *Post-War Jewish Fiction: Ambivalence, Self-Explanation and Transatlantic Connections*. Basingstoke: Palgrave/Macmillan, 2001.

Furman, Andrew. *Contemporary Jewish American Writers and the Multicultural Dilemma: The Return of the Exiled*. New York: Syracuse UP, 2000.

Shechner, Mark. *After the Revolution: Studies in the Contemporary Jewish American Imagination*. Bloomington: Indiana UP, 1987.

Wirth-Nesher, Hana, ed. *The Cambridge Companion to Jewish American Literature*. Cambridge: Cambridge UP, 2003.

——. *What is Jewish Literature?* Philadelphia: Jewish Publication Society, 1994.

Notes on Contributors

David Brauner is Reader in English and American Literature at the University of Reading. He is the author of three books: *Post-War Jewish Fiction: Ambivalence, Self-Explanation and Transatlantic Connections* (2001), *Philip Roth* (2007), and *Contemporary American Fiction* (2010). His recent publications include "Twentieth-Century Jewish Fiction" (*Blackwell Companion to Twentieth-Century American Fiction*, ed. David Seed, 2009); "'The days after' and 'the ordinary run of hours': Counternarratives and Double Vision in Don DeLillo's *Falling Man*" (*Review of International American Studies* 4.1–2, 2009); and "Fifty Ways to See Your Lover: Vision and Revision in the Fiction of Amy Bloom" (*Anglophone Jewish Literature*, ed. Axel Stähler, 2007).

Dean Franco is Associate Professor of English at Wake Forest University. He is the author of *Ethnic American Literature: Comparing Chicano, Jewish, and African American Writing* (2006) as well as articles on American literature, culture, and ethnicity appearing in *Contemporary Literature, Prooftexts, Modern Fiction Studies*, and *PMLA*. He is currently working on a book on race, rights, and cultural recognition in contemporary Jewish-American literature.

Jennifer Glaser is Assistant Professor of English and Comparative Literature at the University of Cincinnati. She is presently completing a manuscript titled "Exceptional Differences: Race and the Postwar Jewish American Literary Imagination." She has published, and has publications forthcoming, in a variety of venues, including *PMLA, MELUS, Safundi, Prooftexts*, and the *New York Times*, as well as an anthology of essays from Random House.

Andrew Gordon is Professor Emeritus of English at the University of Florida and coeditor of *Studies in American Jewish Literature*. His publications include *An American Dreamer: A Psychoanalytic Study of the Fiction of Norman Mailer* (1980); *Psychoanalyses/Feminisms*, coedited with Peter Rudnytsky (2000); *Screen Saviors: Hollywood Fictions of Whiteness*, coauthored with Hernan Vera (2003); and *Empire* *of Dreams: The Science Fiction and Fantasy Films of Steven Spielberg* (2008). He also has many essays on Jewish-American writers in *Modern Fiction Studies, Literature and Psychology, Saul Bellow Journal,* and *Philip Roth Studies.*

Brett Ashley Kaplan is Associate Professor in the Program in Comparative and World Literature and the Program in Jewish Culture and Society at the University of Illinois, Urbana-Champaign. She received her Ph.D. from the Rhetoric Department at the University of California, Berkeley, an M.A. in English Literature-Critical Theory from the University of Sussex, and a B.A. from the University of California, Santa Cruz. Her book on Holocaust art and literature, *Unwanted Beauty: Aesthetic Pleasure in Holocaust Representation,* was published in 2007. She has also published articles in *Journal of Modern Jewish Studies, Comparative Literature Studies, International Studies in Philosophy, Philip Roth Studies, Comparative Literature, Images: Journal of Jewish Art and Culture,* and *Camera Austria,* among edited collections and other venues. Her next book, *Landscapes of Holocaust Postmemory,* is forthcoming from Routledge.

Elaine M. Kauvar is Professor of English at Baruch College (CUNY). She is the author of *Cynthia Ozick's Fiction: Tradition and Invention* (1993) and the editor of the *Cynthia Ozick Reader* (1996). She has published articles on Philip Roth, Cynthia Ozick, William Blake, Jane Austen, and James Joyce as well as on the future of Jewish-American literature. She sits on the editorial board of *Contemporary Literature.* Currently, she is working on the meaning of exile in Jewish autobiographies, especially those of Jewish-American writers.

Catherine Morley is Lecturer in American Literature at the University of Leicester and Secretary of the British Association for American Studies. She is the author of *The Quest for Epic in Contemporary American Fiction* (2008) and *Modern American Literature* (2010). She is also the coeditor of *American Thought and Culture in the 21st Century* (2008) and *American Modernism: Cultural Transactions.* She has published numerous scholarly chapters and articles on John Updike, Philip Roth, Don DeLillo, Paul Auster, Willa Cather, and American writing after 9/11. She is currently working on a new study of American naturalism and modernism titled *The Ache of Modernism.*

Timothy Parrish, Professor of English at Florida State University, is the author of *Walking Blues: Making Americans from Emerson to Elvis* (2001) and *From the Civil War to the Apocalypse: Postmodern History* *and American Fiction* (2008). He edited *The Cambridge Companion to Philip Roth* (2007). Publishing widely on American fiction in such journals as *Modern Fiction Studies, Contemporary Literature,* and *American Literary History,* he is currently completing a study of Ralph Ellison, titled *Ralph Ellison: The Genius of America.*

Jeffrey Rubin-Dorsky is Professor Emeritus of English at the University of Colorado. In his academic days, he wrote extensively on Jewish-American literature and culture. Currently, he is working on a memoir of his boyhood, happily spent watching the Brooklyn Dodgers playing baseball at Ebbets Field.

Gabrielle Seeley lives and teaches in the Black Hills of South Dakota. She writes on individualized instruction and twentieth-century American literature.

Debra Shostak is Professor of English and Chair of Film Studies at the College of Wooster. She is the author of *Philip Roth—Countertexts, Counterlives* (2004). Her articles on contemporary American novelists, including Paul Auster, Jeffrey Eugenides, John Irving, Maxine Hong Kingston, and Philip Roth, have appeared in *Contemporary Literature, Critique, Modern Fiction Studies, Shofar, Studies in the Novel,* and *Twentieth Century Literature.* She also writes on film and is currently working on three adaptations of contemporary American novels.

Index